Declarations

```
// declaration of a simple type
[const] type objName [ = expression]; // declaration of a class object
[const] type objName[(argument list)]; // if no arguments, then the
                                       // default constructor is invoked
// declaration of a function
type fnName([argument list]); // if empty, the argument list is
                              // assumed to be void
```

Declarations have one of the following forms. The intrinsic types are

```
[<signed | unsigned >]char
[<signed | unsigned>] [<short | long>] int
float
double
long double
```

Users may also define their own types using the `class` or `struct` keywords:

```
<struct | class> ClassName [ : [public] BaseClass]
{
public:
  // public data members
  type dataMemberName;
  // public member functions
  type memberFunctionName([arg list]) [{...}]
  // const member function
  type memberFunctionName([arg list]) const [{...}]
  // virtual member functions
  virtual type memberFunctionName([arg list]) [{...}];
  // pure virtual member functions
  virtual type memberFunctionName([arg list]) = 0;
protected:
  // repeat for any protected members};
};
```

C++ For Dummies, 4th Edition

Cheat Sheet

Here, in a nutshell, are a few rules to live by. I've used the following contractions in these rules:

`[feature]`	feature is optional
`<feature1	feature2>`	either feature1 or else feature2
`...`	unspecified number of statements or expressions

Expressions

Expressions have both a value and a type. Expressions take one of the following forms:

```
objName                      // for a simple object
operator expression          // for unary operators
expr1 operator expr2         // for binary operators
expr1 ? expr2 : expr3        // for the ternary operator
funcName([argument list]);   // for function calls
```

Operators

	Operator	Cardinality	Associativity
Highest precedence	() [] -> .		left to right
	! ~ + - ++ — & * (cast) sizeof	unary	left to right
	* / %	binary	left to right
	+ -	binary	left to right
	<< >>	binary	left to right
	< <= > >=	binary	left to right
	== !=	binary	left to right
	&	binary	left to right
	^	binary	left to right
	|	binary	left to right
	&&	binary	left to right
	||	binary	left to right
	?:	ternary	right to left
	= *= /= %= += -= &= ^= |= <<= >>=	binary	right to left
Lowest precedence	,	binary	left to right

The IDG Books Worldwide logo is a registered trademark under exclusive license to IDG Books Worldwide, Inc., from International Data Group, Inc. The ...For Dummies logo is a trademark, and For Dummies is a registered trademark of IDG Books Worldwide, Inc. All other trademarks are the property of their respective owners.

For Dummies®: Bestselling Book Series for Beginners

C++

FOR

DUMMIES®

4TH EDITION

by Stephen R. Davis

IDG
BOOKS
WORLDWIDE

IDG Books Worldwide, Inc.
An International Data Group Company

Foster City, CA ◆ Chicago, IL ◆ Indianapolis, IN ◆ New York, NY

C++ For Dummies® 4th Edition

Published by
IDG Books Worldwide, Inc.
An International Data Group Company
919 E. Hillsdale Blvd.
Suite 400
Foster City, CA 94404
www.idgbooks.com (IDG Books Worldwide Web site)
www.dummies.com (Dummies Press Web site)

Library of Congress Control Number: 00-102505

ISBN: 0-7645-0746-X

Printed in the United States of America

10 9 8 7 6 5 4 3

4B/QV/QX/QQ/IN

Distributed in the United States by IDG Books Worldwide, Inc.

Distributed by CDG Books Canada Inc. for Canada; by Transworld Publishers Limited in the United Kingdom; by IDG Norge Books for Norway; by IDG Sweden Books for Sweden; by IDG Books Australia Publishing Corporation Pty. Ltd. for Australia and New Zealand; by TransQuest Publishers Pte Ltd. for Singapore, Malaysia, Thailand, Indonesia, and Hong Kong; by Gotop Information Inc. for Taiwan; by ICG Muse, Inc. for Japan; by Intersoft for South Africa; by Eyrolles for France; by International Thomson Publishing for Germany, Austria and Switzerland; by Distribuidora Cuspide for Argentina; by LR International for Brazil; by Galileo Libros for Chile; by Ediciones ZETA S.C.R. Ltda. for Peru; by WS Computer Publishing Corporation, Inc., for the Philippines; by Contemporanea de Ediciones for Venezuela; by Express Computer Distributors for the Caribbean and West Indies; by Micronesia Media Distributor, Inc. for Micronesia; by Chips Computadoras S.A. de C.V. for Mexico; by Editorial Norma de Panama S.A. for Panama; by American Bookshops for Finland.

For general information on IDG Books Worldwide's books in the U.S., please call our Consumer Customer Service department at 800-762-2974. For reseller information, including discounts and premium sales, please call our Reseller Customer Service department at 800-434-3422.

For information on where to purchase IDG Books Worldwide's books outside the U.S., please contact our International Sales department at 317-596-5530 or fax 317-572-4002.

For consumer information on foreign language translations, please contact our Customer Service department at 1-800-434-3422, fax 317-572-4002, or e-mail rights@idgbooks.com.

For information on licensing foreign or domestic rights, please phone +1-650-653-7098.

For sales inquiries and special prices for bulk quantities, please contact our Order Services department at 800-434-3422 or write to the address above.

For information on using IDG Books Worldwide's books in the classroom or for ordering examination copies, please contact our Educational Sales department at 800-434-2086 or fax 317-572-4005.

For press review copies, author interviews, or other publicity information, please contact our Public Relations department at 650-653-7000 or fax 650-653-7500.

For authorization to photocopy items for corporate, personal, or educational use, please contact Copyright Clearance Center, 222 Rosewood Drive, Danvers, MA 01923, or fax 978-750-4470.

is a registered trademark under exclusive license to IDG Books Worldwide, Inc. from International Data Group, Inc.

About the Author

Stephen R. Davis (Dallas, TX) and his family have written numerous books including *C++ For Dummies, More C++ For Dummies* and *Windows 95 Programming For Dummies.* Stephen works for Valtech, a PC training and mentoring company.

Dedication

To my friends and family who help me to be the best Dummy I can be.

ABOUT IDG BOOKS WORLDWIDE

Welcome to the world of IDG Books Worldwide.

IDG Books Worldwide, Inc., is a subsidiary of International Data Group, the world's largest publisher of computer-related information and the leading global provider of information services on information technology. IDG was founded more than 30 years ago by Patrick J. McGovern and now employs more than 9,000 people worldwide. IDG publishes more than 290 computer publications in over 75 countries. More than 90 million people read one or more IDG publications each month.

Launched in 1990, IDG Books Worldwide is today the #1 publisher of best-selling computer books in the United States. We are proud to have received eight awards from the Computer Press Association in recognition of editorial excellence and three from Computer Currents' First Annual Readers' Choice Awards. Our best-selling ...For Dummies® series has more than 50 million copies in print with translations in 31 languages. IDG Books Worldwide, through a joint venture with IDG's Hi-Tech Beijing, became the first U.S. publisher to publish a computer book in the People's Republic of China. In record time, IDG Books Worldwide has become the first choice for millions of readers around the world who want to learn how to better manage their businesses.

Our mission is simple: Every one of our books is designed to bring extra value and skill-building instructions to the reader. Our books are written by experts who understand and care about our readers. The knowledge base of our editorial staff comes from years of experience in publishing, education, and journalism — experience we use to produce books to carry us into the new millennium. In short, we care about books, so we attract the best people. We devote special attention to details such as audience, interior design, use of icons, and illustrations. And because we use an efficient process of authoring, editing, and desktop publishing our books electronically, we can spend more time ensuring superior content and less time on the technicalities of making books.

You can count on our commitment to deliver high-quality books at competitive prices on topics you want to read about. At IDG Books Worldwide, we continue in the IDG tradition of delivering quality for more than 30 years. You'll find no better book on a subject than one from IDG Books Worldwide.

John Kilcullen
Chairman and CEO
IDG Books Worldwide, Inc.

Eighth Annual Computer Press Awards ≥1992

Ninth Annual Computer Press Awards ≥1993

Tenth Annual Computer Press Awards ≥1994

Eleventh Annual Computer Press Awards ≥1995

IDG is the world's leading IT media, research and exposition company. Founded in 1964, IDG had 1997 revenues of $2.05 billion and has more than 9,000 employees worldwide. IDG offers the widest range of media options that reach IT buyers in 75 countries representing 95% of worldwide IT spending. IDG's diverse product and services portfolio spans six key areas including print publishing, online publishing, expositions and conferences, market research, education and training, and global marketing services. More than 90 million people read one or more of IDG's 290 magazines and newspapers, including IDG's leading global brands — Computerworld, PC World, Network World, Macworld and the Channel World family of publications. IDG Books Worldwide is one of the fastest-growing computer book publishers in the world, with more than 700 titles in 36 languages. The "...For Dummies®" series alone has more than 50 million copies in print. IDG offers online users the largest network of technology-specific Web sites around the world through IDG.net (http://www.idg.net), which comprises more than 225 targeted Web sites in 55 countries worldwide. International Data Corporation (IDC) is the world's largest provider of information technology data, analysis and consulting, with research centers in over 41 countries and more than 400 research analysts worldwide. IDG World Expo is a leading producer of more than 168 globally branded conferences and expositions in 35 countries including E3 (Electronic Entertainment Expo), Macworld Expo, ComNet, Windows World Expo, ICE (Internet Commerce Expo), Agenda, DEMO, and Spotlight. IDG's training subsidiary, ExecuTrain, is the world's largest computer training company, with more than 230 locations worldwide and 785 training courses. IDG Marketing Services helps industry-leading IT companies build international brand recognition by developing global integrated marketing programs via IDG's print, online and exposition products worldwide. Further information about the company can be found at www.idg.com.   1/26/00

Author's Acknowledgments

I find it very strange that only a single name appears on the cover of any book, but especially a book like this. In reality, many people contribute to the creation of a *For Dummies* book. From the beginning, editorial manager Mary Corder and editorial agent Claudette Moore were involved in guiding and molding the book's content. During development, I found myself hip-deep in edits, corrections, and suggestions from project editors Kelly Ewing and Colleen Williams (third edition), and Susan Pink (first and second editions); and technical reviewers Jeff Bankston (third edition), Garrett Pease (second edition), and Greg Guntle (first edition) — this book would have been a poorer work but for their involvement. And nothing would have made it into print without the aid of the person who coordinated the first and second editions of the project, Suzanne Thomas. Nevertheless, one name does appear on the cover and that name must take responsibility for any inaccuracies in the text.

I also have to thank my wife, Jenny, and son, Kinsey, for their patience and devotion. I hope we manage to strike a reasonable balance.

Finally, a summary of the animal activity around my house. For those of you who have not read any of my other books, I should warn you that this has become a regular feature of my *For Dummies* books.

My two dogs, Scooter and Trude, continue to do well although Trude is all but blind now. Our two mini-Rex rabbits, Beavis and Butt-head, passed on to the big meadow in the sky after living in our front yard for almost a year and a half. We acquired two cats, Bob and Marly (both female, by the way), during the writing of *MORE C++ For Dummies*. Marly died of kitty leukemia, but Bob and the family have carried on.

A friend of my sister-in-law was secretly harboring a pot-bellied pig named Penny in her (the friend's, not Penny's) apartment last winter. Due to some sort of piggy indiscretions, the cover was blown and the apartment manager threatened Penny with bodily harm (apparently he didn't keep kosher). We were forced to spirit Penny away in the back of my Explorer under the cover of darkness. Penny arrived safely at her new quarters (outside this time), where she continues to thrive.

If you would like to contact me concerning C++ programming, pot-bellied pigs, semi-blind dogs, or free-roaming rabbits, feel free to drop me a line at srdavis@ACM.org.

Publisher's Acknowledgments

We're proud of this book; please register your comments through our IDG Books Worldwide Online Registration Form located at http://my2cents.dummies.com.

Some of the people who helped bring this book to market include the following:

Acquisitions, Editorial, and Media Development

Project Editor: Jade L. Williams

(Previous Edition: Colleen Williams, Kelly Ewing*)*

Acquisitions Editor: Sherri Morningstar

Copy Editor: Christine Berman

Proof Editor: Teresa Artman

Technical Editor: Namir Shammas

Permissions Editor: Carmen Krikorian

Associate Media Development Specialist: Megan Decraene

Editorial Manager: Kyle Looper

Media Development Manager: Heather Heath Dismore

Editorial Assistant: Sarah Shupert

Production

Project Coordinator: Maridee Ennis

Layout and Graphics: Tracy K. Oliver, Brent Savage, Jacque Schneider, Janet Seib, Brian Torwelle

Proofreaders: Laura Albert, Corey Bowen, Susan Moritz, York Production Services, Inc.

Indexer: York Production Services, Inc.

Special Help
Amanda M. Foxworth

General and Administrative

IDG Books Worldwide, Inc.: John Kilcullen, CEO

IDG Books Technology Publishing Group: Richard Swadley, Senior Vice President and Publisher; Walter R. Bruce III, Vice President and Publisher; Joseph Wikert, Vice President and Publisher; Mary Bednarek, Vice President and Director, Product Development; Andy Cummings, Publishing Director, General User Group; Mary C. Corder, Editorial Director; Barry Pruett, Publishing Director

IDG Books Consumer Publishing Group: Roland Elgey, Senior Vice President and Publisher; Kathleen A. Welton, Vice President and Publisher; Kevin Thornton, Acquisitions Manager; Kristin A. Cocks, Editorial Director

IDG Books Internet Publishing Group: Brenda McLaughlin, Senior Vice President and Publisher; Sofia Marchant, Online Marketing Manager

IDG Books Production for Branded Press: Debbie Stailey, Director of Production; Cindy L. Phipps, Manager of Project Coordination, Production Proofreading, and Indexing; Tony Augsburger, Manager of Prepress, Reprints, and Systems; Laura Carpenter, Production Control Manager; Shelley Lea, Supervisor of Graphics and Design; Debbie J. Gates, Production Systems Specialist; Robert Springer, Supervisor of Proofreading; Trudy Coler, Page Layout Manager; Troy Barnes, Page Layout Supervisor, Kathie Schutte, Senior Page Layout Supervisor; Michael Sullivan, Production Supervisor

Packaging and Book Design: Patty Page, Manager, Promotions Marketing

◆

The publisher would like to give special thanks to Patrick J. McGovern, without whom this book would not have been possible.

◆

Contents at a Glance

Cartoons at a Glance

By Rich Tennant

Fax: 978-546-7747
E-mail: richtennant@the5thwave.com
World Wide Web: www.the5thwave.com

Table of Contents

Introduction

About This Book

Welcome to *C++ For Dummies,* 4th Edition. Think of this book as C++: *Reader's Digest Edition,* bringing you everything you need to know without the boring stuff.

What's in This Book

C++ For Dummies is an introduction to the C++ language.

C++ For Dummies starts from the ground floor: It doesn't assume that you have any knowledge of programming (this is different from previous editions, which assumed a prior knowledge of C).

Unlike other C++ programming books, *C++ For Dummies* considers the "why" just as important as the "how." The features of C++ are like pieces of a jigsaw puzzle. Rather than just present the features, I think it's important that you understand how they fit together.

If you don't understand why a particular feature is in the language, you won't truly understand how it works. After you finish this book, you'll be able to write a reasonable C++ program, and, just as important, you'll understand why and how it works.

C++ For Dummies doesn't cover Windows programming. Finding out how to program Windows in C++ is really a two-step process. First, you need to master C++. That accomplished, you can move on to Windows. And for that, you could do worse than (watch out for shameless plugs) *Windows 98 Programming For Dummies* (of course, published by IDG Books Worldwide, Inc.).

What's on the CD

The CD-ROM included with *C++ For Dummies* contains the source code to the examples in this book. This can spare you considerable typing.

The CD-ROM also contains the GNU C++ development environment.

Your computer can't execute a C++ program directly (not even a Pentium III). You first need to run your C++ programs through a C++ development environment, which spits out an executable program. (Don't worry, this procedure is explained in Chapter 1.) The GNU C++ contained on the enclosed CD-ROM is just such an environment.

GNU C++ is not some reduced capability, time-limited shareware package. The enclosed GNU C++ is a fully functional, American National Standards Institute (ANSI) standard compliant development tool. GNU C++ can generate the same programs that the big boy can.

Of course, the examples contained in *C++ For Dummies* are compatible with GNU C++. The examples are just as compatible with any other standard ANSI C++ environment — feel free to use your favorite C++ tool, such as Microsoft Visual C++ — to build the programs in this book.

What Is C++?

C++ is an object-oriented, low-level ANSI and ISO standard programming language. *Object-oriented* means that C++ supports programming styles that simplify the building of large-scale, extensible programs. As a low-level language, C++ can generate very efficient, very fast programs. The ANSI and International Standards Organization (ISO) certifications make C++ a portable language. C++ programs are compatible with almost all modern development environments.

C++, as the name implies, is the next generation of the C programming language: the result of adding New Age academic computer linguistic thinking to that old workhorse C. Anything C can do, C++ can do, too. C++ can even do it the same way. But C++ is more than just C with a new coat of paint slapped on. The extensions to C++ are significant and require some thought and some getting used to, but the results are worth it.

The experienced C programmer will find C++ both exciting and frustrating. Just like a German reading Dutch — there's enough similarity that the C programmer can almost make sense out of a C++ program but just enough difference that it isn't quite possible. This book will help you get from C to C++ as painlessly as possible; however, *C++ For Dummies,* 4th Edition, doesn't assume that the reader knows anything about C language.

Conventions Used in This Book

When I describe a message or information that you see on screen, it appears like this:

```
Hi mom!
```

In addition, code listings appear as follows:

```
// some program
void main()
{
    ...
}
```

If you are entering these programs by hand, you must enter the text exactly as shown with one exception: The number of spaces is not critical, so don't worry if you enter one too many or one too few spaces.

Words that are not really English words but are computer words, such as commands or function names, appear like this. Function names are always followed by an open and closed parenthesis like myFavoriteFunction().

Sometimes the book directs you to use specific keyboard commands to get things done. For example, when the text instructs you to press Ctrl+C, it means that you should hold down the Ctrl key while pressing the C key, and then release both together. Don't type the plus sign.

Sometimes I'll tell you to use a menu command, like this:

File➪Open

This line means to use the keyboard or mouse to open the File menu and then choose the Open command. (The underlined letters are the keyboard hot keys, which let you use the menus without reaching for your mouse. To use them, first press the Alt key. In the preceding example, you would press and release the Alt key, press and release the F key, and then press and release the O key.)

What You're Not to Read

C++ is a big pill to swallow. There are the easy parts and the not-so-easy parts. To keep from swamping you with information that you may not be interested in at the moment, technical stuff is flagged with a special icon. (See the section "Icons Used in This Book.")

In addition, certain background information is stuck into sidebars. If you feel the onset of information overload, feel free to skip these sections during the first reading. (Remember to read them sometime, though. In C++, what you don't know will hurt you — eventually.)

Foolish Assumptions

C++ For Dummies, 4th Edition, makes no assumptions about the reader's programming experience, or lack thereof. Of course, it would help if you had turned a computer on before, but it's not an absolute necessity.

Previous versions of *C++ For Dummies* assumed that you already know at least some C. The feeling was that the C++ student should learn C first. Assuming a background in C turned out to be a mistake. First of all, many of the principles of C++ are fundamentally different than those behind C, even though the syntax looks deceptively similar. In addition, most students of C++ today are programming newcomers rather than C retreads.

This fourth edition of *C++ For Dummies* begins with basic programming concepts. The book works its way through simple syntax into the care and feeding of basic programs right into object-oriented concepts. The reader who has digested the entire contents of the book should have no trouble impressing his friends and acquaintances at parties.

How This Book Is Organized

Each new feature is introduced by answering the following three questions:

- ✔ *What* is this new feature?
- ✔ *Why* was it introduced into the language?
- ✔ *How* does it work?

Small pieces of code are sprinkled liberally throughout the chapters. Each demonstrates some newly introduced feature or highlights some brilliant point I'm making. These snippets may not be complete and certainly don't do anything meaningful.

Note: Due to the margins of the book, very long lines of code continue to a second line. This arrow appears at the end of those lines of code to remind you to keep on typing — don't press the Enter key yet! I have tried diligently to keep these run-on coding sentences to a minimum (even if I don't do the same in my English sentences).

At The End of Each Part. . .

In addition, a series of BUDGET programs appears at the end of Parts II, III, and IV. These programs are large enough that you can see a "real" program in action.

I think it's important to see the features of C++ working together in a complete program. I get distracted, however, when I'm forced to wade through many different example programs. I spend more time figuring out what each program does than understanding the language features it contains. In addition, I have difficulty comparing them because they don't do the same thing.

I use one simple example program, BUDGET. This program starts life as a simple, functionally oriented program. Subsequent versions incorporate the features presented in each new part.

By the time you reach the end of the book, BUDGET has blossomed into a complete C++ debutante ready for the object-oriented cotillion. Some may find this a ghastly waste of time. (If so, just skip it and keep it to yourself — I convinced my editor that it was a really neat idea.) However, I hope that as you see BUDGET evolve, you'll see how the features of C++ work together.

Part I: Introducing C++ Programming

Part I starts you on your journey. You begin by examining what it means to write a computer program. From there, you step through the syntax of the language (the meaning of the C++ commands).

Part II: Becoming a Functional Programmer

In this part, you expand upon your newly gained knowledge of the basic commands of C++ by adding the capability to bundle sections of C++ code into modules and reusing these modules in programs.

In this section, I also introduce that most dreaded of all topics, the C++ pointer. If you don't know what that means, don't worry — you'll find out soon enough.

Part III: Programming with Class

The plot thickens in this part. Part III begins the discussion of object-oriented programming. Object-oriented programming is really the reason for the existence of C++. Take the OO features out of C++ and you're left with its predecessor language, C. I discuss things such as classes, constructors, destructors, and making nachos (I'm not kidding, by the way). Don't worry if you don't know what these concepts are (except for nachos — if you don't know what nachos are, we're in big trouble).

Part IV: Class Inheritance

Inheritance is where object-oriented programming really comes into its own. Understanding this most important concept is the key to effective C++ programming and the goal of Part IV. There's no going back now — after you've completed this part, you can call yourself an Object-Oriented Programmer, First Class.

Part V: Optional Features

By the time you get to Part V, you know all you need to program effectively in C++. I touch on remaining, optional issues. You may want to hold off reading these chapters until you stop feeling lightheaded from information overload.

Part VI: The Part of Tens

What *For Dummies* book would be complete without The Part of Tens? In the first chapter in Part VI, you find out the best ways to avoid introducing bugs into your programs.

Have you noticed how many different compiler options there are these days? How do I know whether I want my v_table pointer to follow my member pointer? And what's the alternative to fast floating point? Slow floating point? I guide you through these options, pointing out those that are important and those that are better left alone.

Icons Used in This Book

This is technical stuff that you can skip on the first reading.

Tips highlight a point that can save you a lot of time and effort.

Alerts you to examples and software that appear in this book's CD-ROM.

Remember this. It's important.

Remember this, too. This one can sneak up on you when you least expect it and generate one of those really hard-to-find bugs.

Where to Go from Here

Finding out about a programming language is not a spectator sport. I'll try to make it as painless as possible, but you have to power up the ol' PC and get down to some serious programming. Limber up the fingers, break the spine on the book so that it lies flat next to the keyboard (and so that you can't take it back to the bookstore), and dive in.

Part I
Introducing C++ Programming

The 5th Wave   By Rich Tennant

Re'al Pro'gram·mers

ONE DAY IT REALLY HIT BERTHA JUST HOW OBSESSED HER HUSBAND
HAD BECOME WITH HIS COMPUTER.

In this part . . .

Both the newest, hottest flight simulator and the simplest yet most powerful accounting programs use the same basic building blocks. In this part, you discover the basic features you need to write your killer application.

Chapter 1

Writing Your First C++ Program

· ·

In This Chapter

▶ Finding out about C++

▶ Installing the GNU C++ program from the enclosed CD-ROM

▶ Creating your first C++ program

▶ Executing your program

· ·

*O*kay, so here we are. No one here but just you and me. Nothing left to do but to get started. First, let's begin with a few fundamental concepts.

A computer is this amazingly fast but incredibly stupid machine. A computer can do anything you tell it (within reason) but it does exactly what it's told — nothing more and nothing less.

Perhaps unfortunately for us, computers don't understand any reasonable human language — they don't speak English either. Okay, I know what you're going to say: "I've seen computers that could understand English." What you really saw was a computer executing a program that could meaningfully understand English. (I'm still a little unclear on this computer-understanding-language concept, but then I don't know that my son understands my advice, either, so I'll let it slide.)

Computers understand a language variously known as computer language or machine language. It's possible but extremely difficult for humans to speak machine language. Therefore, computers and humans have agreed to sort of meet in the middle using intermediate languages such as C++. Humans can speak C++ (sort of) and C++ is converted into machine language for the computer to understand.

Grasping C++ Concepts

In the early seventies, a consortium of really clever people worked on a computer system called Multix. The goal of Multix was to provide inexpensive computer access in all houses to graphics, e-mail, stock data, and pornography (okay, I slipped in the pornography part). Of course, this was a completely crazy idea and the entire concept failed.

A small team of engineers working for Bell Labs decided to save some portion of Multix in a very small, lightweight operating system that they dubbed Unix (Un-ix, Mult-ix, get it?).

Unfortunately for these engineers, they didn't have one large machine but a number of smaller machines each from a different manufacturer. The standard development tricks of the day were all machine dependent — they would have to rewrite the same program for each of the available machines. Instead, these engineers invented a small, powerful language, named C.

C was indeed a powerful language, and it caught on like wildfire. However, new programming techniques were devised (most notably object-oriented programming) that left the C programming language behind. Not to be outdone, the engineering community added these new features to the C language, and the result was called C++.

The C++ language consists of:

- A vocabulary of commands that humans can understand and that can be converted into machine language fairly easily

  and

- A language structure (or *grammar*) that allows humans to combine these C++ commands into a program that actually does something (well, maybe does something)

Note: The vocabulary is often known as the semantics, while the grammar is the syntax.

What's a program?

A C++ program is a text file containing a sequence of C++ commands put together according to the laws of C++ grammar. This text file is known as the *source file* (probably because it's the source of all frustration). A C++ source file carries the extension .CPP just as a Microsoft Word file ends in .DOC or an MS-DOS batch file ends in .BAT. The concept extension .CPP is just a convention, but it's used almost exclusively in the PC world.

The point of programming is to write a sequence of C++ commands that can be converted into a machine language program that does whatever it is that we want done. Such machine executable programs carry the extension .EXE. The act of creating an executable program from a C++ program is called *compiling* (or building — there is a difference, but it's small).

That sounds easy enough — what's the big deal? Keep going.

How do I program?

To write a program, you need two things: an editor to build your *.CPP* source file with and a program that converts your source file into a machine executable *.EXE* file to carry out your commands. The tool that does the conversion is known as a *compiler*.

Nowadays, tool developers generally combine the compiler with an editor into a single work-environment package. After entering your program, you need only click a button to create the executable file.

The most popular of all C++ environments is Microsoft's Visual C++.. All of the programs in this book compile and execute with Visual C++; however, many of you may not already own Visual C++ and at $250 bucks a pop, street price, this may be a problem.

Fortunately, there are public domain C++ environments — the most popular of which is GNU C++. The most recent version of GNU C++ environment is included on CD-ROM enclosed at the back of this book. (You can download the absolute most recent version off the Web at www.deloreon.com, if you prefer.)

You can download public domain programs from the Internet. Some of these programs are not free — you are either encouraged to or required to pay some usually small fee. You do not have to pay to use GNU C++.

GNU is pronounced "guh – new." GNU stands for the circular definition "GNU is Not UNIX." This joke goes way back to the early days of C++ — just accept it as is. GNU is a series of tools built by the Free Software Foundation.

GNU C++ is not some bug-ridden, limited edition C++ compiler from some fly-by-night group of developers. GNU C++ is a full-fledged C++ environment. GNU C++ supports the entire C++ language and executes all of the programs in this book (and all other C++ book).

GNU C++ is not a Windows development package for the Windows environment. You'll have to break open the wallet and go for a commercial package like Visual C++.

Follow the steps in the next section to install GNU C++ and build your first C++ program. This program's task is to convert a temperature entered by the user in degrees Celsius into degrees Fahrenheit.

Installing GNU C++

The CD-ROM that accompanies this book contains the GNU C++ package you need to edit and compile your C++ programs. All of the program examples in this book are compatible with Standard C++ compilers, including GNU C++.

To install the GNU C++ on your machine:

1. **Create a directory C:\DJGPP. Of course, you may use whatever disk you prefer instead of C.**

2. **Copy the complete set of GNU C++ ZIP files from the CD-ROM into \DJGPP.**

3. **Unzip the files in the folder itself.**

4. **Add the following commands to your AUTOEXEC.BAT files:**

   ```
   set PATH=C:\DJGPP\BIN;%PATH%
   set DJGPP=C:\DJGPP\DJGPP.ENV
   ```

5. **Reboot to complete the installation.**

Check the READ.ME file for up-to-date information concerning GNU C++.

Creating Your First C++ Program

In this section, you create your first C++ program. You first enter the C++ code into a file called CONVERT.CPP, and then convert the C++ code into an executable program.

Entering the C++ code

The first step to creating any C++ program is to enter C++ instructions using a text editor. The heart of the GNU C++ package is a utility known as *rhide*. At its core, rhide is an editor that links the other facilities of GNU C++ into an integrated package. You use rhide to create Convert.cpp later in this chapter.

1. **Open an MS-DOS window by clicking the MS-DOS icon under the Programs menu.**

   GNU C++ is a command line utility. You will always start rhide from an MSDOS prompt.

2. **Create the directory** `c:\CPP_For_Dummies\Chap01` **(assuming that your main drive is drive C).**

You can use whatever directory name you like, but it's a lot easier to manipulate MS-DOS directory names that don't contain any spaces. It's easier yet to use directory names that are eight characters or fewer in length, but even I have to draw the line somewhere.

Within Chap01, enter the command **rhide** at the MS-DOS prompt.

Create an empty file by entering **New** under the File menu. A blank window opens. Enter the following program exactly as written.

Don't worry too much about indentation or spacing — it isn't critical whether a given line is indented two or three spaces, or whether there are one or two spaces between two words. C++ is case sensitive, however, so you need to make sure everything is lowercase.

The rhide interface

The rhide interface looks fundamentally different than a Windows-oriented program. Windows programs "paint" their output to the screen. This gives Windows programs a more refined appearance.

By comparison, the rhide interface is based on characters. rhide uses a number of blocking characters available in the PC arsenal to simulate a Windows interface — simulate is a strong word here. This gives rhide a less than elegant appearance. For example, rhide doesn't support

resizing the window away from the 80x25 character display which is the standard for MS-DOS programs. rhide does support most of the features you're used to — drop-down menus, multiple windows, mouse interface, and speed keys, for example.

For those of you old enough to remember, the rhide interface looks virtually identical to the interface of the now-defunct Borland suite of programming tools.

TIP

You can cheat and copy the Conversion.cpp file contained on the enclosed CD-ROM in directory \programs\Chap01.

```
//
//  Program to convert temperature from Celsius degree
//  units into Fahrenheit degree units:
//  Fahrenheit = Celsius  * (212 - 32)/100 + 32
//
#include <stdio.h>
#include <iostream.h>

int main(int nNumberofArgs, char* pszArgs[])
{
    // enter the temperature in Celsius
    int celsius;
    cout << "Enter the temperature in Celsius:";
    cin >> celsius;

    // calculate conversion factor for Celsius
    // to Fahrenheit
    int factor;
    factor = 212 - 32;

    // use conversion factor to convert Celsius
    // into Fahrenheit values
    int fahrenheit;
    fahrenheit = factor * celsius/100 + 32;

    // output the results
    cout << "Fahrenheit value is:";
    cout << fahrenheit;

    return 0;
}
```

After you enter the code shown, choose Save As under the File menu to save the file under the name Conversion.cpp.

I know that it may not seem all that exciting, but you've just created your first C++ program!

Building your program

After you've saved your Conversion.cpp C++ source file to disk, it's time to generate the executable machine instructions.

To build your Conversion.cpp program, select the Make option under the Compile menu, or simply click F9. rhide opens a small window at the bottom of the window to display the progress of the build process. If all goes well, the message `Creating Conversion.exe` is followed by `no errors`.

GNU C++ installation errors

A number of common errors might happen during the installation process to spoil your out-of-the-box programming experience. The two most common error messages don't become obvious until you try to compile your program.

The message `Bad command or file name` means that MS-DOS can't find gcc.exe, the GNU C++ compiler. Either you didn't install GNU C++ properly or your path doesn't include `c:\djgpp\bin` where `gcc.exe` resides. Try reinstalling GNU C++ and make sure that the command `SET PATH=c:\djgpp\bin;%PATH%` is in your `autoexec.bat` file. Reboot.

The message `gcc.exe: Conversion.cpp: No such file or directory (ENOENT)` indicates that gcc doesn't know that you're using long file names (as opposed to old MS-DOS 8.3 file names). To correct this problem, edit the file `c:\djgpp\djgpp.env`. Set the `LFN` property to `Y`.

One final warning, GNU C++ doesn't understand file names containing spaces no matter what the value of the long-file-name flag.

GNU C++ generates an error message if it finds any type of error in your C++ program. Coding errors are about as common as snow in Alaska. You'll undoubtedly encounter numerous warnings and error messages, probably even when entering the simple Conversion.cpp. To demonstrate the error reporting process, let's change Line 14 from `cin >> celsius;` to `cin >>> celsius;`

This seems like an innocent enough offense — forgivable to you and me perhaps, but not to C++. *rhide* generates the following messages during the build process:

```
Compiling: Conversion.cpp
In function 'int main(int, char **)':
Conversion.cpp(14) Error: parse error before '>'
There were some errors
```

This error indicates that GNU C++ can't understand what the ">>>"on Line 14 means.

The term *parse* means to convert the C++ commands into something that the machine code generation part of the process can work with.

Edit the file and remove the extra '>' to fix the problem. Press F9 to build Conversion.exe successfully.

Why is C++ so picky?

C++ was able to determine without a doubt that I had screwed up in the previous example. However, if GNU C++ can figure out what I did wrong, then why doesn't it just fix the problem and go on?

The answer is simple but profound. GNU C++ thinks that I mistyped the '">>" symbol but it may be mistaken. What could have been a mistyped command may actually be some other, completely unrelated error. Had the compiler simply corrected the problem, GNU C++ would have masked the real problem.

Finding an error buried in a program that builds without error is difficult and time consuming. It's far better to let the compiler find the error if at all possible. Generating a compiler error is a waste of the computer's time — forcing me to find a mistake that GNU C++ could have caught is a waste of my time. Guess which one I vote for?

Executing Your Program

It's now come time to execute your new creation . . . that is, to run your program. You will run the CONVERT.EXE program file and provide it input to see how well it works.

To execute the Conversion program, click the Run item of the Run menu or press Ctrl+F9.

A window opens immediately, requesting a temperature in Celsius. Enter a known temperature, such as 100 degrees. After you press Enter, the program returns with the equivalent temperature of 212 degrees Fahrenheit. However, because rhide closes the window as soon as the program terminates, you do not have time to see the output before the window closes. *Rhide* opens an alert box with the message that the program terminated with an error code of zero. Despite the name "error code," a zero means that no error actually occurred.

To see the output from the now-terminated program, click the User Screen menu item in the Windows menu or press Alt+5. This window displays the current MS-DOS window. In this window, you see the last 25 lines of output of the program, including the calculated Fahrenheit temperature.

Congratulations! You just entered, built, and executed your first program by using GNU C++.

GNU is guh-not Windows

Notice that GNU C++ is not intended for developing Windows programs. In theory, you could write a Windows application by using GNU C++, but it wouldn't be easy without the help provided by external library such as those that come with Visual C++.

Windows programs have a very visually oriented, windows based output. Convesion.exe is a 32-bit program that executes under Windows, but it's not a "Windows" program in the visual sense.

If you don't know what 32-bit program means, don't worry about it. As I said earlier, this book isn't about writing Windows programs. The C++ programs you write in this book have a command line interface executing within an "MS-DOS box."

Budding Windows programmers shouldn't despair — you didn't waste your money. Learning C++ is a prerequisite to writing Windows programs.

GNU C++ help

GNU C++ provides a help system through the rhide user interface. Place your cursor on a construct that you don't understand and press F1. A window pops up. Alternatively, choose Help⇨Index to display a list of help topics. Click on a topic of interest to display help.

The help that GNU C++ provides isn't nearly as comprehensive as the help you get from other tools, such as Microsoft Visual C++. For example, place the cursor on the 'int' statement and press F1. A window appears describing the editor — not exactly what I was looking for. The help provided by GNU C++ tends to center on library functions and compiler options. Fortunately, after you master the C++ language itself, GNU C++ help is satisfactory for most applications.

Reviewing the Annotated Program

Entering in someone else's program isn't very exciting. You can recognize a few features of Conversion.cpp even at this early date. We can review the Conversion program looking for the elements that are common to all programs.

Examining the framework for all C++ programs

Every C++ program you write for this book uses the same basic framework:

```
// this is some comment that the computer ignores
#include <stdio.h>
#include <iostream.h>
int main(int nNumberofArgs, char* pzArgs[])
{
    ...your code goes here...
    return 0;
}
```

Without going into all the boring details, execution begins with the code contained in the open and closed braces.

Clarifying source code with comments

The first few lines in Conversion.cpp appear to be freeform text. Either this code was meant for human eyes or GNU C++ is a lot smarter than I give it credit for. These first six lines are known as comments. *Comments* are the programmer's explanation of what he or she is doing or thinking when writing a particular code segment. The compiler ignores comments.

A C++ comment begins with a double slash (//) and ends with a newline. You can put any character you want in a comment. A comment may be as long as you want, but it's customary to keep comments to 80 characters so that comments fit on your computer screen.

A newline was known as a carriage return back in the days of typewriters — back when the act of entering characters into a machine was called typing and not keyboarding. A *newline* is the character that terminates a command line.

C++ allows a second form of comment in which everything appearing after a /* and before a */ is ignored; however, this form of comment isn't normally used in C++ anymore.

It may seem odd to have a command in C++ (or any other programming language) that's specifically ignored by the computer. However, all computer languages have some version of the comment. It's critical that the programmer explains what was going through her mind when she wrote the code. A programmer's thoughts may not be obvious to the next guy who picks up her program to use it or modify it. In fact, the programmer herself may forget what her program meant if she looks at it months later.

Basing programs on C++ statements

All C++ programs are based upon what are known as C++ statements. This section reviews the statements that make up the program framework used by the Convert program.

A *statement* is a single set of commands. All statements other than comments end with a semicolon (There's a reason that comments don't end with a semicolon but it's obscure. To my mind, comments should end in a semicolon as well, for consistency's sake if nothing else.)

Program execution begins with the first C++ statement after the open brace and continues through the listing, one statement at a time.

As you look through the program, you can see that spaces, tabs, and new lines appear throughout the program. In fact, I place a newline after every statement in this program. These characters are collectively known as *white space* because you can't see them on the monitor.

You may add white space anywhere you like in your program to enhance readability except in the middle of a word.

Although C++ may ignore white space, it doesn't ignore case. The variable fullspeed and the variable FullSpeed have nothing to do with each other. While the command `int` may be understood completely, C++ has no idea what INT means.

Writing declarations

The line `int nCelsius;` is a declaration statement. A *declaration* is a statement that defines a variable. A *variable* is a "holding tank" for a value of some type. A variable contains a value, such as a number or a character.

The term variable stems from algebra formulae of the following type:

```
x = 10
y = 3 * x
```

In the second expression, y is set equal to 3 times x, but what is x? The variable x acts as a holding tank for a value. In this case, the value of x is 10, but we could have just as well set the value of x to 20 or 30 or -1. The second formula makes sense no matter what the value of x.

In algebra you're allowed to begin with a statement, such as x = 10. In C++, the programmer must first define the variable x before she can use it.

In C++, a variable has a type and a name. The variable defined on Line 11 is called *celsius*. celsius is declared to hold an integer. (Why they couldn't have just said integer instead of *int*, I'll never know. It's just one of those things that you learn to live with.)

The name of a variable has no particular significance to C+. A variable must begin with the letters A through Z or a through z. All subsequent characters must be a letter, a digit 0 through 9 or an underscore (_). Variable names can be as long as you want to make them.

It's convention that variable names begin with a lowercase letter. Each new word within a variable begins with a capital letter, as in myVariable. I explain the significance of the *n* in celsius in Chapter 5.

Try to make variable names short but descriptive. Avoid names such as x because x has no meaning. A variable name such as lengthOfLineSegment is much more descriptive.

Generating output

The lines beginning with cout and cin are known as input/output statements, often contracted to I/O statements. (Like all engineers, programmers love contractions and acronyms.)

The first I/O statement says output the phrase *Enter the temperature in Celsius* to *cout* (pronounced "see-out"). cout is the name of the standard C++ output device. In this case, the standard C++ output device is your monitor.

The next line is exactly the opposite. This says extract a value from the C++ input device and store it into the integer variable celsius. The C++ input device is normally the keyboard. This is the C++ analogue to the algebra formula *x = 10* mentioned above. For the remainder of the program, the value of celsius is whatever the user enters here.

Calculating Expressions

All but the most basic programs perform calculations of one type or another. In C++ an expression is a statement that performs a calculation. Said another way, an expression is a statement that has a value. An operator is a command that generates a value.

For example, in the Conversion example program, the two lines marked as a "calculation expression," the program declares a variable *factor* and assigns it the value resulting from a calculation. This command calculates the difference of 212 and 32. In this example, the operator is the minus sign "–" while the expression is "212–32."

Storing the results of expression

The spoken language can be very ambiguous. The term *equals* is one of those ambiguities. The word equals can mean that two things have the same value as in "5 cents equals a nickel." Equals can also imply assignment as in math when you say that "y equals 3 times x."

To avoid ambiguity, C++ programmers call "=" the *assignment operator*. The assignment operator says store the results of the expression on the right of the "=" into the variable to the left. Programmers say that "factor is assigned the value 212–32."

Examining the remainder of Conversion

The second expression in Conversion.cpp presents a slightly more complicated expression than the first. This expression uses the same mathematical symbols: "*" for multiplication, "/" for division and, "+" for addition. In this case, however, the calculation is performed on variables and not simply constants.

The value contained in the variable `factor` (calculated immediately prior, by the way) is multiplied by the value contained in `nCelsius` (which was input from the keyboard). The result is divided by 100 and summed with 32. The result of the total expression is assigned to the integer variable `fahrenheit`.

The final two commands output the string "Fahrenheit value is:" to the display followed by the value of `fahrenheit`.

Chapter 2

Declaring Variables Constantly

● ●

● ●

*T*he most fundamental of all concepts in C++ is the *variable*. A variable is like a small box. You can store things in the box for later use, in particular numbers. The concept of a variable is borrowed from mathematics. A statement like:

```
x = 1
```

stores the value 1 into the variable *x*. From that point forward the mathematician can use the variable *x* in place of the constant 1 — until she changes the value of *x* to something else.

Variables work the same way in C++. You can make the assignment:

```
x = 1;
```

From that point forward in the program until the value of x is changed any references to x are the same as referencing 1. We say that the value of x is 1.

Unfortunately, C++ has a few more concerns about variables than the mathematician does. This chapter deals with the care and feeding of variables in C++.

Declaring Variables

C++ saves numeric values in small storage boxes known as variables. Mathematicians throw variables around with abandon. A mathematician might write down something like the following:

```
(x + 2) =  y / 2
x + 4 = y
solve for x and y
```

The reader realizes that the mathematician has introduced the variables x and y without explicitly being told. C++ isn't that smart (I told you that computers are stupid).

You have to announce each variable to C++ before you can use it. You have to say:

```
int x;
x = 10;

int y;
y = 5;
```

This declares that there is a variable x and that it is of type `int`. (Variable types are discussed in the next section.) You can declare variables (almost) anywhere you want to in your program as long as you declare the variable before you use it.

Declaring Different Types of Variables

You probably think of a variable in mathematics as just an amorphous box capable of holding whatever you might choose to store in it. You might easily write something like the following:

```
x = 1;
x = 2.3
x = "this is a sentence"
x = Texas
```

C++ is not that flexible. (On the other hand, C++ can do things that you can't do, such as add a million numbers or so in a second, so don't get too uppity.) To C++, there are different types of variables just as there are different types of storage bins. Some storage bins are so small that they can only handle a single number. It takes a larger bin to handle a sentence. Of course, no bin is large enough to hold Texas (maybe Massachussetts, but not Texas).

You have to tell C++ what size bin you need before you can use a C++ variable. In addition, different types of variables have different properties. So far, you have only seen the *int* type of variable.

```
int x;
x = 1;
```

The variable type `int` is the C++ equivalent of an integer. (An *integer* is a number that has no fractional part. Integers are also known as counting numbers or whole numbers.)

Integers are great for most calculations. You can make it up through most (if not all) of grade school with integers. It isn't until 6th grade or so that they start mucking up the waters with fractions. The same is true in C++. Over 90 percent of all variables in C++ are declared to be of type `int`.

Unfortunately, `int` variables don't always work properly in a program. If you worked through the temperature conversion program in Chapter 1, it isn't obvious, but the program has a problem — it can only handle integer temperatures. That is, the conversion program can only handle whole numbers that don't have a fractional part. This limitation of only using integers is not a problem for daily use because it isn't likely that someone (except a meteorologist) would get all excited about entering a fractional temperature, such as 10.5°. A worse problem is that the conversion program lops off the fractional portion of temperatures that it calculates without complaint. This can result in Minnesota getting the credit (again) for having the record low temperature, even though North Dakota beat them out by half a degree just because of an error caused by ignoring the fractional part of a number.

Reviewing the limitations of integers in C++

The `int` variable type is the C++ version of an integer. `int` variables suffer the same limitations as their counting integer equivalents in math do.

Integer round off

Consider the problem of calculating the average of three numbers. Given three `int` variables — nValue1, nValue2, and nValue3 — an equation for calculating the average is

```
(nValue1 + nValue2 + nValue3) / 3
```

Because all three values are integers, the sum is assumed an integer. Given the values 1, 2,and 2, the sum is 5. Five divided by 3 is 1⅔ ,or 1.666. Given that all three variables nValue1, nValue2, and nValue3 are integers, the sum is also assumed to be an integer. Unlike people (who are reasonable), computers (which are not always reasonable) force the quotient to be an integer by forcing 1.666 into 1.

Lopping off the fractional part of a number is called *truncation,* or rounding off. For many applications, truncation isn't a big deal. In fact, some might go so far as to consider it reasonable (not mathematicians or bookies, of course). However, integer truncation in computer programs can be much worse. Consider the following equivalent formulation:

```
nValue1/3 + nValue2/3 + nValue3/3
```

Plugging in the same 1, 2, and 2 values, you get a result of 0. To see how this can occur, consider that ⅓ truncates to 0, ⅔ truncates to 0, and ⅔ truncates to 0. The sum of 0, 0, and 0 is zero. (Sort of like that old song: "Nothing from nothing leaves nothing, ya gotta be something. . .") You can see that integer truncation can be completely unacceptable.

Limited range

A second problem with the int variable type is its limited range. A normal int variable can store a maximum value of 2,147,483,647 and a minimum value of -2,147,483,648 — more or less, plus 2 billion to minus 2 billion, for a total range of 4 billion.

Solving the truncation problem

The limitations of int variables can be unacceptable in some applications. Fortunately, C++ understands decimal numbers. A decimal number can have a nonzero fractional part. (Mathematicians also call these *real numbers.*) Decimal numbers avoid many of the limitations of int type integers. Notice that a decimal number "can have" a nonzero fractional part. In C++ the number 1.0 is just as much a decimal number as 1.5. The equivalent integer is written simply as 1.

C++ refers to decimal numbers as floating-point numbers or simply floats. The term floating point stems from the fact that the decimal point is allowed to float back and forth as necessary to express the value. Floating-point variables are declared in the same way as int variables:

```
float fValue1;
```

From this point forward the variable fValue1 is declared to be a float. Once declared, you cannot change the type of a variable. fValue1 is now a float and will be a float for the remainder of its natural instructions. To see how floating-point numbers fix the truncation problem inherent with integers, convert all the `int` variables to `float`:

```
1/3 + 2/3 + 2/3
```

is equivalent to

```
0.333... + 0.666... + 0.666...
```

which equals

```
1.666...
```

The programs `IntAverage` and `FloatAverage` are available on the enclosed CD to demonstrate this averaging example.

Examining the limitations of floating point

While floating point variables can solve many calculation problems such as truncation, they have a number of limitations themselves. These problems are sort of the reverse of those associated with integer variables. `float` variables cannot be used as counting numbers, they are more difficult for the computer, and they also suffer from round-off error (though not nearly to the same degree as `int` variables).

Counting

You cannot use floating-point variables in applications where counting is important. This includes C++ constructs, which requires counting ability. C++ can't verify which whole number value is meant by a given floating-point number.

For example, it's clear that 1.0 is 1. But what about 0.9 or 1.1? Should these also be considered as 1? C++ simply avoids the problem by insisting on using `int` values when counting is involved.

Calculation speed

Historically, a computer processor can process integer arithmetic quicker than floating-point arithmetic. Thus, while a processor can add 1,000 integer numbers in a given amount of time, the same processor can perform only 200 floating-point calculations.

Calculation speed is becoming less of a problem as microprocessors increase in ability. Most modern processors contain special calculation circuitry for performing floating-point calculations almost as fast as integer calculations.

Loss of accuracy

Floating-point variables cannot solve all computational problems. Floating-point variables have a limited precision of about 6 digits — an extra-economy size, double-strength version of float can handle some 15 significant digits with room left over for lunch.

To evaluate the problem, consider that ⅓ is expressed as 0.333 . . . in a continuing sequence. The concept of an infinite series makes sense in math, but not to a computer. The computer has a finite accuracy. Average 1, 2, and 2 and you get 1.666667.

C++ can correct for many forms of round off error. For example, in output, C++ can determine that instead of 0.999999, that the user really meant 1. In other cases, even C++ cannot correct for round-off error.

Not so limited range

The float data type also has a limited range though the range of a float is much larger than that of an integer. The maximum value for an int is a skosh more than 2 billion. The maximum value of a float variable is roughly 10 to the 38th power. That's 1 followed by 38 zeroes.

Only the first 6 digits have any meaning as the remaining 32 digits suffer from floating-point round-off error. Thus, a floating-point variable can hold the value 123,000,000 without round-off error but not 123,456,789.

Declaring Variable Types

You have seen that variables must be declared and that they must be assigned a type. C++ provides a number of different variable types. See Table 2-1 for a list of variables, their advantages and limitations.

Table 2-1	C++ Variables	
Variable	*Example*	*Purpose*
int	1	A simple counting number, either positive or negative.
float	1.0F	A real number.
double	1.0	A larger version of float that takes more memory but has more accuracy and greater range.

Variable	Example	Purpose
char	c	A single char variable stores a single alphabetic or digital character. Not suitable for arithmetic.
string	"this is a string"	A string of characters forming a sentence or phrase.
long	10L	A potentially larger version of int. There is no difference between long and int with GNU C++ and Microsoft Visual C++.

The following statement declares a variable lVariable as type long and sets it equal to the value 1, while dVariable is a double set to the value 1.0.

```
// declare a variable and set it to 1
long lVariable;
lVariable = 1;

// declare a variable of type double and set it to 1.0
double dVariable;
dVariable = 1.0;
```

You can declare a variable and initialize it in the same statement:

```
int nVariable = 1;   // declare a variable and
                     // initialize it to 1
```

The only benefit to initializing a variable in the declaration is that it saves typing; however, such declarations are common.

A char variable can hold a single character, whereas a string holds a string of characters. Thus, a is the character a, whereas a is a string containing just the letter a. (String is not actually a variable type but for most purposes you can treat it as such. Chapter 9 describes strings in detail.)

The character a and the string a are not the same thing. If an application requires a string, you cannot provide a character, even if the string contains only the single character.

Types of constants

A constant is an explicit number or character (such as 1, 0.5, or 'c'). Constants have a type just like variables. In an expression such as n = 1;, the constant 1 is an int. To make 1 a long integer, write the statement as n = 1L;. The analogy is as follows: 1 represents a single ball in the bed of a pickup truck, while 1L is a single ball in a dump truck. The ball is the same, but the capacity of its container is much larger.

Following the *int* to *long* comparison, 1.0 represents the value 1, but in a floating-point container. Notice, however, that the default for floating point constants is double. Thus, 1.0 is a double number and not a float.

Special characters

You can store any printable character you want in a char or string variable. You can also store a set of non-printable characters that is used as character constants. See Table 2-2 for a description of these important nonprintable characters.

Table 2-2	Special Characters
Character Constant	*Action*
\n	new line
\t	tab
\0	null
\\	backslash

You have already seen the newline character at the end of strings. This character breaks a string up onto separate lines. However, a newline may appear anywhere within a string. For example,

```
"This is line 1\nThis is line 2"
```

appears on the output as:

```
This is line 1
This is line 2
```

Similarly, the \t tab character moves output to the next tab position. This position can vary, depending on the type of computer you are using to run the program. Because the backslash character is used to signify special characters, a character pair for the backslash itself is required. The character \\ represents the backslash.

C++ collision with MS-DOS file names

MS-DOS uses the backslash character to separate folder names in the path to a file. Thus, root\folderA\file represents File within FolderA which is a subdirectory of Root.

Unfortunately, MS-DOS's use of backslash conflicts with the use of backslash to indicate an escape character in C++. The character \ \ is a backslash in C++. The MS-DOS path root\folderA\file is represented in C++ string as root\\folderA\\file.

Mixed Mode Expressions

C++ allows you to mix variable types in a single expression. That is, you are allowed to add an integer with a double. The following expression where nValue1 is an int is allowed:

```
// in the following expression the value of nValue1
// is converted into a double before performing the
// assignment
int nValue1 = 1;
nValue1 + 1.0;
```

An expression in which the two operands are not the same type is called a *mixed mode expression*. Mixed mode expressions generate a value whose type is equal to the more capable of the two operands. In this case, nValue1 is converted to a double before the calculation proceeds. Similarly, an expression of one type may be assigned to a variable of a different type as in the following statement:

```
// in the following assignment, the whole
// number part of fVariable is stored into nVariable
float fVariable = 1.0;
int nVariable;
nVariable = fVariable;
```

You can loose precision or range if the variable on the left-hand side of the assignment is smaller. In the previous example, you must truncate the value of fVariable before storing in nVariable.

Naming conventions

You may have noticed that the name of each variable begins with a special character that seems to have nothing to do with the name. These special characters are shown in the following table. You can immediately recognize dVariable as a variable of type double by using this convention.

These leading characters help the programmer keep track of the variable type. Thus, you can immediately identify the following as a mixed mode assignment of a long variable to an int variable.

    nVariable = lVariable;

Although this book uses some special characters in variable names, these characters have no significance to C++. You can use the letter

q to signify int, if you desire. I used this first-letter-naming convention in this chapter to simplify the discussion; however, many programmers use this naming scheme all the time.

Character	Type
n	int
l	long
f	float
d	double
c	character
sz	string

Converting a larger size value into a smaller type is called *demotion*, while converting values in the opposite direction is known as *promotion*. Programmers say that the value of int variable nVariable1 is promoted to a double as in the following:

```
int nVariable1 = 1;
double dVariable = nVariable1;
```

Mixed mode expressions are not a good idea. Avoid forcing C++ to do your conversions for you.

Chapter 3

Performing Mathematical Operations

· ·

· ·

A mathematician uses more than just the variables described in Chapter 2. A mathematician must do something with those variables: She can add them together, subtract them, multiply them, an almost endless list of other operations.

C++ offers the same set of basic operations: C++ programs can multiply, add, divide, and so forth. Programs have to be able to perform these operations in order to get anything done. What good is an insurance program if it can't calculate how much you're supposed to (over) pay?

C++ operations look like the arithmetic operations you would perform on a piece of paper, except for the fact that variables must be declared before they can be used (as detailed in Chapter 2):

```
int var1;
int var2 = 1;
var1 = 2 * var2;
```

Two variables, var1 and var2, are declared. var2 is initialized to 1. var1 is assigned the value resulting from the calculation 2 times the value of var2.

This chapter describes the complete set of C++ mathematical operators.

Performing Simple Binary Arithmetic

A binary operator is one that has two arguments. If you can say `var1 op var2`, then op must be a binary operator. The most common binary operators are the simple operations you performed in grade school. The binary operators are flagged in Table 3-1.

Table 3-1	Mathematical Operators in Order of Precedence	
Precedence	*Operator*	*Meaning*
1	+ (unary)	Effectively does nothing
1	- (unary)	Returns the negative of its argument
2	++ (unary)	Increment
2	-- (unary)	Decrement
3	* (binary)	Multiplication
3	/ (binary)	Division
3	% (binary)	Module
4	+ (binary)	Addition
4	- (binary)	Subtraction
5	=, *=,%=,+=,-= (special)	Assignment types

Multiplication, division, modulus, addition, and subtraction are the operators used to perform arithmetic. In practice, they work just like the familiar arithmetic operations as well:

```
float var = 133 / 12;
```

Each of these binary operators has the conventional meaning that you studied in grammar school with one exception. You may not have encountered modulus in your studies.

The modulus operator (%) is similar to the remainder after division. For example, 4 goes into 15 three times with a remainder of 3. Expressed in C++ terms, 15 modulus 4 is 3.

```
int var = 15 % 4; // var is initialized to 3
```

Because programmers are always trying to impress nonprogrammers with the simplest things, C++ programmers define modulus as follows:

```
IntValue % IntDivisor
```

is equal to

```
IntValue - (IntValue / IntDivisor) * IntDivisor
```

Try this out on this example:

```
15 % 4 is equal to 15 - (15/4) * 4
                   15 - 3 * 4
                   15 - 12
                   3
```

Modulus is not defined for floating point variable because it depends on the round-off error inherent in integers. (I discuss round-off errors in Chapter 2.)

Decomposing Expressions

The most common type of statement in C++ is the expression. An *expression* is a C++ statement with a value. All expressions also have a type such as int, double, char, and so on. A statement involving any of the mathematical operators is an expression since all these operators return a value. For example, 1 + 2 is an expression whose value is 3 and type is int. (Remember that constants without decimal points are ints.)

Expressions can be complex or extremely simple. In fact, the statement 1 is an expression because it has a value (1) and a type (int). There are five expressions in the following statement:

```
z = x * y + w;
```

The expressions are:

```
x * y + w
x * y
x
y
w
```

An unusual aspect of C++ is that an expression is a complete statement. Thus, the following is a legal C++ statement:

```
1;
```

All expressions have a type. The type of the expression 1 is int.

Determining the Order of Operations

All operators perform some defined function. In addition, all operators have a precedence. The precedence of the operator determines the order in which the expressions are evaluated. This solves the following problem:

```
int var = 2 * 3 + 1;
```

If the addition is performed before the multiplication then the value of the expression is 2 times 4 or 8. If the multiplication is performed first, the value is 6 + 1 or 7.

The precedence of the operators determines who goes first. Table 3-1 shows that multiplication has higher precedence than addition, so the result is 7. (The concept of precedence is also present in arithmetic. C++ adheres to the common arithmetic precedence.)

So what happens when we use two operators of the same precedence in the same expression?

```
int var = 8 / 4 / 2;
```

Is this 8 divided by 2 or 4, or is it 2 divided by 2 or 1? When operators of the same precedence appear in the same expression, they are evaluated from left to right (this is also the same common rule applied in arithmetic). Thus, the answer is 8 divided by 4, which is 2 divided by 2 (which is 1).

The expression

```
x / 100 + 32
```

divides x by 100 before adding 32. But what if the programmer wanted to divide x by 100 plus 32? The programmer can bundle expressions together using parentheses as follows:

```
x/(100 + 32)
```

This has the same effect as dividing x by 132.

The original expression

```
x / 100 + 32
```

is identical to the expression

```
(x/100) + 32
```

Why did C++ bundle the expressions the way it did? In a given expression, C++ performs multiplication and division before addition or subtraction. Multiplication and division have higher precedence than addition and subtraction.

In summary: Precedence refers to the order in which operators are evaluated. An operator with higher precedence is executed first. You can override the precedence of an operator by using parentheses.

Performing Unary Operations

Arithmetic binary operators, those operators that take two arguments, are familiar. You've probably been doing binary operations since the first grade in school. Unary operators are those operators that take a single argument: for example, -a. Many of these operations are not so well known.

The unary mathematical operators are +, -, ++ and −−. Thus:

```
int var1 = 10;
int var2 = -var1;
```

The latter expression uses the unary operator — to calculate the value negative 10.

The minus operator changes the sign of its argument. Positive numbers become negative and vice versa. The plus operator does not change the sign of its argument. Effectively, the plus operator has no effect at all.

The ++ and the −− operators might be new to you. These operators increment and decrement their arguments by one. The increment and decrement operators are limited to non-floating point variables. The value of var after executing the following expression is 11.

```
int var = 10;    // initalize var
var++;           // now increment it
                 // value of var is now 11
```

The increment and decrement operators are peculiar in that both come in two flavors: a prefix version and a postfix version. Consider the increment operator (the decrement is exactly analogous).

Suppose that the variable n has the value 5. Both ++n and n++ increment n to the value 6. The difference between the two is that the value of ++n in an expression is 6 while the value of n++ is 5. This is demonstrated in the following example:

```
// declare three integer variables
int n1, n2, n3;

// the value of both n1 and n2 is 6
n1 = 5;
n2 = ++n1;

// the value of n1 is 6 but the value of n3 is 5
n1 = 5;
n3 = n1++;
```

Thus, n2 is given the value of n1 after n1 has been incremented using the pre-increment operator, while n3 gets the value of n1 before it is incremented using the post-increment operator.

Using Assignment Operators

The assignment operators are binary operators that change the value of their left argument. The simple assignment operator, the =, is an absolute necessity in any programming language. This operator stores the value of the right-hand argument into the left argument. However, the other assignment operators appear to be someone's whim.

The creators of C++ noticed that assignments often follow the form:

```
variable = variable # constant
```

where # is some binary operator. Thus, to increment an integer operator by two, the programmer might write:

```
nVariable = nVariable + 2;
```

This says "add two to the value of nVariable and store the results back into nVariable."

It is common to see the same variable on both the right and left side of an assignment.

Because the same variable appears on both sides of the = sign, they decided to add the operator to the assignment operator. All of the binary operators have an assignment version. Thus, the assignment above could have been written:

```
nVariable += 2;
```

Once again this says "add 2 to the value of nVariable."

Why define a separate increment operator?

The authors of C++ noted that programmers add 1 more than any other constant. As a convenience factor, a special add 1 instruction was added to the language.

In addition, most computer processors have an increment instruction that is faster than the addition instruction. When C++ was created with microprocessors being what they were, saving a few instructions was a big deal.

Other than assignment itself, these assignment operators are not used that often. In certain cases, they can actually make the resulting program easier to read.

Chapter 4

Performing Logical Operations

● ●

In This Chapter

▶ Using sometimes illogical logical operators

▶ Defining logical variables

▶ Operating with bitwise logical operators logically a bit at a time

● ●

*T*he most common statement in C++ is the expression. Most expressions involve the arithmetic operators such as addition (+), subtraction (-) and multiplication (*). This chapter describes these types of expressions.

There is a whole other class of operators known as the *logical operators*. By comparison with the arithmetic operators, most people don't think about operations.

It isn't that people don't deal with logical operations. People compute AND and OR constantly. I won't eat cereal without cereal AND milk AND sugar (lots of sugar). I'll have a bourbon OR scotch. People use logical operations all the time, it's just that they don't write them down or think of them in that light.

Logical operators fall into two types. The AND and OR operators are what I will call simple logical operators. There is a second type of operator, the bit-wise operator, which is unique to the computer world. This type of operator looks at each of the bits that make up the computer's internal representation of a number.

Why Mess with Logical Operations?

If I could get through this much of my life without worrying about logical operations, then why start now? C++ programs have to make decisions. A program that can't make decisions is of limited use. The Conversion program (see Chapter 1) is about as complex you can get without some type of decision-making. Do this if the input variable is negative, do this if it's positive. Making decisions requires the use of logical operators.

Using the Simple Logical Operators

C++ programs must be able to make decisions. The Convert program from Chapter 1 that did nothing more than convert one temperature from Fahrenheit to Celsius was particularly unexciting because it did not make any decisions based on the input. C++ programs use the logical operators to make these decisions.

The simple logical operators, shown in Table 4-1, evaluate to true or false.

Table 4-1	Simple Operators Representing Daily Logic
Operator	*Meaning*
==	Equality; true if the left-hand argument has the same value as the right
! =I	Inequality; opposite of equality
>, <	Greater than, less than; true if the left-hand argument is greater than/less than the right-hand argument
>=, <=	Greater than or equal to, less than or equal to; true if either > or == is true/< or == is true
&&	AND; true if both the left-and right-hand arguments are true
||	OR; true if either the left-or the right-hand arguments are true
!	NOT; true if its argument is false

The first six entries in Table 4-1 are comparison operators. The equality operator is used to compare two numbers. For example, the following is true if the value of n is 0 and is false otherwise.

```
n == 0;
```

Don't confuse the equality operator == with the assignment operator =. Not only is this a common mistake, but it's a mistake that the C++ compiler generally cannot catch — that makes it more than twice as bad.

```
n = 0;    // programmer meant to say n == 0
```

The greater than (>) and less than (<) operators are similarly common in everyday life. The following expression logical comparison is true:

```
int n1 = 1;
int n2 = 2;
n1 < n2
```

It's easy to forget which is greater than and which is less than. Just remember that the operator is true if the arrow points to the smaller of the two.

You may think that n1 is greater than or less than n2; however, this ignores the possibility that n1 and n2 are equal. The greater than or equal to operator (<=) and less than or equal to operator (>=) are similar to the less than and greater than operators except that they include equality whereas the other operators do not.

The & (AND) and || (OR) are equally common. These operators are typically combined with the other logic operators:

```
// true if n2 is greater than n1 but smaller than nV3
(n1 < n2)& & (n2 < n3);
```

Just as an aside, you can define the greater than or equal to operator as follows:

```
n1 <= n2 is the same as (n1 < n2) || (n1 == n2)
```

Be careful performing logical operations on floating point variables

Real numbers are those numbers that can have a fractional part. Because of this, real numbers cannot be counting numbers. That is, you can say the first (1st), second (2nd), third, fourth, etc. because the relationship of 1, 2, and 3 are known exactly. It does not make sense to speak of the 4.5th number in a sequence. (This brings to mind the number between the fourth and fifth, but it has no real meaning).

Similarly the C++ type float, which is the C++ representation, is not a counting number. Even worse, unlike a real number, a floating number does not have an infinite number of digits beyond the decimal point. Because of this, you must be careful when using the comparison operators on floating-point numbers. Consider the following example:

```
float f1 = 10.0;
float f2 = f1 / 3;
f1 == (f2 * 3.0);    // are these two equal?
```

The comparison in the preceding example is not necessarily true. A floating-point variable cannot hold an unlimited number of significant digits. Thus, f2 is not equal to 3 and a third, but 3.3333. Unlike the mathematical concept, the number of threes after the decimal point is finite. After multiplying 3.3333 by 3, you are more likely to get 9.9999 than 10. Such small differences may be unnoticeable to a person but not to the computer. Equality means exactly that, exact equality.

Modern processors are very sophisticated in performing such calculations. The processor may, in fact, accommodate the round-off error, but from C++, you can't tell exactly what the processor will do.

Problems can arise even in a straightforward calculation, such as the following:

```
float f1 = 10.0;
float f2 = 100 % 10;
f1 == f2;                 // are these two equal?
```

Theoretically, f1 and f2 should be equal (refer to Chapter 3 if you don't remember the modulus operator). There doesn't appear to be any problem with round off; however, you can't be sure — you have no idea how the computer represents floating numbers internally. To flatly claim that 100 percent, 10 has no round-off error makes assumptions about the CPU internals.

The safer comparison is as follows:

```
float f1 = 10.0;
float f2 = f1 / 3;
float f3 = f2 * 3.0;
(f1 - f3) < 0.0001 && (f3 - f1) < 0.0001;
```

This comparison is true if f1 and f3 are within some delta of each other, which should be true even accounting for some small round-off error.

Short circuits and C++

The & & and || perform what is called *short circuit evaluation*. Consider the following:

```
condition1 && condition2
```

If condition1 is not true, then the result is not true no matter what the value of condition2 (for example., condition2 could be true or false without changing the result). Similarly in the following:

```
condition1 || condition2
```

If `condition1` is true, then the result is true no matter what the value of `condition2`.

To save time, C++ evaluates `condition1` first. C++ does not evaluate `condition2` if `condition1` is false in the case of & & or `condition1` is true in the case of | |.

Logical variable types

If `>` is an operator, then a comparison such as `a > 10` must be an expression. Clearly, the result of such an expression must be either TRUE or FALSE.

You may have noticed already that there was no Boolean variable type mentioned in our discussion of variable types back in Chapter 2. That is, there is no variable type that can have the value TRUE or FALSE. Then what is the type of an expression such as `a > 10`?

C++ uses the type `int` to store Boolean values. The value 0 is taken to be FALSE. Any value other than zero is TRUE. An expression such as `a > 10` evaluates to 0 (FALSE) or 1 (TRUE).

Microsoft Visual Basic also uses an integer to hold TRUE and FALSE values; however, in Visual Basic, a comparison operation returns either a 0 (FALSE) or a -1 (TRUE).

The new ANSI C++ standard does define a type `bool` to handle Boolean variables; however, it is not supported in the GNU C++, which comes on the enclosed CD-ROM.

Expressing Binary Numbers

C++ variables are stored internally as so-called binary numbers. Binary numbers are stored as a sequence of 1 and 0 values known as bits. Most of the time, you don't really need to deal with numbers at the bit level; however, there are occassions when doing so is convenient. C++ provides a set of operators for this purpose.

Because it is not often that you have to deal with C++ variables at the bit level, the remainder of this chapter should be considered a Techie section.

The so-called bitwise logical operators operate on their arguments at the bit level. To understand how they work, let's first examine how computers store variables.

The decimal number system

The numbers that we are familiar with are known as *decimal numbers* because they are based on the number 10. In general, the programmer expresses C++ variables as decimal numbers. Thus, you would say that the value of var is 123, for example.

A number such as 123 refers to $1 * 100 + 2 * 10 + 3 * 1$. Each of these base numbers — 100, 10, and 1 — are powers of 10.

```
123 = 1 * 100 + 2 * 10 + 3 * 1
```

Expressed in a slightly different but equivalent way:

```
123 = 1 * 10₂ + 2 * 10₁ + 3 * 10₀
```

Remember that any number to the zero power is 1.

Other number systems

The use of a base number of 10 for our counting system stems in all probability from the fact that humans have 10 fingers, the original counting tools. The alternative would have been base 20.

If our numbering scheme had been invented by dogs, it might well be based on the numeral eight (one digit of each paw is out of sight on the back part of the leg). Such an octal system would have worked just as well:

```
123₁₀ = 1 * 8² + 7 * 8¹ + 3 * 8A⁰ = 173₈
```

The small 10 and 8 here refer to the numbering system, 10 for decimal (base 10) and 8 for octal (base 8). A counting system may use any positive base.

The binary number system

Computers have essentially two fingers. (Maybe that's why computers are so stupid: without an opposable thumb, they can't grasp anything. And then again, maybe not.) Computers prefer counting using base 2. The number 123_{10} would be expressed as:

```
123₁₀ = 0*128 + 1*64 + 1*32 + 1*16 + 1*8 + 0*4 +1*2 + 1*1
      = 01111011₂
```

It is always convention to express binary numbers by using 4, 8, 32, or 32 binary digits even if the leading digits are zero. This is also because of the way computers are built internally.

Because the term *digit* refers to a multiple of ten, a *binary digit* is called a bit. The terms stem from binary digit. Four bits make up a byte. A word is usually either two or four bytes.

With such a small base, it is necessary to use a large number of bits to express numbers. It is inconvenient to use an expression such as 01111011_2 to express such a mundane value as 123_{10}. Programmers prefer to express numbers by units of bytes, or four bits.

A single four-bit digit is essentially base 16 beause four bits can express up any value from 0 to 15. Base 16 is known as the hexadecimal counting system. Hexadecimal is often contracted to simply, hex.

Hexadecimal uses the same digits for the numbers 0 through 9. For the digits between 9 and 16, hexadecimal uses the first six letters of the alphabet: A for 10, B for 11, etc. Thus, 123_{10} becomes $7B_{16}$.

```
123 = 7 * 16^1 + B (i.e. 11) * 16^0 = 7B_16
```

Because programmers prefer to express numbers in 4, 8, 32, or 64 bits, they similarly prefer to express hexadecimal numbers in 1, 2, 4, or 8 hexadecimal digits even when the leading digits are 0.

Finally, it is inconvenient to express a hexadecimal number such as $7B_{16}$ using a subscript because terminals don't support subscripts. Even on a word processor such as the one I am using now, it is inconvenient to change fonts to and from subscript mode just to type two digits. Therefore, programmers use the convention of beginning a hexadecimal number with a 0x (the reason for such a strange conviction goes back to the early days of C). Thus, 7B becomes 0x7B. Using this convention, 0x7B is equal to 123 while 0x123 is equal to 291.) Once I learned this, those computer nerds had a hard time losing me at dinner parties (until they start bring out that *.com* nonsense, anyway).

All of the mathematical operators can be performed on hexadecimal numbers in the same way that they are applied to decimal numbers. The reason that we can not perform a multiplication such as 0xC * 0xE in our head has more to do with the multiplication tables we learned in school than on any limitation in the number system.

Roman numeral expressions

It is interesting to note that some numbering systems do hinder computations. The Roman numeral system greatly hindered the development of math.

Adding two Roman numerals isn't too difficult:

XIX + XXVI = XLV

Think this one out:

a) IX + VI: The I after the V cancels out the I before the X so the result is V carry the X.

b) X + XX: Plus the carry X is XXXX, which is expressed as XL.

Subtraction is only slightly more difficult.

However, multiplying to Roman numerals requires a Bachelors degree in Mathematics. (You end up with rules like X promotes the digits on the right by 1 letter so that X IV becomes XL.) Division required a PhD and higher operations such as integration would have been completely impossible.

Performing Bitwise Logical Operations

All C++ numbers can be expressed in binary form. Binary numbers use only the digits 1 and 0 to represent a value. The following Table 4-2 defines the set of operations that work on numbers one bit at a time; hence the term bitwise operators.

Table 4-2	Bitwise Operators
Operator	*Function*
~	NOT: Toggle each bit from 1 to 0 and from 0 to 1
&	AND: Each bit of the left-hand argument with that on the right
|	OR
^	XOR

Bitwise operations can potentially store a lot of information in a small amount of memory. There are a lot of traits in the world that have only two (or, at most, four) possibilities — that are either this way or that way. You are either married or you're not (you might be divorced but you are still not currently married). You are either male or female (at least that's what my driver's license says). In C++, you can store each of these traits in a single bit — in this way, you can pack 32 separate properties into a single `int`, a 32-to-1 savings.

In addition, bit operations can be extremely fast. There is no performance penalty paid for that 32-to-1 savings.

The single bit operators

The bitwise operators (AND (&), OR (|) and NOT (~)) perform logic operations on single bits. If you consider 0 to be false and 1 to be true (it doesn't have to be this way, but that is the common convention), then you can say things like the following for the NOT operator:

```
NOT 1 (true)  is 0 (false)
NOT 0 (false) is 1 (true)
```

Similarly, the AND operator is defined as following:

```
1 (true) AND 1 (true)  is 1 (true)
1 (true) AND 0 (false) is 0 (false)
```

Similarly for the OR operator:

```
1 (true)  OR 0 (false) is 1 (true)
0 (false) OR 0 (false) is 0 (false)
```

The definition of the truth table for the AND and OR operators appear in the following table.

One other logical operation that is not so commonly used in day-to-day living is the or else operator commonly contracted to XOR. XOR is true if either argument is true but not if both are true. The truth table for XOR is shown in Table 4-3.

Table 4-3		Truth Table for the XOR Operator
XOR	*1*	*0*
1	0	1
0	1	0

Armed with these single bit operators, we can take on the C++ bitwise logical operations.

Using the bitwise operators

The bitwise operators operate on each bit separately.

The bitwise operators are used much like any other binary arithmetic operator. The NOT operator is the easiest to understand. To NOT a number is to NOT each bit that makes up that number:

```
~0110₂ (0x6)
 1001₂ (0x9)
```

Thus we say that ~0x6 equals 0x9.

The following calculation demonstrates the & operator:

```
  0110₂
&
  0011₂
  0010₂
```

Beginning with the most significant bit, 0 AND 0 is 0. In the next bit, 1 AND 0 is 0. In bit 3, 1 AND 1 is 1. In the least significant bit, 0 AND 1 is 0.

The same calculation can be performed in hexadecimal by first converting the number in binary, performing the operation and then converting the result back.

```
  0x6            0110₂
&         →  &
  0x3            0011₂
                 0010₂     →   0x₂
```

In shorthand, we say that 0x6 & 0x3 equals 0x2.

(Try this test: was is 0x6 | 0x3? Get this and you'll be in Seventh Heaven. Fail and you're taking the first in the Seven Steps to Hell. I was able to get this in just a little before eight minutes.)

A simple test

The following program serves as an example of the bitwise operators in action. The program initializes two variables and outputs the result of ANDing, ORing, and XORing them.

```cpp
// BitTest - initialize two variables and output the
//           results of applying the ~,& , | and ^
//           operations
#include <stdio.h>
#include <iostream.h>

int main(int nArg, char* pszArgs[])
{
    // set output format to hexadecimal
    cout.setf(ios::hex, ios::hex);

    // initialize two arguments
```

```
    int nArg1;
nArg1 = 0x1234;

    int nArg2;
nArg2 = 0x00ff;

    // now perform each operation in turn
    // first the unary NOT operator
    cout << "Arg1           = 0x" << nArg1 << "\n";
    cout << "Arg2           = 0x" << nArg2 << "\n";
    cout << "~nArg1         = 0x" << ~nArg1 << "\n";
    cout << "~nArg2         = 0x" << ~nArg2 << "\n";

    // now the binary operators
    cout << "nArg1 & nArg2 = 0x"
         << (nArg1 & nArg2)
         << "\n";
    cout << "nArg1 | nArg2 = 0x"
         << (nArg1 | nArg2)
         << "\n";
    cout << "nArg1 ^ nArg2 = 0x"
         << (nArg1 ^ nArg2)
         << "\n";

    return 0;
}
```

The first of statement in our program (the one right after the main keyword) that appears as `cout.setf(ios::hex);` sets the output format from the default decimal to hexadecimal (you'll have to trust me that it works for now).

The remainder of the program is straightforward. The program reads nArg1 and nArg2 from the keyboard and then outputs all combinations of bitwise calculations.

Executing the program on the values 0x1234 and x00ff using the Visual C++environment results in the following output:

```
Arg1           = 0x1234
Arg2           = 0xff
~nArg1         = 0xffffedcb
~nArg2         = 0xffffff00
nArg1 & nArg2 = 0x34
nArg1 | nArg2 = 0x12ff
nArg1 ^ nArg2 = 0x12cb
```

The GNU C++ compiler does not handle hexadecimal input or output. The preceding results are only achievable with Visual C++.

Hexadecimal numbers appear with a preceding 0x.

Why define such a crazy operator?

The purpose for most operators is clear. No one would quarrel with the need for the plus or minus operators. The use for the < or > operators is clear. It may not be so clear to the beginner when and why one would use the bitwise operators.

The AND operator is often used to mask out information. For example, suppose that we wanted to extract the least significant hex digit from a four-digit number:

```
    0x1234           0001 0010 0011 0100
  &            →&
    0x000F           0000 0000 0000 1111
                     0000 0000 0000 0100   →   0x0004
```

Another use is that of setting and extracting individual bits.

Suppose that you were using a single byte to store information about a person in a database that you were building. The most significant bit might be set to 1 if the person is male, the next set to 1 if a programmer, the next set to 1 if the person is handsome, and the least significant bit set to 1 if the person has a dog. See the following Table 4-4.

Table 4-4	Sample Bits and Settings
Bit	*Meaning*
0	1->male
1	1->programmer
2	1->Vulcan
3	1->owns a dog

This byte is encoded for each database and stored along with name, Social Security number, and any number of other illegal information.

A human (that is, non-Vulcan), male programmer who owns a dog would be coded as 1101_2. If you want to test all records in the records, searching for human programmers who don't own dogs irrespective of gender and whether or not they owned a dog, we would use the following comparison:

```
(databaseValue & 0x0110) == 0x0100
            *^^*              ^ ->  0 = not Vulcan
                              ^     1 = is a programmer
                       * -> no interest
                       ^ -> interested
```

In this case, the 0110 value is known as a mask because it masks away bit properties of no interest.

Chapter 5

Controlling Program Flow

● ●

In This Chapter

▶ Controlling the flow through the program

▶ Executing a group of statements repetitively

▶ Avoiding infinite loops

● ●

*T*he simple programs that appear in Chapters 1 through 4 process a fixed number of inputs, output the result of that calculation, and quit. However, these programs lack any form of flow control. They can not make tests of any sort. Computer programs are all about making decisions. If the user presses a key, the computer responds to the command.

For example, if the user presses Ctrl + C, the computer copies the currently selected area to the Clipboard. If the user moves the mouse, the pointer moves on the screen. If the user clicks the right mouse button with the Windows key depressed, the computer crashes. The list goes on and on. Programs that don't make decisions are necessarily pretty boring.

Flow control commands allow the program to decide what action to take based on the results of the C++ logical operations performed (see Chapter 4). There are basically three types of flow control statements: the branch, the loop, and the switch.

Controlling Program Flow with the Branch Commands

The simplest form of flow control is the branch statement. This instruction allows the program to decide which of two paths to take through C++ instructions based on the results on a logical expression (see Chapter 4 for a description of logical expressions).

In C++, the branch statement is implemented using the if statement:

```
if (m > n)
{
    // Path 1
    // ...instructions to be executed if
    // m is greater than n
}
else
{
    // Path 2
    // ...instructions to be executed if not
}
```

First, the logical expression m > n is evaluated. If the result of the expression is true, then control passes down the path marked Path 1 in the previous snippet. If the expression is not true, control passes to Path 2. The else clause is optional. If it is not present, then C++ acts as if it is present but empty.

Actually, the braces are optional if there is only one statement to execute as part of the if. However, it is very easy to make a mistake that the C++ compiler can't catch without the braces as a guide marker. It is always much safer to include the braces. If your friends try to entice you into not using braces, just say no.

The following program demonstrates the if statement:

```
// BranchDemo - input two numbers. Go down one path of the
//              program if the first argument is greater than
//              the first or the other path if not
#include <stdio.h>
#include <iostream.h>

int main(int arg, char* pszArgs[])
{

    // input the first argument...
    int arg1;
    cout << "Enter arg1: ";
    cin  >> arg1;

    // ...and the second
    int arg2;
    cout << "Enter arg2: ";
    cin  >> arg2;

    // now decide what to do:
    if (arg1 > arg2)
    {
        cout << "argument 1 is greater than argument 2\n";
```

```
    }
    else
    {
        cout << "argument 1 is not greater than argument
            2\n";
    }

    return 0;
}
```

Here the program reads two integers from the keyboard and compares them. If the expression "arg1 is greater than arg2" is true, then control flows to the output statement `cout << "argument 1 is greater than argument 2"`. If arg1 is not greater than arg2, control flows to the else clause where the statement `cout << "argument 1 is not greater than argument 2\n"` is executed.

Executing Loops in a Program

Branch statements allow you to control the flow of a program's execution from one path of a program or another. This is a big improvement but still not enough to write full strength programs.

Consider the problem of updating the computer display. On the typical PC display, one thousand pixels are drawn to update the entire display. A program outfit without the ability to execute the same code repetitively would need to include the same set of instructions over and over one thousand times.

What we really need is a way for the computer to execute the same (short) sequence of instructions one thousand times. Executing the same command multiple times requires looping statements.

Looping while a condition is true

The simplest form of looping statement is the `while` loop. The `while` appears as follows:

```
while(condition)
{
    // ...repeatedly executed as long as condition is true
}
```

The `condition` is tested. This condition could be `if var > 10` or `if var1 == var2` or anything else you might think of. If it is true, then the statements within the braces are executed. Upon encountering the closed brace, control returns to the beginning and the process starts over. The effect is that the C++ code within the braces is executed repeatedly as long as the condition is true. (Kind of like how I get to walk around the yard with my dog until she . . . well, until we're done.)

If the condition were true the first time, then what would make it be false in the future? Consider the following example program:

```cpp
// WhileDemo - input a loop count. Loop while
//              outputting astring arg number of times.
#include <stdio.h>
#include <iostream.h>

int main(int arg, char* pszArgs[])
{
    // input the loop count
    int loopCount;
    cout << "Enter loopCount: ";
    cin  >> loopCount;

    // now loop that many times
    while (loopCount > 0)
    {
        loopCount = loopCount - 1;
        cout << "Only " << loopCount << " loops to go\n";
    }
    return 0;
}
```

WhileDemo begins by retrieving a loop count from the user, which it stores in the variable loopCount. The program then executes a while loop. The while first tests loopCount. If loopCount is greater than zero the program enters the body of the loop (the body is the code between the braces) where it decrements loopCount by 1 and outputs the result to the display. The program then returns to the top of the loop to test whether loopCount is still positive.

When executed, the program WhileDemo outputs the results shown below. Here you can see that I entered a loop count of 5. The result is that the program loops 5 times, each time outputting a count down.

```
Only 4 loops to go
Only 3 loops to go
Only 2 loops to go
Only 1 loops to go
Only 0 loops to go
```

If the user enters a negative loop count, the program skips the loop entirely. Because the condition is never true, control never enters the loop. In addition, if the user enters a very large number, the program loops for a long time before completing.

A separate, less frequently used version of the while loop known as the do...while appears identical except that the condition isn't tested until the bottom of the loop:

```
do
{
    // ...the inside of the loop
} while (condition);
```

Because the condition isn't tested until the end, the body of the do...while is always executed at least once.

The condition is only checked at the beginning of the while loop or at the end of the do...while loop. Even if the condition ceases to be true some time during the execution of the loop, control does not exit the loop until the condition is retested.

Using the autoincrement/autodecrement feature

Programmers very often use the autoincrement ++ or the autodecrement -- operators with loops that count something. Notice from the following snippet extracted from the WhileDemo example, that the program decrements the loop count by using the assignment and subtraction statements

```
// now loop that many times
while (loopCount > 0)
{
    loopCount = loopCount - 1;
    cout << "Only " << loopCount << " loops to go\n";
}
```

A more compact version would have been to use autodecrement feature:

```
while (loopCount > 0)
{
    loopCount--;
    cout << "Only " << loopCount << " loops to go\n";
}
```

The logic in this version is the same as the original. The only difference is the way that loopCount is decremented.

Because the autodecrement both decrements its argument and returns its value, the decrement operation can actually be combined with the while loop. In particular, the following version is the smallest loop yet.

```
while (loopCount-- > 0)
{
    cout << "Only " << loopCount << " loops to go\n";
}
```

Believe it or not, the `loopcount-- > 0` is the version that most C++ programmers would use. It's not that C++ programmers like being cute — although they do. You will find the more compact version using the autoincrement or autodecrement feature embedded in the logical comparison easier to read as you gain experience.

Both `loopCount--` and `--loopCount` expressions decrement `loopCount`; however, the former returns the value of `loopCount` before being decremented and the latter after.

How often should the autodecrement version of `WhileDemo` execute when the user enters a loop count of 1? If you use the predecrement version, the value of `--loopCount` is 0 and the body of the loop is never entered. With the postdecrement version, the value of `loopCount--` is 1 and control enters the loop.

You might be fooled into thinking that the version of the program with the autodecrement command executes faster since it contains fewer statements. This is not the case, however. Modern compilers are pretty good at getting the number of machine language instructions down to a minimum no matter which of the above decrement instructions you use.

Using the for loop

A second form of loop is the `for` loop. The `for` loop is preferred over the more basic `while` loop because it is generally easier to read — there is really no other advantage.

The `for` loop has the following format:

```
for (initialization; conditional; increment)
{
    // ...body of the loop
}
```

Execution of the `for` loop begins with the initialization clause.

The initialization clause got its name because this is normally where counting variables are initialized. The initialization clause is only executed once when the `for` loop is first encountered.

Execution continues with the conditional clause. In similar fashion to the `while` loop, the `for` loop continues to execute as long as the conditional clause is true.

After completing execution of the code in the body of the loop, control passes to the increment clause before returning to check the conditional, thereby repeating the process. The increment clause normally houses the autoincrement or autodecrement statements used to update the counting variables.

The `while` equivalent to the `for` loop is:

```
initialization;
while(conditional)
{
    {
        // ...body of the loop
    }
    increment;
}
```

All three clauses are optional. If the initialization or increment clauses are missing, C++ ignores them. If the conditional clause is missing, C++ performs the `for` loop forever (or until something else passes control outside of the loop).

The `for` loop is better understood by example. The following `ForDemo` program is nothing more than the `WhileDemo` converted to use the `for` loop construct.

```
// ForDemo - input a loop count. Loop while
//             outputting astring arg number of times.
#include <stdio.h>
#include <iostream.h>

int main(int arg, char* pszArgs[])
{

    // input the loop count
    int loopCount;
    cout << "Enter loopCount: ";
    cin  >> loopCount;

    // count up to the loop count limit
    for (; loopCount > 0;)
    {
        loopCount = loopCount - 1;
        cout << "Only " << loopCount << " loops to go\n";
    }
    return 0;
}
```

This modified version of WhileDemo loops the same as it did before. However, rather than modify the value of loopCount, this ForDemo version uses a counter variable.

Control begins by declaring a variable and initializing it to the value contained in loopCount. It then checks the variable i to make sure that it is positive. If so, the program executes the output statement decrements i and starts over.

The for loop is also convenient when you need to count from 0 up to the loop count value rather than from the loop count down to 0. This is implemented by a simple change to the for loop:

```
// ForDemo - input a loop count. Loop while
//           outputting astring arg number of times.
#include <stdio.h>
#include <iostream.h>

int main(int arg, char* pszArgs[])
{

    // input the loop count
    int loopCount;
    cout << "Enter loopCount: ";
    cin  >> loopCount;

    // count up to the loop count limit
    for (int i = 1; i <= loopCount; i++)
    {
        cout << "We've finished " << i << " loops\n";
    }
    return 0;
}
```

Rather than begin with the loop count, this version of ForDemo starts with 1 and loops up to the value entered by the user. The use of the variable i for for loop increments is historical (stemming from the early days of the FORTRAN programming language).

When declared within the initialization portion of the for loop, the index variable is only known within the for loop itself. Nerdy C++ programmers say that the scope of the variable is the for loop. In the example above, the variable i is not accessible from the return statement since that statement is not within the loop. Not all compilers stick to this rule, however. You will need to test your own C++ compiler to see which way it works.

You might be tempted to ask, "If there is a while equivalent to the for command, while mess with the for loop?" (Go ahead . . . ask it.) By forcing the initialization, test, and increment features of any loop into fixed locations and format, the for loop is considerably easier to understand.

Avoiding the dreaded infinite loop

An *infinite* loop is an execution path that continues forever. An infinite loop occurs any time the condition, which would otherwise terminate the loop, cannot occur — usually due to some coding error.

Consider the following minor variation of the earlier loop:

```
while (loopCount > 0)
  {
      cout << "Only " << loopCount << " loops to go\n";
  }
```

The programmer forgot to decrement the variable loopCount as in the loop example below. The result would be a loop counter that never changed. The test condition would either be always false or always true. The program executes in a never ending or infinite loop.

I realize that nothing's infinite. Eventually the power will fail, the computer will break, Microsoft will go bankrupt, and dogs will sleep with cats. . . . Either the loop will stop executing or you won't care anymore.

You can create an infinite loop in many more ways than shown here, most of which are much more difficult to spot than this one.

Applying special loop controls

C++ defines two special flow control commands known as break and continue. It can happen that the condition for terminating the loop occurs neither at the beginning nor at the end of the loop but in the middle. Consider the following program that accumulated number of values entered by the user. The loop terminates when the user enters a negative number.

The challenge with this problem is that the program can't exit the loop until the user has entered a value, but must exit before the value is added to the sum.

For these cases, C++ defines the break command. When encountered, the break causes control to exit the current loop immediately. Control passes from the break statement to the statement immediately following the closed brace.

The format of the break commands is as follows:

```
while(condition) // break works equally well in for loop
  {
     if (some other condition)
```

```
        {
            break;    // exit the loop
        }
    }                 // control passes here when the
                      // program encounters the break
```

Armed with this new `break` command, my solution to the accumulator problem appears as the program BreakDemo.

```
// BreakDemo - input a series of numbers.
//             Continue to accumulate the sum
//             of these numbers until the user
//             enters a 0.
#include <stdio.h>
#include <iostream.h>

int main(int arg, char* pszArgs[])
{
    // input the loop count
    int accumulator = 0;
    cout << "This program sums values entered"
         << "by the user\n";
    cout << "Terminate the loop by entering "
         << "a negative number\n";

    // loop "forever"
    for(;;)
    {
        // fetch another number
        int value = 0;
        cout << "Enter next number: ";
        cin  >> value;

        // if it's negative...
        if (value < 0)
        {
            // ...then exit
            break;
        }

        // ...otherwise add the number to the
        // accumulator
        accumulator = accumulator + value;
    }

    // now that we've exited the loop
    // output the accumulated result
    cout << "\nThe total is "
         << accumulator
         << "\n";

    return 0;
}
```

After explaining the rules to the user (entering a negative number to terminate, etc.), the program enters what looks like an infinite `for` loop. Once within the loop, BreakDemo retrieves a number from the keyboard. Only after the program has read a number can it test to see if the number read matches the exit criteria. If the input number is negative, control passes to the `break` causing the program to exit the loop. If the input number is not negative control skips over the `break` command to the expression that sums the new value into the accumulator. Once the program exits the loop, it outputs the accumulated value and exits.

When performing an operation on a variable repeatedly in a loop, make sure that the variable is initialized properly before entering the loop. In this case, the program zeros `accumulator` before entering the loop where `value` is added to it.

The `continue` command is used less frequently. When the program encounters the `continue` command, it immediately passes back to the top of the loop. The remainder of the statements in the loop are ignored for the current iteration. The following example snippet ignores negative numbers that the user might input:

```
while(1)
{
    // input a value
    cout << "Input a value:";
    cin  >> inputVal;

    // if the value is negative...
    if (inputVal < 0)
    {
        // ...output an error message...
        cout << "Negative numbers are not allowe\n";

        // ...and go back to the top of the loop
        continue;
    }

    // ...process input like normal
}
```

Nesting Control Commands

Return to our PC screen repaint problem. Surely a loop structure of some type is used to write each pixel from left to right on a single line (do Hebrew displays scan from right to left?) What about repeatedly repainting each scan line from top to bottom? (Do PC screens in Australia scan from the bottom to the top?) For this, you need to include the left-to-right scan loop within the top-to-bottom scan line.

A loop command within another loop is known as a nested loop. As an example, you can modify the BreakDemo program into a program that accumulates any number of sequences. In this NestedDemo program, the inner loop sums numbers entered from the keyboard until the user enters a negative number. The outer loop continues accumulating sequences until the sum is 0.

```
// NestedDemo - input a series of numbers.
//              Continue to accumulate the sum
//              of these numbers until the user
//              enters a 0. Repeat the process
//              until the sum is 0.
#include <stdio.h>
#include <iostream.h>

int main(int arg, char* pszArgs[])
{
    // the outer loop
    cout << "This program sums multiple series\n"
         << "of numbers. Terminate each sequence\n"
         << "by entering a negative number.\n"
         << "Terminate the series by entering two\n"
         << "negative numbers in a row\n";

    // continue to accumulate sequences
    int accumulator;
    do
    {
        // start entering the next sequence
        // of numbers
        accumulator = 0;
        cout << "\nEnter next sequence\n";

        // loop forever
        for(;;)
        {
            // fetch another number
            int value = 0;
            cout << "Enter next number: ";
            cin  >> value;

            // if it's negative...
            if (value < 0)
            {
                // ...then exit
                break;
            }

            // ...otherwise add the number to the
            // accumulator
            accumulator = accumulator + value;
        }

        // output the accumulated result...
```

```
        cout << "\nThe total is "
             << accumulator
             << "\n";

        // ...and start over with a new sequence
        // if the accumulated sequence was not zero
    } while (accumulator != 0);
    cout << "Program terminating\n";
    return 0;
}
```

Switching to A Different Subject?

One last control statement is useful in a limited number of cases. The switch statement resembles a compound if statement by including a number of different possibilities rather than a single test:

```
switch(expression)
{
    case c1:
        // go here if the expression == c1
        break;
    case c2:
        // go here if expression == c2
        break;
    else
        // go here if there is no match
}
```

The value of expression must be an integer (int, long, or char). The case values c1, c2, and c3 must be constants. When the switch statement is encountered, the expression is evaluated and compared to the various case constants. Control branches to the case that matches. If none of the cases match, control passes to the else clause.

Consider the following example code snippet:

```
cout << "Enter a 1, 2 or 3:";
cin  >> choice;

switch(choice)
{
  case 1:
    // do "1" processing
    break;

  case 2:
    // do "2" processing
```

```
      break;

  case 3:
    // do "3" processing

  default:
    cout << "You didn't enter a 1, 2 or 3\n";
}
```

Once again, the `switch` statement has an equivalent, in this case the compound `if` statement; however, when there are more than two or three cases, the `switch` structure is much easier to understand.

The `break` statements are necessary to exit the `switch` command. Without the `break` statements, control falls through from one case to the next.

Part II

Becoming a Functional Programmer

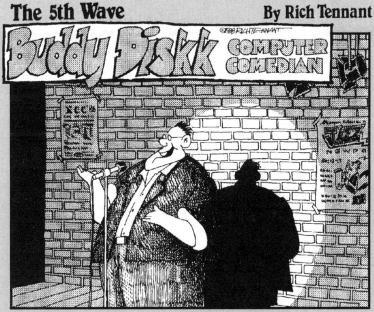

The 5th Wave   By Rich Tennant

Buddy Diskk COMPUTER COMEDIAN

"SO I SAID, 'WAITER! WAITER! THERE'S A BUG IN MY SOUP!' AND HE SAYS, 'SORRY, SIR, THE CHEF USED TO PROGRAM COMPUTERS.' AHH HAHA HAHA THANK YOU! THANK YOU!"

In this part . . .

1t's one thing to perform operations such as addition and multiplication — even when we're logical (AND, OR, and the like). It's another thing to write real programs. This section introduces the features necessary to make this leap into programmerdom.

Chapter 6

Creating Functions

● ●

In This Chapter

▶ Writing functions

▶ Passing data to functions

▶ Naming functions with different arguments

▶ Creating function templates

▶ Determining variable storage class

● ●

*D*evelopers often need the ability to break programs up into smaller chunks that are easier to develop. The programs developed in prior chapters have been small enough that this subdivision was not necessary; however, "real world" programs can be many of thousands (or millions!) of lines long. Without this ability to divide up the program into parts, developing such large programs would quickly become impossible.

C++ allows programmers to divide their code up into chunks known as functions. A function with a simple description and a well-defined interface to the outside world can be written and debugged without worrying about the code that surrounds it.

A good function can be described using a single sentence that contains a minimum number of ORs and ANDs. For example, the function sumSequence accumulates a sequence of integer values entered by the user. This definition is concise and clear.

This divide-and-conquer approach reduces the difficulty of creating a working program of significant size. This is a simple form of encapsulation — see Chapter 12 for more details on encapsulation.

Writing and Using a Function

Functions are best understood by example. This section starts with the example program, FunctionDemo, which simplifies the NestDemo program I discussed in Chapter 5 by defining a function to contain part of the logic. This section then explains how the function is defined and how it is invoked using an example program FunctionDemo as a pattern both of the problem and the solution.

NestDemo involves an inner loop, which accumulates a sequence of numbers surrounded by an outer loop that repeats the process until the user quits. Separating the two loops simplifies the program.

The following FunctionDemo program shows how NestDemo can be simplified by creating the function sumSequence().

Function names are normally written with a set of parentheses immediately following the term.

```
// FunctionDemo - demonstrate the use of functions
//                by breaking the inner loop of the
//                NestedDemo program off into its own
//                function

#include <stdio.h>
#include <iostream.h>

// sumSequence - add a sequence of numbers entered from
//               the keyboard until the user enters a
//               negative number.
//               return - the summation of numbers entered
int sumSequence(void)
{
    // loop forever
    int accumulator = 0;
    for(;;)
    {
        // fetch another number
        int value = 0;
        cout << "Enter next number: ";
        cin  >> value;

        // if it's negative...
        if (value < 0)
        {
            // ...then exit from the loop
            break;
        }

        // ...otherwise add the number to the
        // accumulator
```

```
              accumulator= accumulator+ value;
        }

        // return the accumulated value
        return accumulator;
}

int main(int arg, char* pszArgs[])
{
        cout << "This program sums multiple series\n"
             << "of numbers. Terminate each sequence\n"
             << "by entering a negative number.\n"
             << "Terminate the series by entering two\n"
             << "negative numbers in a row\n";

        // accumulate sequences of numbers...
        int accumulatedValue;
        do
        {
            // sum a sequence of numbers entered from
            // the keyboard
            cout << "\nEnter next sequence\n";
            accumulatedValue = sumSequence();

            // now output the accumulated result
            cout << "\nThe total is "
                 << accumulatedValue
                 << "\n";

        // ...until the sum returned is 0
        } while (accumulatedValue != 0);
        cout << "Program terminating\n";
        return 0;
```

Calling the function sumSequence ( )

First, concentrate on the main program contained in the braces following
main(). This section of code looks similar to NestDemo.

The main difference is the expression accumulatedValue =
sumSequence(); appearing roughly in the middle of the main() section. The
sumSequence() calls a function called sumSequence(). A value returned by
the function is stored in the variable accumulatedValue. This value is sub-
sequently displayed. The main program continues to loop until the sum
returned by the inner function is zero, which indicates that the user has finished calculating sums.

To call a function means to begin executing the code contained in the function. After this code is finished, control returns to the statement immediately
following the function call.

Defining the *sumSequence ( )* function

The statement int sumSequence(void) begins the definition of the
sumSequence() function. The block of code contained in the braces is the
function body. The function body of sumSequence() is identical to that found
in the inner loop of NestDemo.

So the declaration goes like this: The main program enters a loop that looks
like the outer loop in NestedDemo. In the middle of this loop where you
would have found an inner loop, all that is there is the call to
sumSequence(). When execution reaches this inner section, control passes
to the sumSequence() function, which accumulates a sum. This sum is
returned to the main body of code that continues with the remainder of the
outer loop.

Understanding the Details of Functions

Functions are so fundamental to the creating of C++ programs that understanding the details of defining, creating, and testing functions is critical.
With the example FunctionDemo program finished, here's a definition of
function.

A *function* is a logically separated block of C++ code. The function construct
has the following form:

```
<return type> name(<arguments to the function>)
{
    // ...
    return <expression>;
}
```

The *arguments* to a function are values that can be passed for the function to
use as input. The *return value* is a value that the function returns. For example, in the call to the function square(10), the value 10 is an argument to the
function square(). The returned value is 100.

Both the arguments and the return value are optional. If either is absent, the
keyword *void* is used instead. That is, if a function has a void argument list,
the function does not take any arguments when called (this was the case with
the FunctionDemo program). If the return type is void, the function does not
return a value to the caller.

In the example FunctionDemo program, the name of the function is
sumSequence(), the return type is int, and no arguments exist.

The default argument type to a function is `void`, meaning that it takes no arguments. A function `int fn(void)` may be declared as `int fn()`.

The function construct made it possible for me to write two distinct parts of the FunctionDemo program separately. I concentrated on creating the sum of a sequence of numbers when writing the `sumSequence()` function. I didn't think about other code that may call the function.

Similarly, when writing `main()`, I concentrated on handling the summation returned by `sumSequence()` while thinking only of what the function did — not how it worked.

Understanding Simple functions

The simple function `sumSequence()` returns an integer value that it calculates. Functions may return any of the regular types of variables. For example, a function might return a `double` or a `char`. (*int, double,* and *char* are a few of the variable types discussed in Chapter 5.)

If a function returns no value, the return type of the function is labeled void.

A function may be labeled by its return type. Thus, a function that returns an `int` is often known as an `integer function`. A function that returns no value is known as a *void function*.

For example, the following void function performs an operation, but returns no value.

```
void echoSquare()
{
    cout << "Enter a value:";
    cin >> value;
    cout << "\n The square is:" << value * value "\n";
    return;
}
```

Control begins at the open brace and continues through to the return statement. The return statement in a void function is not followed by a value.

The return statement in a void function is optional. If not present, execution returns to the calling function when control encounters the close brace.

Understanding functions with arguments

Simple functions are of limited use because the communication from such functions is one-way — through the return value. Two-way communication is through function arguments.

Functions with arguments

A *function argument* is a variable whose value is passed to the calling function during the call operation. The following example defines and uses a function `square()` that returns the square of a double precision float passed to it:

```
// SquareDemo - demonstrate the use of a function
//              which processes arguments

#include <stdio.h>
#include <iostream.h>

// square - returns the square of its argument
//          doubleVar - the value to be squared
//          returns - square of doubleVar
double square(double doubleVar)
{
    return doubleVar * doubleVar;
}

// sumSequence - add a sequence of numbers entered from
//               the keyboard and squareduntil the
//               user enters a negative number.
//               return - the summation of the square
//               of the numbers entered
int sumSequence(void)
{
    // loop forever
    int accumulator= 0;
    for(;;)
    {
        // fetch another number
        double dValue = 0;
        cout << "Enter next number: ";
        cin  >> dValue;

        // if it's negative...

        if (dValue < 0)
        {
            // ...then exit from the loop
            break;
        }

        // ...otherwise calculate the square
        int value = (int)square(dValue);
```

```
            // now add the square to the
            // accumulator
            accumulator= accumulator+ value;
        }

    // return the accumulated value
    return accumulator;
}

int main(int arg, char* pszArgs[])
{
    cout << "This program sums multiple series\n"
         << "of numbers. Terminate each sequence\n"
         << "by entering a negative number.\n"
         << "Terminate the series by entering two\n"
         << "negative numbers in a row\n";

    // Continue to accumulate numbers...
    int accumulatedValue;
    do
    {
        // sum a sequence of numbers entered from
        // the keyboard
        cout << "\nEnter next sequence\n";
        accumulatedValue = sumSequence();

        // now output the accumulated result
        cout << "\nThe total is "
             << accumulatedValue
             << "\n";

    // ...until the sum returned is 0
    } while (accumulatedValue != 0);
    cout << "Program terminating\n";
    return 0;
}
```

This is the same FunctionDemo() program, except that SquareDemo() adds
the square of the values entered. The function square() returns the value of
its one argument multiplied by itself. The change to the sumSequence() function is simple — rather than accumulate the value entered, the function now
accumulates the result returned from square().

Functions with multiple arguments

Functions may have multiple arguments that are separated by commas. Thus,
the following function returns the product of its two arguments:

```
int product(int arg1, int arg2)
{
    return arg1 * arg2;
}
```

Casting values

Line 38 of the *SquareDemo* program contains an operator never before seen:

```
accumulator = accumulator +
    (int)dValue;
```

The *(int)* in front of the *dValue* indicates that the programmer wants to convert the *dValue* variable from its current type, in this case *double*, into an *int* before performing the addition.

A *cast* is an explicit conversion from one type to another.

Any numeric type may be cast into any other numeric type. Without such a cast, C++ would have converted the types anyway, but would have generated a warning just to make sure that it's doing the correct conversion. The cast reassures the compiler that this conversion is what's wanted.

---

main () exposed

The "keyword" `main()` from our standard program template is nothing more than a function — albeit a function with strange arguments — but a function nonetheless.

When a program is built, C++ adds some boilerplate code that executes before your program ever starts. This code sets up the environment in which your program operates. For example, this boilerplate code opens the default input and output channels.

After the environment has been established, the C++ boilerplate code calls the function `main()`, thereby beginning execution of your code. When your program finishes, it exits from `main()`. This enables the C++ boilerplate to clean up a few things before turning control over to the operating system that kills the program.

Overloading Function Names

C++ allows the programmer to assign the same name to two or more functions. This multiple use of names is known as overloading functions or simply overloading.

In general, two functions in a single program cannot share the same name. If they did, C++ would have no way to distinguish them.

However, the name of the function includes the number and type of its arguments. (The name of the function does not include its return argument.) Thus, the following are not the same functions:

```
void someFunction(void)
{
    // ....perform some function
}
void someFunction(int n)
{
    // ...perform some different function
}
void someFunction(double d)
{
    // ...perform some very different function
}
void someFunction(int n1, int n2)
{
    // ....do something different yet
}
```

C++ still knows that the functions someFunction(void), someFunction(int), someFunction(double), and someFunction(int, int) are not the same. Like so many things that deal with computers, this has an analogy in the human world.

void as an argument type is optional. sumFunction(void) and sumFunction() are the same function. A function has a shorthand name, such as someFunction(), in same way that I have the shorthand name Stephen (actually, my nickname is Randy, but work with me on this one). If there aren't any other Stephens around, then people can talk about Stephen behind his back. If, however, there are other Stephens, no matter how handsome they might be, people have to use their full names — in my case, Stephen Davis. As long as we use the entire name, no one gets confused — no matter how many Stephens there might be. The full name for one of the someFunctions()is someFunction(int). As long as this full name is unique, no confusion occurs.

The analogies between the computer world (where ever that is) and the human world are hardly surprising because humans build computers. I wonder if dogs had built computers, would the standard unit of memory be a gnaw instead of a byte, or would requests group in packs instead of queues?

A typical application may appear as follows:

```
int intVariable1, intVariable2; // equivalent to
                                // int Variable1;
                                // int Variable2;
double doubleVariable;

// functions are distinguished by the type of
// the argument passed
someFunction();                 // calls someFunction(void)
someFunction(intVariable1);     // calls someFunction(int)
someFunction(doubleVariable);   // calls someFunction(double)
```

```
someFunction(intVariable1, intVariable2); // calls
                                  // someFunction(int, int)

// this works for constants as well
someFunction(1);             // calls someFunction(int)
someFunction(1.0);           // calls someFunction(double)
someFunction(1, 2);          // calls someFunction(int, int)
```

In each case, the type of the arguments matches the full name of the three functions.

The return type is not part of the extended name (also known as the function signature) of the function. The following two functions have the same name and, thus, cannot be part of the same program:

```
int someFunction(int n);     // full name of the function
                             // is someFunction(int)
double someFunction(int n);  // same name
```

The following is acceptable:

```
int someFunction(int n);
double d = someFunction(10); // promote returned value
```

The `int` returned by `someFunction()` is promoted into a `double`. Thus, the following would be confusing:

```
int someFunction(int n);
double someFunction(int n);
double d = someFunction(10);// promote returned int?
                             // or use returned double as is
```

C++ would know whether to use the value returned from the `double` version of `someFunction()` or promote the value returned from `int` version.

Defining Function Prototypes

The programmer may provide the remainder of a C++ source file, or module, the extended name (the name and functions) during the definition of the function.

The target functions `sumSequence()` and `square()` appearing earlier in this chapter were both defined in code that appeared before the actual call. This doesn't have to be the case: A function may be defined anywhere in the module. (A *module* is another name for a C++ source file.)

However, something has to tell main() the full name of the function before it can be called. Consider the following code snippet:

```
int main(int argc, char* pArgs[])
{
    someFunc(1, 2);
}
int someFunc(double arg1, int arg2)
{
    // ...do something
}
```

The call to someFunc() from within main() doesn't know the full name of the function. It may surmise from the arguments that the name is someFunc(int, int) and that its return type is void; however, as you can see, this is incorrect.

I know, I know — C++ could be less lazy and look ahead to determine the full name of someFunc()s on its own, but it doesn't. Like my crummy car, I've learned to live with it.

What is needed is some way to inform main() of the full name of someFunc() before it is used. What is needed is a before use function declaration. We need some type of prototype.

A prototype declaration appears the same as a function with no body. In use, a prototype declaration appears as follows:

```
int someFunc(double, int);
int main(int argc, char* pArgs[])
{
    someFunc(1, 2);
}
int someFunc(double arg1, int arg2)
{
    // ...do something
}
```

The prototype declaration tells the world (at least that part of the world after the declaration), that the extended name for someFunc() is someFunction(double, int). The call in main() now knows to cast the 1 to a double before making the call. In addition, main() knows that the value returned by someFunc() is an int.

A function call that returns a value is an expression. As with any other provide expression, you are allowed to throw the value returned by a function.

Variable Storage Types

Function variables are stored in three different places. Variables declared within a function are said to be local. In the following example, the variable localVariable is local to the function fn():

```
int globalVariable;
void fn()
{
    int localVariable;
    static int staticVariable;
}
```

The variable localVariable doesn't exist until the function fn() is called. localVariable ceases to exist when the function returns. Upon return, whatever value that is stored in localVariable is lost. In addition, only fn() has access to localVariable — other functions cannot reach into the function to access it.

By comparison, the variable globalVariable exists as long as the program is running. All functions have access to globalVariable all of the time.

The static variable staticVariable is something of a mix between a local and a global variable. The variable staticVariable is created when execution first reaches the declaration (roughly, when the function fn() is called). In addition, staticVariable is only accessible within fn(). Unlike localVariable, however, staticVariable continues to exist even after the program returns from fn(). If fn() assigns a value to staticVariable once, it will still be there the next time that fn() is called.

In case anyone asks, there is a fourth type, auto, but today it has the same meaning as local, so just ignore them. It's just like I ignore the blue smoke coming from my auto.

Chapter 7

Storing Sequences in Arrays

- -

In This Chapter

▶ Introducing the array data type

▶ Using arrays

▶ Initializing an array

▶ Using the most common type of array — the character string

- -

*A*n *array* is a sequence of variables that share the same name and are referenced using an index. Arrays are useful little critters that allow you to store a large number of values that are related in some way — for example, the batting averages of all the players on the same team might be a good candidate for storage within an array. Arrays can be multidimensional, too, allowing you, for example, to store an array of batting averages within an array of months, which allows you to work with the batting averages of the team as they occur by month. If you think about it long enough, you get a headache.

In this chapter, you find out how to initialize and use arrays for fun and profit. You also find out about an especially useful form of array, a *string,* which in C++ is really just an array of type `char`.

Considering the Need for Arrays

Consider the following problem. You need a program that can read a sequence of numbers from the keyboard. You'll use the now-standard rule that a negative number terminates input. Once the numbers have been read in, and only then, the program shall display them on the standard output device.

You can attempt to store numbers in a set of independent variables, as in:

```
cin >> value1;
if (value1 >= 0)
{
    cin >> value2;
    if (value2 >= 0)
    {
            ...
```

You can see that this approach can't handle sequences involving more than just a few numbers. Besides, it's ugly. What is needed is some type of structure that has a name like a variable but that can contain more than one variable. This is the purpose of the array.

An array solves the problem of sequences nicely. For example, the following snippet declares an array valueArray that has storage for up to 128 int values. It then populates the array with numbers entered from the keyboard.

```
int value;

// declare an array capable of holding up to 128 ints
int valueArray[128];

// define an index used to access subsequent members of
// of the array; don't exceed the 128 int limit
for (int i = 0; i < 128; i++)
{
    cin >> value;

    // exit the loop when the user enters a negative
    // number
    if (value < 0)
    {
        break;
    }
    valueArray[i] = value;
}
```

The second line of this snippet declares an array valueArray. Array declarations begin with the type of the array members: in this case, int. This is followed by the name of the array. The last element of an array declaration is an open and closed bracket containing the maximum number of elements that the array can hold. In this code snippet, valueArray can accommodate up to 128 integers.

This snippet reads a number from the keyboard and stores it into each subsequent member of the array valueArray. An individual element of an array is accessed by providing the name of the array followed by brackets containing the index. The first integer in the array is valueArray[0], the second is valueArray[1], and so on.

In use, `valueArray[i]` represents the `i`'th element in the array. The index variable `i` must be a counting variable — that is, `i` must be a `char`, an `int`, or a `long`. If `valueArray` is an array of `int`s, then `valueArray[i]` is an `int`.

Using an array

The following program inputs a sequence of integer values from the keyboard until the user enters a negative number. The program then displays the numbers input and reports their sum.

```
// ArrayDemo - demonstrate the use of arrays
//             by reading a sequence of integers
//             and then displaying them in order
#include <stdio.h>
#include <iostream.h>

// prototype declarations
int sumArray(int integerArray[], int sizeOfloatArray);
void displayArray(int integerArray[], int sizeOfloatArray);

int main(int nArg, char* pszArgs[])
{

    // input the loop count
    int nAccumulator = 0;
    cout << "This program sums values entered"
         << "by the user\n";
    cout << "Terminate the loop by entering "
         << "a negative number\n";

    // store numbers into an array
    int inputValues[128];
    int numberOfValues = 0;
    for(; numberOfValues < 128; numberOfValues++)
    {
        // fetch another number
        int integerValue;
        cout << "Enter next number: ";
        cin  >> integerValue;

        // if it's negative...
        if (integerValue < 0)
        {
            // ...then exit
            break;
        }

        // ... otherwise store the number
        // into the  storage array
        inputValues[numberOfValues] = integerValue;
    }
```

```
    // now output the values and the sum of the values
    displayArray(inputValues, numberOfValues);
    cout << "The sum is "
         << sumArray(inputValues, numberOfValues)
         << "\n";
    return 0;
}

// displayArray - display the members of an
//                array of length sizeOfloatArray
void displayArray(int integerArray[], int sizeOfArray)
{
    cout << "The value of the array is:\n";
    for (int i = 0; i < sizeOfArray; i++)
    {
        cout.width(3);
        cout << i << ": " << integerArray[i] << "\n";
    }
    cout << "\n";
}

// sumArray - return the sum of the members of an
//            integer array
int sumArray(int integerArray[], int sizeOfArray)
{
    int accumulator = 0;
    for (int i = 0; i < sizeOfArray; i++)
    {
        accumulator += integerArray[i];
    }
    return accumulator;
}
```

The program ArrayDemo begins with a prototype declaration of the functions sumArray() and displayArray() that it will need later. The main body of the program contains an input loop (boring). This time, however, the input values are stored off in the array inputValues.

Input occurs within the initial for loop. The input value is first stored off into the local variable integerValue. If it is found to be negative, control exits the loop through the break. If not, integerValue is copied into the array. The int variable numberOfValues is used as an index into the array.

numberOfValues was initialized to 0 up at the beginning of the for loop. The index is incremented on each iteration of the loop. The test in the for loop keeps the program from storing more than 128 entries because this is the size of the array. (The program goes immediately to the output portion after 128 entries whether the user enters a negative number or not.)

The array `inputValues` is declared as 128 integers long. If you're thinking that this is enough, don't count on it. Writing more data than an array causes your program to perform erratically and often to crash. No matter how large you make the array, always put a check to make sure that you do not exceed the limits of the array.

The main function ends by displaying the contents of the array and the sum. The `displayArray()` function contains the typical `for` loop used to traverse an array. Each entry in the array is added to the variable `accumulator`. The `sizeOfArray` passed to the function indicates the number of values contained in the array.

Notice yet again, that the index is initialized to 0 and not to 1. In additions, notice how the `for` loop terminates before `i` is equal to `sizeOfArray`. You don't want to add all 128 elements of `integerArray` to `accumulator` — none of the elements after the `sizeOfArray` element contains valid data.

Just to keep nonprogrammers guessing, the term *iterate* is used to mean traverse through a set of objects such as an array. Programmers say that the `sumArray()` function iterates through the array. In a similar fashion, the `displayArray()` function iterates through `integerArray`, displaying each element.

Initializing an array

A local variable does not start life with a valid value, including 0. Said another way, a local variable contains garbage until you actually store something into a local variable. Locally declared arrays are the same — each element contains garbage until you actually assign something to it. You should initialize local variables when you declare them. This rule is even more true for arrays. It is far too easy to access uninitialized array elements thinking that they are valid values.

Fortunately, an array may be initialized at the time it is declared. The following code snippets demonstrates how this is done:

```
float floatArray[5] = {0.0, 1.0, 2.0, 3.0, 4.0};
```

This initializes `floatArray[0]` to 0, `floatArray[1]` to 1, `floatArray[2]` to 2 and so on.

The number of initialization constants can determine the size of the array. For example, we could have determined that `floatArray` has 5 elements just by counting the values within the braces. C++ can count as well (here's at least one thing C++ can do for itself).

The following declaration is identical to the one above.

```
float floatArray[] = {0.0, 1.0, 2.0, 3.0, 4.0};
```

You may initialize all of the elements in an array to a common value by listing only that value. For example, the following initializes all 25 locations in floatArray to 1.0.

```
float floatArray[25] = {1.0};
```

Accessing too far into an array

Mathematicians start counting arrays with 1. The first member of a mathematical array x is x(1). Most program languages start with an offset of 1 as well. C++ arrays begin counting at 0. The first member of a C++ array is valueArray[0].

Sometimes I wonder whether they shouldn't call it Contrarion++. In indexing, a C++ array begins with 0; thus, the last element of a 128-integer array is integerArray[127] and not integerArray[128].

Unfortunately for the programmer, C++ does not check to see whether the index you are using is within the range of the array. C++ is perfectly happy giving you access to integerArray[200]. In fact, C++ will even let you access integerArray[-15].

As an analogy, suppose that distances on a highway were measured by equally spaced power line poles. (In Oklahoma this isn't too far from the truth.) We'll call this unit of measure a pole length. The road to my house begins at the turnoff from the main highway and continues to my house in a straight line. The length of this road is exactly nine pole lengths. If we begin numbering poles with the telephone pole at the highway, then the telephone pole next to my house is pole number 10.

You can access any position along the road by counting poles from the highway. If you measure from the highway to the highway, you calculate a distance of 0 pole lengths. The next discrete point is one pole length and so one until you get to my house at nine pole-lengths distance.

You can measure a distance 20 pole lengths away from the highway. Of course, this location is not on the road. (Remember that the road stops at my house.) In fact, there's no telling what you might find there. You might be on the next highway, you might be out in a field, you might even land in my neighbor's living room (that might be fun). Examining that location is bad enough, but storing something there could be a lot worse. Storing something in a field is one thing, but plop something down in my neighbor's living room and it's his. (I know because every time my newspaper misses my yard, it ends up in my neighbor's living room.)

By analogy, reading array[20] of a 10-element array returns a more or less random value. Writing to array[20] has unpredictable results. It may do nothing, it may lead to erratic behavior, or it may crash the program.

The most common incorrect location to access is integerArray[128]. While only one element beyond the end of the array, reading or writing this location is just as dangerous as any other incorrect address.

Using arrays?

On the surface, the ArrayDemo program doesn't do anything more than our earlier, non-array-based programs did. True, this version can replay its input by displaying the set of input numbers before calculating their sum, but this feature hardly seems earth shattering.

Yet, the ability to redisplay the input values hints at a significant advantage to using arrays. Arrays allow the program to process a series of numbers multiple times. The main program was able to pass the array of input values to displayArray() for display and then repass the same numbers to sumArray() for addition.

Defining and using arrays of arrays

Arrays are adept at storing sequences of numbers. Some applications require sequences of sequences. A classic example of this matrix configuration is the spreadsheet. Laid out like a chessboard, each element in the spreadsheet has both an x and a y offset.

C++ implements the matrix as follows:

```
int intMatrix[10][5];
```

This matrix is 10 elements in 1 dimension, and 5 in another, for a total of 50 elements. In other words, intMatrix is a 10-element array, each element of which is a 5-int array. As you might expect, one corner of the matrix is in intMatrix[0][0] while the other corner is intMatrix[9][4].

Whether you consider intMatrix to be ten elements long in the x dimension and in the y dimension is a matter of taste. A matrix may be initialized in the same way that an array is:

```
int intMatrix[2][3] = {{1, 2, 3}, {4, 5, 6}};
```

This initializes the three-element array intMatrix[0] to 1, 2, and 3 and the three-element array intMatrix[1] to 4, 5, and 6, respectively.

Using Arrays of Characters

The elements of an array are of any type. Arrays of floats, doubles, and longs are all possible; however, arrays of characters have particular significance.

Human words and sentences can be expressed as an array of characters. An array of characters containing my first name would appear as:

```
char sMyName[] = {'S', 't', 'e', 'p', 'h', 'e', 'n'};
```

The following small program displays my name:

```
// CharDisplay - output a character array to
//               standard output, the MS-DOS window
#include <stdio.h>
#include <iostream.h>

// prototype declarations
void displayCharArray(char stringArray[],
                      int sizeOfloatArray);

int main(int nArg, char* pszArgs[])
{
    char charMyName[] = {'S', 't', 'e', 'p', 'h', 'e', 'n'};
    displayCharArray(charMyName, 7);
    cout << "\n";
    return 0;
}

// displayCharArray - display an array of characters
//                    by outputing one character at
//                    a time
void displayCharArray(char stringArray[],
                      int sizeOfloatArray)
{
    for(int i = 0; i< sizeOfloatArray; i++)
    {
        cout << stringArray[i];
    }
}
```

The program declares a fixed array of characters charMyName containing — you guessed it — my name (what better name?). This array is passed to the function displayCharArray() along with its length. The displayCharArray() function is identical to the displayArray() function in our earlier example program except that this version displays chars instead of ints.

This program works fine; however, it is inconvenient to pass the length of the array around with the array itself. If we could come up with some rule, we wouldn't need to pass the size of the array — we would know that the array was complete when we encountered the special code character.

Let's use the code that 0 marks the end of a character array.

The character whose value is 0 is not the same thing as 0. The value of 0 is 0x10. The character whose value is 0 is often written as \0, whose value is 0x0, just to make it clear that this is a character.

The character \y is the character whose numeric value is y. The character \0 is known as the null character. Using that rule, the previous small program becomes:

```cpp
// DisplayString - output a character array to
//                 standard output, the MS-DOS window
#include <stdio.h>
#include <iostream.h>

// prototype declarations
void displayString(char stringArray[]);

int main(int nArg, char* pszArgs[])
{
    char charMyName[] =
            {'S', 't', 'e', 'p', 'h', 'e', 'n', 0};
    displayString(charMyName);
    cout << "\n";
    return 0;
}

// displayString - display a character string
//                 one character at a time
void displayString(char stringArray[])
{
    for(int i = 0; stringArray[i] != 0; i++)
    {
        cout << stringArray[i];
    }
}
```

The declaration of charMyName declares the character array with the extra null character \0 on the end. The displayString program iterates through the character array until a null character is encountered.

The function displayString() is simpler to use than its displayCharArray() predecessor. It is no longer necessary to pass along the length of the character array.

Further, `displayString()` works when the size of the character string is not known at compile time. This case occurs more often than you might think (see Chapter 9 for details).

This code of terminating a character array with a null is so convenient that it is used throughout the C++ language. C++ even gives such an array a special name.

A *string* is a null terminated character array.

C++ provides a more convenient means of initializing a string using double quotes rather than the single quotes used for characters. The following is exactly equivalent to Lines 11 and 12 in the previous example.

```
char szMyName[] = "Stephen";
```

The naming convention used here is exactly that, a convention. C++ does not care. The prefix `sz` stands for *zero-terminated string*.

The string `Stephen` is eight characters long and not seven — the null character after the `n` is assumed.

Manipulating Strings

The C++ programmer is often required to manipulate strings. C++ provides a number of standard string-manipulation functions to make the job easier. Try writing your own first to get an idea of how these functions work.

Writing our own concatenate function

You can write your own example string manipulation function to concatenate function by using array semantics and adding the test for a null at the end of the array. Consider the following example:

```
// Concatenate - concatenate two strings
//                with a " - " in the middle
#include <stdio.h>
#include <iostream.h>

// the following include file is required for the
// str functions
#include <string.h>

// prototype declarations
void concatString(char szTarget[], char szSource[]);
```

```
int main(int nArg, char* pszArgs[])
{
    // read first string...
    char szString1[256];
    cout << "Enter string #1:";
    cin.getline(szString1, 128);

    // ...now the second string...
    char szString2[128];
    cout << "Enter string #2:";
    cin.getline(szString2, 128);

    // ...concatenate a " - " onto the first...
    concatString(szString1, " - ");
    // strcat(szString1, " - ");

    // ...now add the second string...
    concatString(szString1, szString2);
    // strcat(szString1, szString2);

    // ...and display the result
    cout << "\n" << szString1 << "\n";

    return 0;
}

// concatString - concatenate the szSource string
//                onto the end of the szTarget string
void concatString(char szTarget[], char szSource[])
{
    // find the end of the first string
    int targetIndex = 0;
    while(szTarget[targetIndex])
    {
        targetIndex++;
    }

    // tack the second onto the end of the first
    int sourceIndex = 0;
    while(szSource[sourceIndex])
    {
        szTarget[targetIndex] =
            szSource[sourceIndex];
        targetIndex++;
        sourceIndex++;
    }

    // tack on the terminating null
    szTarget[targetIndex] = '\0';
}
```

The main function reads two strings using the `getline()` function. The alternate `cout >> szString` reads up to the first space. Here, you want to read until the Enter key.

Function `main()` concatenates the two strings using our `concatString()` function before outputting the result. The `concatString()` concatenates the second argument, `szSource`, onto the end of the first argument, `szTarget`. It does this in several stages.

The first loop within `concatString()` finds the end of the `szTarget` string. `concatString()` iterates through the string `szTarget` until `targetIndex` references the null at the end of the string. At this point, `targetIndex` now references the last character in the target string.

The loop `while(value == 0)` is the same as `while(value)` because value is considered false if it's equal to 0 and true otherwise. Also, this common shorthand takes a little getting use to.

The second loop iterates through the `szSource` string, copying each element from that string into `szTarget` starting with the first character in `szSource` and the last character in `szTarget`. The loop stops when `sourceIndex` references the null character in `szSource`.

The `concatString()` function tacks a final null character onto the resulting target string before returning.

Don't forget to terminate the strings that you construct programmatically. You will generally know that you forgot to terminate your string if the string appears to contain *garbage* at the end when displayed or if the program crashes inexplicably.

Make sure that the target array has enough room to handle the resulting concatenated string. It is very tempting to write C++ statements such as the following:

```
char dash[] = " - ";
concatString(dash, szMyName);
```

This doesn't work because `dash` is provided just enough room to store four characters. The function will undoubtedly overrun the end of the `dash` array.

Reviewing the C++ string handling functions

The C++ library provides a set of simple functions for manipulating strings. Some of these functions are more complicated than they might appear to be.

You can write your own versions — it can even be instructional, as was the case with the example of the *concatenate()* function. Using these functions can save you a lot of trouble and heartache, see Table 7-1.

Table 7-1	String-Handling Functions
Name	*Operation*
`int strlen(string)`	Returns the number of characters in a string
`void strcat(target, source)`	Concatenates the source string onto the end of the target string
`void strcpy(target, source)`	Copy a string into a buffer
`int strstr`	Find the first occurrence of one string in another
`int strcmp(source1, source2)`	Compare two strings
`int stricmp(source1, source2)`	Compare two strings without regard to case

You need to add the statement #include `<strings.h>` to the beginning of any program that uses the `str...` functions.

In the Concatenate program, the call to `concatString()` could have been replaced with a call to the standard C++ `strcat()` saving us the need to write our own version:

```
strcat(szString1, " - ");
```

These functions may seem somewhat backwards to any reasonable individual (this is an acid test for the reader). The second string is concatenated onto the end of the first argument. Our own `concatString()` was written the same way in order to mimic the C++ standard.

Handling wide characters

The standard C++ `char` type is an 8-bit field capable of representing the values from 0 to 255. There are 10 digits, as well as 26 lowercase letters plus 26 uppercase letters. Even if you add various umlaut and accented characters, you still have more than enough range to represent the Roman alphabet set and still have room left over for the Cyrillic alphabet.

Problems with the char type don't arise until you begin to include the oriental character sets, in particular the Chinese and Japanese kanjis. There are literally thousands of these symbols — much more than the lowly eight-bit character set.

C++ includes support for a newer character type called wchar, or wide characters. While this is not an intrinsic type like char, numerous C++ functions treat it as if it were. For example, wstrstr() compares two wide character sets. If you are writing international applications and need access to oriental languages, you will need to use these wide character functions.

Because this is an added level of complexity, I don't speak any more of it in this book.

Avoiding Obsolescent Output Functions

C++ provides a set of lower level input and output functions. The most useful is the printf() output function. In it's most basic form, printf() outputs a string to the default display.

```
printf("This string is output to display");
```

The printf() function performs output using a set of embedded format control commands each of which begins with a % sign. For example, the following prints out the value of an integer and a double variable.

```
int nInt = 1;
double doubleVar = 3.5;
printf("The int value is %i; the float value is %f",
        nInt, doubleVar);
```

The integer value is inserted at the point of the %i, while the double appears at the location of the %f:

```
The int value is 1; the float value is 3.5
```

The printf() function is not as difficult to use as it appears once you get used to its quirks. However, the stream version of output that the remainder of this book uses is easier (and less likely to be used incorrectly, as we see in later chapters — remember to always practice safe hex).

Chapter 8

Taking a First Look at C++ Pointers

· ·

In This Chapter

▶ Addressing variables in memory

▶ Declaring and using pointer variables

▶ Recognizing the inherent dangers of pointers

▶ Passing pointers to functions

▶ Allocating objects off of the heap (whatever that is)

· ·

*T*he C++ language is fairly conventional compared with other programming languages. Some computer languages lack (il) logical operators (see Chapter 4). C++ certainly presents its own unique syntax. C++ really separates itself from the crowd in definition and use of pointer variables. *Pointers* are variables that "point at" other variables. This is to say that pointer variables contain the addresses of locations in memory.

This chapter introduces the pointer variable type. It begins with some concept definitions, flows through pointer syntax, and then introduces some of the reasons for the pointer mania, which grips the C++ programming world.

What's in an Address?

Just as the saying goes, "Everyone has to be somewhere," every C++ variable is stored somewhere in the computer's memory. Memory is broken into individual bytes with each byte carrying its own address numbered 0, 1, 2, and so on.

A variable `intRandy` might be at address 0x100 while `floatReader` might be over at location 0x180. (By convention, memory addresses are expressed in hexadecimal.)

Just like a person, a variable takes a certain amount of room. Again, just like a person, some variable types take up more room than others. (I'm not going into whether I'm one of the large volume or small volume types.) The amount of storage consumed by the different variable types appears in the following table (these values are for Visual C++ 6 and GNU C++ executing on a Pentium processor).

Table 8-1	Variables and Storage Space
Variable Type	*Memory Consumed [Bytes]*
int	4
long	4
float	4
double	8

Consider the following Layout test program that demonstrates the layout of variables in memory. (Ignore the new & operator — let's just say for now that &n returns the address of the variable n.)

```
// Layout - this program tries to give the
//          reader an idea of the layout of
//          local memory in her compiler
#include <stdio.h>
#include <iostream.h>

int main(int intArgc, char* pszArgs[])
{
    int     m1;
    int     n;
    long    l;
    float   f;
    double  d;
    int     m2;

    // set output to hex mode
    cout.setf(ios::hex);

    // output the address of each variable
    // in order to get an idea of the size
    // of each variable
    cout << "--- = 0x" << (long)&m1 << "\n";
    cout << "&n  = 0x" << (long)&n  << "\n";
    cout << "&l  = 0x" << (long)&l  << "\n";
    cout << "&f  = 0x" << (long)&f  << "\n";
    cout << "&d  = 0x" << (long)&d  << "\n";
    cout << "--- = 0x" << (long)&m2 << "\n";

    return 0;
}
```

WARNING!

Don't worry if the values you see when running this program are different. Your program is storing its variables in a different memory range, which is expected. The relationship between the locations is the prime importance.

From the comparison of locations, we can also infer that the size of n is four bytes (0x65fdf4 - 0x65fdf0), the size of the long l is also four bytes (0x65fdf0 - 0x65fdec), and so forth.

GNU C++ and Visual C++ choose the same variable layout.

Using Pointer Variables

A *pointer variable* is a variable that contains an address, usually the address of another variable. See Table 8-2 for an example.

Table 8-2	Pointer Operators
Operator	*Meaning*
& (unary)	The address of
* (unary)	(in an expression) The thing pointed at by
	(in a declaration) Pointer to

You can see the use of these new operators in the following example:

```
void fn()
{
    int  intVar;
    int* pintVar;

    pintVar  = &intVar;  // pintVar now points to intVar
    *pintVar = 10;       // stores 10 into int location
                         // pointed at by pintVar
}
```

The function fn() begins with the declaration of intVar. The next statement declares the variable pintVar to be a variable of type pointer to an int. (By the way, pintVar is pronounced pee-int-Var, not pint-Var.)

Pointer variables are declared like normal variables except for the addition of the unary * character. This * character can appear anywhere between the base type name — in this case int —, and the variable name; however, it is becoming increasingly common to add the * to the end of the variable type.

The * character is called the *asterisk character* (that's logical enough), but because asterisk is hard to say, many programmers have come to call it the *splat character*. Thus, they would say splat pintVar.

Many programmers adopt a naming convention in which the first character of the variable name indicates the type of the variable, such as n for int, d for double, and so on. A further aspect of this naming convention is to place a p on the beginning of a pointer variable name.

In an expression, the unary operator & means the address of. Thus, we would read the first assignment as store the address of intVar in pintVar.

To make this more concrete, let's assume that the memory for function fn() starts at location 0x100. In addition, we'll assume that intVar is at address 0x102 and that pintVar is at 0x106. The layout here is simpler than the actual results from the Layout program; however, the concepts are identical.

The first assignment stores the value of &intVar (0x102) in the pointer variable pintVar. The second assignment in the small program snippet says store 10 in the location pointed at by pintVar. The value 10 is stored in the address contained in pintVar, which is 0x102 (the address of intVar).

Comparing pointers and houses

A pointer is much like a house address. Your house has a unique address. Each byte in memory has an address that is unique. A house address is made up of both numbers and letters. For example, my address is 123 Main Street (of course, it isn't — I lied — I don't want stalkers, unless, of course, they were female stalkers). An address in memory is just a series of numbers (like 123456). For reasons of convenience, computer addresses are generally written in hexadecimal, but that's immaterial.

You can store a couch in the house at 123 Main Street — you can store a number in the byte located at 0x123456. Alternatively, you can take a piece of paper and write down an address — I don't know, say, 123 Main Street. You can now store a couch at the house with the address written down on the piece of paper. In fact, this is the way delivery people work — their job is to deliver a couch to the address written down on the shipping orders whether it's 123 Main Street or not. (I'm not maligning delivery people — they have brains — it's just that this is more or less the way things work.)

In C++, this is written (loosely speaking):

```
House myHouse;
House* houseAddress;
houseAddress = &myHouse;
*houseAddress = couch;
```

In humanspeak, you would say myHouse is a House. houseAddress is the address of a House. Assign the address of myHouse to the House pointer, houseAddress. Now store a couch at the house located at the address stored in houseAddress.

Having said all that, let's look at the `int` and `int*` version of that:

```
int myInt;
int* intAddress;
intAddress = &myInt;
*intAddress = 10;
```

That is, `myInt` is an `int`. `intAddress` is a pointer to an `int`. Assign the address of `myInt` into the pointer `intAddress`. Finally, assign 10 to the `int` pointed at by `intAddress`.

Using different types of pointers

Every expression has a type as well as a value. The type of the expression `intVar` expression is pointer to an integer, written as `int*`. Comparing this with the declaration of `pintVar`, you see that the types match exactly:

```
int* pintVar = &intVar; // both sides of the assignment are
                        // of type int*
```

Similarly, because `pintVar` is of type `int*`, the type of `*pintVar` is `int`.

```
*pintVar = 10;     // both sides of the assignment are
                   // of type int
```

The type of the thing pointed to by `pintVar` is `int`. This is equivalent to saying that if `houseAddress` is the address of a house, then the thing pointed at by `houseAddress` must be a house. Amazing, but true.

Pointers to other types of variables are expressed the same way:

```
double doubleVar;
double* pdoubleVar = &doubleVar;
*pdoubleVar = 10.0;
```

A pointer on a Pentium class machine takes four bytes no matter what it points to. That is, an address on a Pentium is four bytes long, period.

Matching pointer types is extremely important. Consider what might happen if the following were allowed:

```
int   n1;
int*  pintVar;
pintVar  = &n1;
*pintVar = 100.0;
```

The second assignment attempts to store the eight-byte double value 100.0 into the four-byte space allocated for n1. Actually, this isn't as bad as it looks — C++ is smart enough to demote the constant 100.0 to an `int` before making the assignment.

It is possible to cast one type of variable into another:

```
int iVar;
double dVar = 10.0;
iVar = (int)dVar;
```

Similarly, it is possible to cast one pointer type into another.

```
int* piVar;
double dVar = 10.0;
double* pdVar;
piVar = (int*)pdVar;
```

Consider, however, what catastrophes can arise if this type of casting about of pointers were to get loose. Save a variable into an area of the wrong size and nearby variables can be wiped out. This is demonstrated graphically in the following LayoutError program.

```
// LayoutError - demonstrate the results of
//                 a messing up a pointer usage
#include <stdio.h>
#include <iostream.h>

int main(int intArgc, char* pszArgs[])
{
    int    upper = 0;
    int    n     = 0;
    int    lower = 0;

    // output the values of the three variables before...
    cout << "upper = " << upper << "\n";
    cout << "n     = " << n     << "\n";
    cout << "lower = " << lower << "\n";

    // now store a double into the space
    // allocated for an int
    cout << "\nPerforming assignment of double\n";
    double* pD = (double*)&n;
    *pD = 13.0;

    // display the results
     cout << "upper = " << upper << "\n";
    cout << "n     = " << n     << "\n";
    cout << "lower = " << lower << "\n";

    return 0;
}
```

The first three lines in main() declare three integers in the normal fashion. The assumption made here is that these three variables are laid out next to each other.

The next three executable lines output the value of the three variables. Not surprisingly, all three variables display as 0. The assignment *pD = 13.0; stores the double value 13.0 into the integer variable n. The three output statements display the values of all three variables after the assignment.

After assigning the double value 13.0 into the integer variable n, n itself is not modified at all; however, the nearby variable upper is filled with a garbage value. This is not good.

The house equivalent goes something like this:

```
House* houseAddress = &"123 Main Street";
Hotel* hotelAddress;
hotelAddress = (Hotel*)houseAddress;
*hotelAddress = TheRitz;
```

houseAddress is initialized to point to my house. The variable hotelAddress is a pointer to a hotel. Now, the house address is cast into the address of a hotel and saved off. Finally, The Ritz is plopped down on top of my house. Because The Ritz is a lot bigger than my house (Okay, slightly bigger than my house), it isn't surprising that TheRitz wipes out my neighbors' houses as well.

The type of the pointer saves the programmer from stuffing an object into a space that is too big or too small. The assignment *pintVar = 100.0; actually causes no problem — because C++ knows that pintVar points to an int, C++ knows to demote the 100.0 into an int before making the assignment.

Passing Pointers to Functions

One of the uses of pointer variables is in passing arguments to functions. To understand why this is important, you need to understand how arguments are passed to a function.

Passing by value

You may have noticed that it is not normally possible to change the value of a variable passed to a function from within the function. Consider the following example code segment:

```
void fn(int intArg)
{
    intArg = 10;
    // value of intArg at this point is 10
}

void parent(void)
{
    int n1 = 0;
    fn(n1);
    // value of n1 at this point is 0
}
```

Here the parent() function initializes the integer variable n1 to zero. The value of n1 is then passed to fn(). Upon entering the function, intArg is equal to 10, the value passed. fn() changes the value of intArg before returning to parent(). Perhaps surprisingly, upon returning to parent(), the value of n1 is still 0.

The reason is that C++ doesn't pass a variable to a function. Instead, C++ passes the value contained in the variable at the time of the call. That is, the expression is evaluated, even if it just a variable name, and the result is passed.

It is easy for a speaker to get lazy and say something like, "Pass the variable x to the function fn()." This really means to pass the value of the expression x.

Passing pointer values

Like any other intrinsic type, a pointer may be passed as an argument to a function:

```
void fn(int* pintArg)
{
    *pintArg = 10;
}

void parent(void)
{
    int n = 0;

    fn(&i);         // this passes the address of i
                    // now the value of n is 10
}
```

In this case, the address of n is passed to the function fn() rather than the value of n. The significance of this difference is apparent when you consider the assignment within fn().

Suppose n is located at address 0x102. Rather than the value 10, the call fn(&n) passes the value 0x106. Within fn(), the assignment *pintArg = 10 stores the value 10 into the int variable located at location 0x102, thereby overwriting the value 0. Upon returning to parent(), the value of n is 10 because n is just another name for 0x102.

Passing by reference

C++ provides a shorthand for the above — a shorthand that doesn't involve the hassle of dealing with pointers yourself. In the following example, the variable n is passed by reference.

In passed by reference, the parent function passes a reference to the variable rather than the value. *Reference* is another word for address.

```
void fn(int& intArg)
{
    intArg = 10;
}

void parent(void)
{
    int n = 0;
    fn(n)
                        // here the value of n is 10
}
```

In this case, a reference to n is passed to fn() rather than the value. The fn() function stores the value 10 into int location referenced by intArg.

Notice that reference is not an actual type. Thus, the function's full name is fn(int) and not fn(int&).

Making Use of a Block of Memory Called the Heap

The *heap* is an amorphous block of memory that your program can access as necessary. This section describes why it exists and how to use it.

Just as it is possible to pass a pointer to a function, it is also possible for a function to return a pointer. A function that returns the address of a double would be declared as follows:

```
double* fn(void);
```

However, one must be very careful when returning a pointer. In order to understand the dangers, you must know something about variable scope. (No, I don't mean a variable zoom rifle scope.)

Limiting scope

C++ variables have a property in addition to their value and type known as scope. *Scope* is the range over which a variable is defined (and not a mouthwash!).

Consider the following code snippet:

```
// the following variable is accessible to
// all functions and defined as long as the
// program is running(global scope)
int intGlobal;

// the following variable intChild is accessible
// only to the function and is defined only
// as long as C++ is executing child() or a
// function which child() calls (function scope)
void child(void)
{
    int intChild;
}

// the following variable intParent has function
// scope
void parent(void)
{
    int intParent = 0;
    fn();

    int intLater = 0;
    intParent = intLater;
}

int main(int nArgs, char* pArgs[])
{
    parent();
}
```

Execution begins with main(). The function main() immediately invokes parent(). The first thing that the processor sees in parent() is the declaration of intParent. At that point, intParent goes into scope — that is, intParent is defined and available for the remainder of the function parent().

The second statement in parent() is the call to child(). Once again, the function child() declares a local variable, this time intChild. The variable intChild is within the scope of child(). Technically intParent is not within the scope of child()because child() doesn't have access to intParent; however, the variable intParent continues to exist.

When child() exits, the variable intChild goes out of scope. Not only is intChild no longer accessible, but it no longer even exists. (The memory occupied by intChild is returned to the general pool to be used for other things.)

As parent() continues executing, the variable intLater goes into scope at the declaration. At the point that parent() returns to main(), both intParent and intLater go out of scope. The programmer may declare a variable outside of any function. This type of variable, known as a global variable, remains in scope for the duration of the program.

Because intGlobal is declared globally in this example, it is available to all three functions and remains available for the life of the program.

Examining the scope problem

The following code segment compiles without error but does not work:

```
double* child(void)
{
    double dLocalVariable;
    return &dLocalVariable;
}

void parent(void)
{
    double* pdLocal;
    pdLocal  = child();
    *pdLocal = 1.0;
}
```

The problem with this function is that dLocalVariable is defined only within the scope of the function fn(). Thus, by the time that the memory address of dLocalVariable is returned from child(), it refers to a variable that no longer exists. The memory that dLocalVariable formerly occupied is probably being used for something else.

This is a very common error because it can creep up in a number of different ways. Unfortunately, this error does not cause the program to instantly stop. In fact, the program may work perfectly well most of the time — as long as the memory formerly occupied by dLocalVariable is not reused immediately, the program continues to work. Such intermittent problems are the most difficult to solve.

Providing a solution using the heap

The scope problem originated from the fact that C++ returned the locally defined memory before the programmer was ready. What is needed is a block of memory controlled by the programmer. She can allocate the memory and put it back when she wants to — not because C++ thinks it a good idea. Such a block of memory is called the *heap*.

Heap memory is allocated using the `new` command followed by the type of object to allocate. For example, the following allocates a `double` variable off the heap.

```
double* child(void)
{
    double* pdLocalVariable = new double;
    return pdLocalVariable;
}
```

Although the variable `pdLocalVariable` goes out of scope when the function `child()` returns, the memory to which `pdLocalVariable` refers does not. A memory location returned by `new` does not go out of scope until it is explicitly returned to the heap using the `delete` command:

```
void parent(void)
{
    // child() returns the address of a block
    // of heap memory
    double* pdMyDouble = child();

    // store a value there
    *pdMyDouble = 1.1;

    // ...

    // now return the memory to the heap
    delete pdMyDouble;
    pdMyDouble = 0;

    // ...
}
```

Here the pointer returned by `child()` is used to store a double value. Once the function is finished with the memory location, it is returned to the heap. The function *parent()* sets the pointer to zero once the heap memory has been returned — this is not a requirement, but a very good idea. If the programmer mistakenly attempts to store something in `* pdMyDouble` after the `delete`, the program will crash immediately.

A program that crashes immediately upon encountering an error is much easier to fix that one that is intermittent in its behavior.

Chapter 9

Taking a Second Look at C++ Pointers

C++ allows the programmer to operate on pointer variables much as she would on simple types of variables. (The concept of pointer variables is introduced in Chapter 8.) Applying operations on pointers has some profound implications that will be presented in this chapter.

Defining Operations on Pointer Variables

Some of the same operators discussed in Chapter 3 may be applied to pointer types. This section examines the implications of this both to pointers and to the array types (arrays are presented in Chapter 7). Table 9-1 lists the three fundamental operations that are defined on pointers.

Table 9-1	The Three Operations Defined on Pointer Types	
Operation	*Result*	*Meaning*
`pointer + offset`	pointer	Calculate the address of the object integer entries `from` `pointer`

(continued)

Table 9-1 *(continued)*		
Operation	*Result*	*Meaning*
pointer - offset	pointer	The opposite of addition
pointer2 - pointer1	offset	Calculate the number of entries between pointer2 and pointer1

Here offset is of type int. (Although not listed in Table 9-1, operators closely related to addition and subtraction, such as ++ and += are also defined.)

The real estate memory model (used so effectively in Chapter 8, if I don't say so myself) is useful to explain how mathematical operations on pointers work. Consider a city block in which all houses are numbered sequentially. The house next to 123 Main Street would have the address 124 Main Street (or 122 if you go backward, like the left-handed and the British).

Now it's pretty clear that the house four houses down from 123 Main Street must be 127 Main Street; thus, it would be called 123 Main + 4 = 127 Main. Similarly, if I were to say how many houses are there from 123 Main to 127 Main, the answer would be four — 127 Main - 123 Main = 4. Just as an aside, a house is zero houses from itself: 123 Main - 123 Main = 0.

Re-examining arrays in light of pointer variables

Let's consider the strange and mysterious world of arrays. Once again, my neighborhood comes to mind. An array is just like my city block. Each element of the array corresponds to a house on that block. Here, however, the array elements are measured by the number of houses from the beginning of the block (the street corner). The house right on the corner is 0 houses from the corner, the house next to it is 1 house from the corner, etc. Thus, cityBlock[0] is the first house on the block, etc.

Now consider an array of 32 one-byte characters called charArray. If the first byte of this array were stored at address 0x110, then the array would extend over the range 0x110 through 0x12f. While charArray[0] is located at address 0x110, charArray[1] is at 0x111, charArray[2] at 0x112 and so forth.

Make the next step to a pointer ptr variable. After executing the expression:

```
ptr = &charArray[0];
```

the pointer ptr contains the address 0x110. Addition of an integer offset to a pointer is defined such that the relationships shown in Table 9-2 are true.

Table 9-2 also demonstrates why adding an offset *n* to *ptr* calculates the address of the *n*th element in *charArray*.

Table 9-2	Adding Offsets	
Offset	*Result*	*Corresponds to*
+ 0	0x110	charArray[0]
+ 1	0x111	charArray[1]
+ 2	0x112	charArray[2]
...	...	...
+ n	0x110+ n	charArray[n]

The addition of an offset to a pointer is similar to applying an index to an array.

Thus, given that:

```
char* ptr = &charArray[0];
```

then

```
*(ptr + n) fl corresponds with ‡ charArray[n]
```

Because * has higher precedence than addition, * ptr + n adds n to the character that ptr points to. The parentheses are needed to force the addition to occur before the indirection. The expression *(ptr + n) retrieves the character pointed at by the pointer ptr plus the offset n.

In fact, the correspondence between the two forms of expression is so strong that C++ considers array[n] nothing more than a simplified version of *(ptr + n) where ptr points to the first element in array.

```
array[n] -- C++ interprets as → *(&array[0] + n)
```

In order to complete the association, C++ takes a second short cut. Given

```
char charArray[20];
```

then

```
charArray is defined as &charArray[0];
```

That is, the name of an array without any subscript present is the address of the array itself. Thus, we can further simplify the association to

```
array[n] --> C++ interprets as --> *(array + n)
```

Applying operators to the address of an array

The correspondence between indexing an array and pointer arithmetic is a useful concept. (If it weren't a powerful concept, would I have brought it up? Okay, you got me on that one, but it's powerful none the less.)

For example, a `displayArray()` function used to display the contents of an array of integers could be written as follows:

```
// displayArray - display the members of an
//                array of length nSize
void displayArray(int intArray[], int nSize)
{
    cout << "The value of the array is:\n";

    for(int n; n < nSize; n++)
    {
        cout << n << ": " << intArray[n] << "\n";
    }
    cout << "\n";
}
```

This version uses the array operations with which you are familiar. A pointer version of the same appears as follows:

```
// displayArray - display the members of an
//                array of length nSize
void displayArray(int intArray[], int nSize)
{
    cout << "The value of the array is:\n";

    int* pArray = intArray;
    for(int n; n < nSize; n++, pArray++)
    {
        cout << n << ": " << *pArray << "\n";
    }
    cout << "\n";
}
```

The new `displayArray()` begins by creating a pointer to an integer pArray that points at the first element of `intArray`.

The p in the variable name indicates that the variable is a pointer.

The function then loops through each element of the array. On each loop, `displayArray()` outputs the current integer, that is, the integer pointed at by pArray before incrementing the pointer to the next entry in `intArray`.

You may think that such a conversion is silly; however, the pointer version of displayArray() is more common that the array version. For some reason, C++ programmers avoid the use of arrays.

The use of pointers to access arrays is nowhere more common than in the accessing of character arrays.

Expanding pointer operations to a string

A string is simply a character array whose last character is a null. C++ uses the null character at the end to serve as a terminator. This null terminated array serves as a quasi-variable type of its own. (See Chapter 7 for an explanation of string arrays.) Often C++ programmers use character pointers to manipulate such strings. The following code examples compare this technique to the earlier technique of indexing in the array.

Contrasting pointer-based with array-based string manipulation

Character pointers enjoy the same relationship with a character array that any other pointer and array share. However, the fact that strings end in a terminating null makes them especially amenable to pointer-based manipulation.

The concatString() function in Chapter 7 concatenated two character string arrays. The prototype for this function was declared as follows:

```
void concatString(char szTarget[], char szSource[]);
```

The prototype declaration describes the type of arguments, which the function accepts, as well as the return type. This declaration appears the same as a function definition with no function body.

In order to find the null at the end of the szTarget array, the concatString() function iterated through szTarget string using the following while loop:

```
void concatString(char szTarget[], char szSource[])
{
    // find the end of the first string
    int intTargetIndex = 0;
    while(szTarget[intTargetIndex])
    {
        intTargetIndex++;
    }

    // ...
```

Using the relationship between pointers and arrays, concatString() could have been prototyped as follows:

```
void concatString(char* pszTarget, char* pszSource);
```

The sz refers to a string of characters that ends in a zero (null).

The pointer version of concatString() contained in the program ConcatenatePtr is written:

```
void concatString(char* pszTarget, char* pszSource)
{
    // find the end of the first string
    while(*pszTarget)
    {
        pszTarget++;
    }

    // ...
```

The while loop in the array version of concatString() looped until szTarget[intTargetIndex] was equal to zero. This version iterates through the array by incrementing pszTarget on each pass through the loop until the character pointed at by pszTarget is *null*.

The expression ptr++ is a shortcut for ptr = ptr + 1.

Upon exiting the while loop, pszTarget points to the null character at the end of the szTarget string. It is no longer correct to say the array pointed at by pszTarget since pszTarget no longer points to the beginning of the array.

Completing the concatString ( ) example

The following displays the complete ConcatenatePtr program:

```
// ConcatenatePtr - concatenate two strings
//                  with a " - " in the middle
//                  using pointer arithmetic
//                  rather than array subscripts
#include <stdio.h>
#include <iostream.h>

void concatString(char* pszTarget, char* pszSource);

int main(int nArg, char* pszArgs[])
{
    // read first string...
    char szString1[256];
    cout << "Enter string #1:";
    cin.getline(szString1, 128);
```

```
        // ...now the second string...
        char szString2[128];
        cout << "Enter string #2:";
        cin.getline(szString2, 128);

        // ...concatenate a " - " onto the first...
        concatString(szString1, " - ");

        // ...now add the second string...
        concatString(szString1, szString2);

        // ...and display the result
        cout << "\n" << szString1 << "\n";

        return 0;
}

// concatString - concatenate* pszSource onto the
//                 end of* pszTarget
void concatString(char* pszTarget, char* pszSource)
{
        // find the end of the first string
        while(*pszTarget)
        {
            pszTarget++;
        }

        // tack the second onto the end of the first
        // (copy the null at the end of the source array
        // as well - this terminates the concatenated
        // array)
        while(*pszTarget++ = *pszSource++)
        {
        }
}
```

The `main()` portion of the program does not differ from its array based cousin. The `concatString()` function is significantly different, however.

As noted, the equivalent declaration of `concatString()` is now based on **char*** type pointers. In addition, the initial `while()` loop within `concatString()` searches for the terminating null at the end of the `pszTarget` array.

The extremely compact loop that follows copies the `pszSource` array onto the end of the `pszTarget` array. The `while()` clause does all the work, executes as follows:

1. Fetch the character pointed at by `pszSource`.

2. Increment `pszSource` to the next character.

3. Save the character in the character position pointed at by `pszTarget`.

4. Increment `pszTarget` to the next character.

5. Execute the body of the loop if the character is not null.

After executing the empty body of the while loop, control passes back up to the `while()` clause itself. This loop is repeated until the character copied to* `pszTarget` is the null character.

Justifying pointer-based string manipulation

The sometimes-cryptic nature of pointer-based manipulation of character strings might lead the reader to wonder, "Why?" That is, what advantage does the `char*` pointer version of `concatString()` have over the easier to read index version?

The pointer version of `concatenate()` is much more common in C++ programs that the array version.

The answer is partially historic and partially human nature. When C, the progenitor to C++, was invented, compilers were pretty simplistic. These compilers could not perform the complicated optimizations that modern compilers can. As complicated as it might appear to the human reader, a statement such as Line 48 can be converted into an amazingly small number of machine level instructions even by a stupid compiler.

Older computer processors were not very fast by today's standards. In the old days of C, saving a few computer instructions was a big deal. This gave C a big advantage over other languages of the day, notably Fortran, which did not offer pointer arithmetic.

In addition to the efficiency factor, programmers like to generate clever program statements to combat what can be a repetitively boring job. Once C++ programmers learn how to write compact and cryptic but efficient statements, there is no getting them back to searching arrays with indices.

Do not generate complex C++ expressions in order to create a more efficient program. There is no obvious relationship between the number of C++ statements and the number of machine instructions generated. Compare the following two sets of expressions:

```
// this expression...
*pszArray1++ = '\0';

// ...and this expression might generate the same
// amount of machine code
*pszArray2 = '\0';
pszArray2 = pszArray2 + 1;
```

In the old days, when compilers were simpler, the first version might have generated fewer instructions but the code generated should be identical using today's optimizing compilers.

Applying operators to pointer types other than char

It is not too hard to convince yourself that szTarget + n points to szTarget [n] when szTarget is an array of chars. After all, a char occupies a single byte. If szTarget were stored at 0x100, then the sixth element is located at 0x105.

It is not so obvious that pointer addition works in exactly the same way for an int array because an int takes four bytes for each char's one byte. If the first element in intArray were located at 0x100, then the sixth element would be located at 0x114 (0x100 + (5 * 4) = 0x114).

Fortunately for us, array + n points at array[n] no matter how large a single element of array might be. C++ takes care of the element size for us.

Once again our dusty old house analogy works here as well. (I mean dusty analogy, not dusty houses.) The third house down from 123 Main is 126 Main, no matter how large the houses might be.

Contrasting a pointer with an array

There are some differences between the address of an array and a pointer. For one, the array allocates space for the data while the pointer does not:

```
void arrayVsPointer()
{
    // allocate storage for 128 characters
    char charArray[128];

    // allocate space for a pointer but not for
    // the thing pointed at
    char* pArray;
}
```

Here charArray occupies 128 characters. pArray occupies only four bytes, the amount of storage required by a pointer.

The following function does not work:

```
void arrayVsPointer()
```

```
// this works fine
char charArray[128];
charArray[10] = '0';
*(charArray + 10) = '0';

// this does not work
char* pArray;
pArray[10] = '0';
*(pArray + 10) = '0';
}
```

The expressions charArray[10] and *(charArray + 10) are equivalent and legal. The two expressions involving pArray don't make sense. While they are both legal to C++, the uninitialized pointer pArray contains some random value. pArray has not been initialized to point to an array such as charArray so that both pArray[10] and the equivalent *(pArray + 10) reference garbage.

The mistake of referencing memory with an uninitialized pointer variable is generally caught by the CPU when the program executes, resulting in the dreaded *segment violation* error that you see from time to time issuing from your favorite applications under your favorite, or not so favorite, operating system.

A second difference between a pointer and the address of an array is the fact charArray is a constant while pArray is not. Thus, the following for loop used to initialize the array charArray does not work:

```
void arrayVsPointer()
{
char charArray[10];
for (int i = 0; i < 10; i++)
{
    *charArray = '\0';     // this makes sense...
    charArray++;           // ...this does not
}
}
```

The expression charArray++ makes no more sense than 10++. The following version is correct:

```
void arrayVsPointer()
{
char charArray[10];
char* pArray = charArray;
for (int i = 0; i < 10; i++)
{
    *pArray = '\0';    // this works great
    pArray++;
}
}
```

Declaring and Using Arrays of Pointers

If pointers can point to arrays, then it seems only fitting that the reverse should be true. Arrays of pointers are a type of array of particular interest.

Just as arrays may contain other data types, an array may contain pointers. The following declares an array of pointers to ints.

```
int* pInts[10];
```

Given the above declaration, pnInt[0] is a pointer to an int value. Thus, the following is true:

```
void fn()
{
    int n1;
    int* pInts[3];
    pInts[0] = &n1;
    *pInts[0] = 1;
}
```

or

```
void fn()
{
    int n1, n2, n3;
    int* pInts[3] = {&n1,&n2,&n3};
    for (int i = 0; i < 3; i++)
    {
        *pInts[i] = 0;
    }
}
```

or even

```
void fn()
{
    int* pInts[3] = {(new int),
                     new int),
                     new int)};
    for (int i = 0; i < 3; i++)
    {
        *pInts[i] = 0;
    }
}
```

The latter declares three int objects off the heap.

The most common use for arrays of pointers is to create arrays of character strings. The following two examples show why arrays of character strings are useful.

Utilizing arrays of character strings

If C++ supports arrays of pointers, then arrays of pointers to arrays must be possible. You could take this recursion as far as you want ("arrays of pointers to arrays of pointers to. . . "). A case of particular interest is an array of pointers to character strings. (Remember that a string is nothing more than a special type of character array.)

Suppose I need a function that returns the name of the month corresponding to an integer argument passed it. For example, if the program is beyond the value 1, it responds by returning a pointer to the string January. The month 0 is assumed to be invalid as are any numbers greater than 12.

I could write the function as follows:

```
// int2month() - return the name of the month
char* int2month(int nMonth)
{
    char* pszReturnValue;

    switch(nMonth)
    {
        case 1: pszReturnValue = "January";
                break;
        case 2: pszReturnValue = "February";
                break;
        case 3: pszReturnValue = "March";
                break;
        // ...and so forth...
        default: pszReturnValue = "invalid";
    }
    return pszReturnValue;
}
```

The switch() control command is like a sequence of if statements.

A more elegant solution uses the integer value for the month as an index into an array of pointers to the names of the months. In use, this appears as follows:

```
// int2month() - return the name of the month
char* int2month(int nMonth)
{
    // first check for a value out of range
    if (nMonth < 1 || nMonth > 12)
    {
        return "invalid";
    }

    // nMonth is valid - return the name of the month
```

```
        char* pszMonths[] = {"invalid",
                             "January",
                             "February",
                             "March",
                             "April",
                             "May",
                             "June",
                             "July",
                             "August",
                             "September",
                             "October",
                             "November",
                             "December"};
        return pszMonths[nMonth];
}
```

Here int2month() first checks to make sure that nMonth is a number between 1 and 12, inclusive (the default clause of the switch statement handled that for us in the previous example). If nMonth is valid, the function uses it as an offset into an array containing the names of the months.

Accessing the arguments to main ( )

First argument to *main()* is an array of pointers to strings. These strings contain the arguments to the program itself. The arguments to a program are the strings that appear with the program name when you launch it. For example, suppose I entered the following command at the MS-DOS prompt:

```
MyProgram file.txt /w
```

MS-DOS executes the program contained in the file MyProgram.exe, passing it the arguments file.txt, and /w. Switch arguments beginning with a slash (/) or a dash (-) are treated like any other — it is left up to the program to interpret them. However, arguments beginning with <, >, >>, or || have special interest to MS-DOS and Unix and are not passed as arguments to the program.

The use of the term arguments is a little confusing. The arguments to a program and the arguments to a C++ function follow a different syntax but the meaning is the same.

The variable pszArgs passed to main() is an array of pointers to the arguments to the program while nArg is the number of arguments.

Consider the following simple program:

```
// PrintArgs - write the arguments to the program
//             to the standard output
```

```
#include <stdio.h>
#include <iostream.h>

int main(int nArg, char* pszArgs[])
{
    // print a warning banner
    cout << "The arguments to " << pszArgs[0] << "\n";

    // now write out the remaining arguments
    for (int i = 1; i < nArg; i++)
    {
        cout << i << ":" << pszArgs[1] << "\n";
    }

    // that's it
    cout << "That's it\n";
    return 0;
}
```

As always, the function main() accepts two arguments. The first argument is an int that I have been calling nArgs. This variable is the number of arguments passed to the program. The second argument is an array of pointers of type char* which I have been calling pszArgs. Each one of these char* elements points to an argument passed to the program.

If I executed the PrintArgs program as follows:

```
PrintArgs arg1 arg2 arg3 /w
```

from the command line of an MS-DOS window nArgs would be 5 (one for each argument). The first argument is the name of the program itself. Thus, pszArgs[0] points to PrintArgs. The remaining elements in pszArgs point to the program arguments. The element pszArgs[1] points to arg1, pszArgs[2] to arg2, for example. Because MS-DOS does not place any significance on /w, this string is also passed as an argument to be processed by the program.

Chapter 10

Remaining Functional Features

●●●

●●●

*M*any programs are small enough that they can fit comfortably in a single .cpp source file. For most "industrial strength" programs, this would be a severe limitation. This chapter examines how to break up a program into multiple .cpp files, each of which can be written, examined, and compiled on its own.

Breaking Programs Apart?

The programmer can break a single program into separate source files generally known as modules. These modules are compiled separately and then combined during the build process to generate a single program.

The process of combining separately compiled modules into a single executable is called *linking*.

Breaking programs into smaller, more manageable pieces has several advantages. First, breaking a program into modules reduces the compile time. Both GNU C++ and Visual C++ take but seconds to gobble up the small programs that appear in this book and spit out an executable program. Very large programs can take quite some time to build. I've worked on projects that took most of the night to rebuild.

Rebuilding an entire program every time even a single function changes is an awful waste. It's much better to recompile a single module (which may contain more than just the one function, but not that many more).

Second, it's easier to comprehend and, therefore, easier to write and debug a program that consists of a number of well-thought-out modules, each of which represents a logical grouping of functions. A large, single source module full of all the functions that a program might use quickly becomes hard to keep straight ("hard to get your arms around," so to speak).

Finally comes reuse. A module full of common routines that have been separated from the main application may find application in future programs.

Looking at a Large Program

I can't really include a large program in a book like this . . . well, I could, but there wouldn't be enough room left in the book for my dry and subtle yet humorous wit. (Maybe I should have just put in the large program and left it at that.) The FunctionDemo program from Chapter 6 will serve as an example large program.

The module FunctionDemo.cpp appears as follows:

```cpp
// FunctionDemo - demonstrate the use of functions
//                by breaking the inner loop of the
//                NestedDemo program off into its own
//                function

#include <stdio.h>
#include <iostream.h>

// sumSequence - add a sequence of numbers entered from
//               the keyboard until the user enters a
//               negative number.
//               return - the summation of numbers entered
int sumSequence(void)
{
    // loop forever
    int nAccumulator = 0;
        for(;;)
        {
        // fetch another number
            int nValue = 0;
            cout << "Enter next number: ";
            cin  >> nValue;

        // if it's negative...
            if (nValue < 0)
            {
        // ...then exit from the loop
                break;
            }
```

```
                // ...otherwise add the number to the
                // accumulator
                nAccumulator = nAccumulator + nValue;
                }

        // return the accumulated value
        return nAccumulator;
}

int main(int nArg, char* pszArgs[])
{
        cout << "This program sums multiple series\n"
             << "of numbers. Terminate each sequence\n"
             << "by entering a negative number.\n"
             << "Terminate the series by entering two\n"
             << "negative numbers in a row\n";

        // accumulate sequences of numbers...
        int nAccumulatedValue;
        do
        {
                // sum a sequence of numbers entered from
                // the keyboard
            cout << "\nEnter next sequence\n";
            nAccumulatedValue = sumSequence();

                    // now output the accumulated result
                    cout << "\nThe total is "
                 << nAccumulatedValue
                 << "\n";

        // ...until the sum returned is 0
        } while (nAccumulatedValue != 0);
        cout << "Program terminating\n";
        return 0;
}
```

As with many other programs in this book, FunctionDemo adds a sequence of
numbers that the user types. It differs from some of its brethren in that
main() calls a function sumSequence() to actually perform the work of
adding up the sequence of numbers entered.

Examining the Divided FunctionDemo Program

The module FunctionDemo.cpp is logically divided into two functions that
perform different roles. The function main() prompts the user with an entire
paragraph before entering into a loop that accumulates and outputs the sum

of a sequence of numbers. The function sumSequence() sums the sequence of numbers and returns their sum.

The program could be divided along these lines: the module that actually accumulates sums of numbers and that which uses this function to add a sequence of numbers input from the keyboard and output this information to the user.

To demonstrate the point, I break the following version of the FunctionDemo program into two parts: the first containing the function sumSequence(), and the second containing the function main().

The example program here is pretty small. Although the sumSequence() function may be worth separating for use in the future, you certainly wouldn't break FunctionDemo into two parts in order to reduce compile time or reduce complexity. This example merely demonstrates the mechanics of dividing a program into multiple modules.

Separating off the sumSequence() module

The sumSequence() function is easily separable from the rest of the FunctionDemo module. The following SeparateModule.cpp file contains the sumSequence() function in a single, standalone module:

```
// SeparateModule - demonstrate how programs can be
//                  broken into multiple modules to
//                  make them easier to write and test;
//                  this module contains the function
//                  that main() calls

#include <stdio.h>
#include <iostream.h>

// sumSequence - add a sequence of numbers entered from
//               the keyboard until the user enters a
//               negative number.
//               return - the summation of numbers entered
int sumSequence(ostream& out, istream& in)
{
    // loop forever
    int nAccumulator = 0;
        for(;;)
        {
        // fetch another number
            int nValue = 0;
            out << "Enter next number: ";
            in  > nValue;

        // if it's negative...
```

```
            if (nValue < 0)
            {
        // ...then exit from the loop
                break;
        }

        // ...otherwise add the number to the
        // accumulator
        nAccumulator = nAccumulator + nValue;
            }

    // return the accumulated value
    return nAccumulator;
}
```

The framework for SeparateModule.cpp is the same as the one I use for all of the programs (maybe SeparateModule isn't all that separate). The only real difference is the absence of a main() function. If you tried to build this module, it would compile fine, but it would generate a "can't find no main() function" error during the final build phase.

The final phase of the build process is known as the link phase because this is where the different modules are linked together into one executable.

The function sumSequence() appears almost the same as it did in the FunctionDemo program from Chapter 9 with one difference. The older version input its data from cin and output to cout. We want sumSequence() to be as generic as possible. Rather than input from a fixed object, this version accepts input from an input object and outputs to the output object passed to it.

The cin object you've seen up to now is a type of istream but so are input files other than standard input. By specifying a generic istream object that the calling function provides, this version of sumSequence() can be used to read other types of input including external files. The same flexibility is true of the ostream object as well. See Chapter 26 for a more detailed discussion.

It may seem like unnecessary confusion to pass the input and output objects to sumSequence().

Don't forget, eschew obfuscation!

You should go out of your way to write functions as flexible as possible if you think that you may be reusing them in future programs.

Generating the remnant MainFunction.cpp module

With `sumSequence()` safely stored off in a separate module, MainModule.cpp is left with only the main() function:

```
// MainModule - demonstrate how programs can be
//              broken into multiple modules to make
//              them easier to write and test;
//              this module contains the main() function

#include <stdio.h>
#include <iostream.h>

// provide prototypes for external functions
int sumSequence(ostream& out, istream& in);

int main(int nArg, char* pszArgs[])
{
    cout << "This program sums multiple series\n"
         << "of numbers. Terminate each sequence\n"
         << "by entering a negative number.\n"
         << "Terminate the series by entering two\n"
         << "negative numbers in a row\n";

    // accumulate sequences of numbers...
    int nAccumulatedValue;
    do
    {
        // sum a sequence of numbers entered from
        // the keyboard
        cout << "\nEnter next sequence\n";
        nAccumulatedValue = sumSequence(cout, cin);

            // now output the accumulated result
            cout << "\nThe total is "
         << nAccumulatedValue
         << "\n";

    // ...until the sum returned is 0
    } while (nAccumulatedValue != 0);
    cout << "Program terminating\n";
    return 0;
}
```

Other than the absence of the `sumSequence()` function, the only difference is the addition of the function prototype.

```
int sumSequence(ostream& out, istream& in);
```

Chapter 6 describes the function prototype.

Without the presence of the actual function, the programmer must include a prototype to describe the interface to sumSequence().

Creating the project file

You can now open the two source files SeparateModule.cpp and MainModule.cpp in the rhide editor. With both files open, click the Make command from the Compile menu (or press F9). rhide compiles both files and links them into a single program which is gives the unlikely name of aout.exe. (You can rename it to whatever you want later.)

Creating a project file under GNU C++

The approach of keeping all relevant modules open in the rhide editor has one advantage: It's very easy. This can be a disadvantage, however, if the number of modules that make up the program is large.

A more flexible approach is to create a file that tells rhide which files to link together to build the program. Such a file is called the *project file*.

Follow these steps to create a project file under rhide:

1. **Close any open files and then choose Project⇨Open Project.**

2. **Type Separate for the project name (the name isn't actually important — you can choose any name you want).**

   A project window with the single entry <empty> opens along the bottom of the display.

3. **Choose Project⇨Add Item.**

   A window opens, showing you the files in the current directory.

4. **Click the file MainModule.cpp to open it.**

   Repeat for SeparateModule.cpp.

5. **Click Cancel to close the add window. This completes the creation of the Project Separate.**

6. **Select Make under the Compile menu to create the program Separate.exe.**

Another advantage to project files is that they give rhide a place to store off properties about the program. rhide project files don't include a lot of information, however, Visual C++ stores a lot of information.

Creating a project file under Visual C++

You may be using your own Visual C++ environment to build the programs in this book. Here are the steps for creating a Visual C++ project file:

1. **Choose File⇨Close Workspace to close any project files you opened previously. (A workspace is the Microsoft name for a collection of project files.)**

2. **Open the MainModule.cpp source file and click the compile button. (Notice that I did not say "the make button.")**

   If you do accidentally click Make, it won't hurt anything but the program won't link properly.

3. **Visual C++ now asks you whether you want to create a Project file. This is because Visual C++ cannot operate on a C++ file without a project file of some type. Click Yes.**

   You now have a project file containing the single source file SeparateModule.cpp.

4. **If it's not already opened, open the Workspace window and select Workspace under View.**

   You should see a window open up with two tabs at the bottom: one marked Class View and the other marked File View. These two tabs provide two different ways of looking at the contents of the project. The file view lists the .CPP modules which make up the program.

5. **Switch to the File view by clicking on the tab marked FileView within the Project window.**

6. **Right-click on MainModule files. A drop-down window appears.**

   This drop-down lists the files that make up the MainModule project. Right now MaiModule.cpp is the only file list.

7. **Select Add Files to Project. An "Open File" menu appears.**

   This menu is similar to that which appears when you open a file in Microsoft Word.

8. **From the menu, open the SeparateModule.cpp source file to add the file to the project.**

   Both MainModule.cpp and SeparateModule.cpp should now appear in the list of functions that make up the project.

9. **Click Build to build the program with the new project.**

Including the #include Directive

MainModule had to include a prototype for the `sumSequence()` function in order to let `main()` know how to call it. Unfortunately, it's all too easy to make a mistake when including such a prototype. Worse yet, what if multiple modules use `sumSequence()`? The programmer needs to enter a prototype declaration into each of the using modules. And what if the various prototypes disagree, probably due to some careless error?

C++ provides a mechanism to handle such a situation. The programmer can create a single file that can be "included" into other files at compile time. Include files work as follows:

1. Create a file SeparateModule.h containing the prototype declaration for sumSequence(). It's a convention that the name of an include file end in .h:

```
// SeparateModule.h - include the prototype declarations
//                    for functions contained within
//                    SeparateModule.cpp
int sumSequence(ostream& out, istream& in);
```

2. Edit MainModule.cpp to include SeparateModule.h in place of the prototype declaration. (This file is included on the enclosed CD-ROM as MainModuleInclude.cpp.)

```
// MainModule- demonstrate how programs can be
//             broken into multiple modules to make
//             them easier to write and test;
//             this module contains the main() function

#include <stdio.h>
#include <iostream.h>

// include external prototypes and declarations
#include "SeparateModule.h"

int main(int nArg, char* pszArgs[])
{
```

The *#include* directive tells C++ to insert the contents of the file SeparateModule.h into the file being compiled. Thus, what the compiler sees after the insertion is identical to what it saw before.

The directive *#include* must start in column one.

Including the same .h file more than once in the same module can happen more often that you would think. One include includes another that includes a third and a fourth and before you know it, you've included the same file.

This is not a problem as long as the .h file includes only #defines and function prototypes. It is considered bad form for an include file to define a global variable or contain the implementation of a function.

You can avoid the multiple include problem by using another pound command called #ifdef. This command says include the remainder of the commands up to an #endif, if the following #define has been defined. (Alternatively, #ifndef is the inverse operations: if NOT def.)

```
// MyInclude.h
// check to see if some #define has already been
// defined if not then this is the first time that
// this include file has been encountered during
// compilation
#ifndef MyModule_h

// now define MyModule_h to signal that we've been by
// this way before
#define MyModule_h

// now put whatever you want in your include file

// close the #ifndef at the end of the file
#endif
```

These checks are performed during the compilation of the module and not during the execution of the program.

Using the Standard C++ Library

Now you can see why I include the directives *#include <stdio. h>* and *#include <iostream.h>* in my programs. These include files contain the definitions for functions that I've been using, such as *cin>*.

Notice that the standard C++ defined *.h* files are included using the <> brackets while locally defined *.h* files are defined using the quote commands. The only difference between the two is that C++ looks for files contained in quotes starting with the "current" directory (the directory containing the project file) while C++ begins the search for bracketed files in the C++ include file directories. Either way, the programmer controls the directories searched via project file settings.

Chapter 11

Debugging C++

· ·

· ·

*Y*ou may have noticed that your programs often don't work the first time. In fact, I have seldom, if ever, written a nontrivial C++ program that didn't have some type of error the first time I tried to execute it.

That leaves you with two alternatives: You can abandon a program that has an error or find and fix the error. This chapter assumes you'll use the latter approach: In this chapter, you find out how to track down and eradicate software bugs.

Identifying Types of Errors

Two types of errors exist — those that the C++ compiler can catch on its own and those that the compiler can't catch. Errors that C++ can catch are known as *compile-time errors*. Compile-time errors are relatively easy to fix because the compiler generally points you to the problem. Sometimes the description of the problem isn't quite correct (it's easy to confuse a compiler) but after you learn the quirks of your own C++ environment, understanding its complaints isn't too difficult.

Errors that C++ can't catch show up as you try to execute the program. These are known as *run-time errors*. Run-time errors are harder to find than compile-time errors because you have no hint of what's gone wrong except for whatever errant output the program might generate. "Errant" is the key word here.

You can use two different techniques for finding bugs. You can add output statements at key points. You can get an idea of what's gone wrong with your program as these different output statements are executed. A second approach is to use a separate program called a debugger. A debugger enables you to control your program as it executes.

Both of these debugging techniques are covered in this chapter.

Choosing the WRITE Technique for the Problem

Adding output statements to the C++ source code to find out what's going on within the program is known as using the WRITE statement approach. It gained this name back in the days of early programs, which were written in FORTRAN. Fortran's output is through its WRITE command.

The following "buggy" program shows how the WRITE approach works.

The following program is supposed to read a series of numbers from the keyboard and return their average. Unfortunately, the program contains two errors, one that makes the program crash and one that causes the program to generate incorrect results.

```
// ErrorProgram - this program averages a series
//                of numbers, except that it contains
//                at least one fatal bug
#include <stdio.h>
#include <iostream.h>

int main(int argc, char* pszArgs[])
{
    cout << "This program is designed to crash!\n";

    // accumulate input numbers until the
    // user enters a negative number, then
    // return the average
    int nSum;
    for (int nNums = 0; ;)
    {
        // enter another number to add
        int nValue;
        cout << "\nEnter another number:";
        cin  >> nValue;

        // if the input number is negative...
        if (nValue < 0)
        {
```

```
            // ...then output the average
            cout << "\nAverage is: "
                 << nSum/nNums
                 << "\n";
            break;

        }

        // not negative, add the value to
        // the accumulator
        nSum += nValue;
    }
    return 0;
}
```

After entering this program, build the executable ErrorProgram.exe file (press F9). (This version of the program appears on the enclosed CD-ROM as ErrorProgram1.cpp.)

Execute the program by double-clicking the program name from Windows Explorer. Enter the values of **1**, **2**, and **3** followed by **–1** to terminate input. However, instead of producing the much-anticipated value of 2 (even I can calculate the average of 1, 2, and 3), the program terminates with the not-very-friendly error message shown in Figure 11-1.

Catching bug #1

The error message shown in Figure 11-1 seems rather imposing. The fact is that most of the information provided in this message is useless to us. (This extra information probably not useful to anyone.) However, the second line gives us one very useful piece of information: "Division by zero at. . . ." Apparently someone divided some number by zero (pretty astute, huh?).

This isn't always so straightforward. For example, suppose that the program lost its way and began executing instructions that aren't part of the program? (That happens a lot more often than you think.) The CPU may just happen to execute a divide instruction, thereby generating a divide by zero error message, and thereby masking the source of the problem. (An errant program is like a train that's jumped the track — the program doesn't stop executing until it hits something really big.)

A program "losing its way" is so common that it has names: "jumping into space" or "driving into the weeds." Both of these phrases generate descriptive images.

NextExecute the program from within the environment — sometimes environments such as Visual C++ and GNU C++ can make some sense out of some of those error numbers.

The examples shown here are from GNU C++; however, the output from Visual C++ is very similar.

From within `rhide`, load the program, rebuild it, and execute it by using the Run command (Ctrl+F9). Again, enter the same **1**, **2**, **3**, and **–1** values, and again the program crashes (at least something is predictable).

One of the first things you need to do when tracking down a problem is find the set of operations that causes the program to fail every time. By reproducing the problem, you know not only how to recreate it for debug purposes, but you also know when it's fixed.

`rhide` opens a window containing the message "Program exit code 255 (0xff)", as shown in Figure 11-2. I may not know much (this is true, by the way, I *don't* know much), but the normal, "no error" return code is 0. The fact that the return code isn't zero means that something went wrong; however, the actual value 0xff doesn't do much for me.

Figure 11-2:
The return code of 0xFF indicates that the program exited abnormally, but it doesn't indicate why.

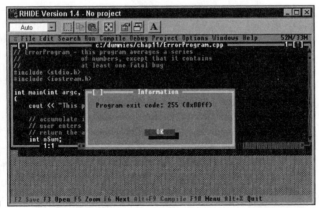

Click the OK button. `rhide` opens two windows in addition to the source code window.

You may not see all three windows because one window may be covering one of the others. Cycle through the available windows by pressing the F6 key.

In Window 3, you see the same error message that you saw when executing the previous program, but what's this behind curtain number 2? Window 2 appears in Figure 11-3.

Figure 11-3: rhide is able to calculate the location of the failure.

```
RHIDE Version 1.4 - No project                              _□×
 Auto  ▼  □ ◩ ◧ ⬚ ◫ A
 ≡ File Edit Search Run Compile Debug Project Options Windows Help    51H/33M
                c:/dummies/chap11/ErrorProgram.cpp         1
 // ErrorProgram - this program averages a series
 //                of numbers, except that it contains
 //                at least one fatal bug
 #include <stdio.h>
 #include <iostream.h>

 int main(int argc, char* pszArgs[])
 {
     cout << "This program is designed to crash!\n";

     // accumulate input numbers until the
     // user enters a negative number, then
     // return the average
     int nSum;
 ▌─[■]──────────── Message Window ──────────── 2─[↑]
 Call frame traceback:
 ErrorProgram.cpp(28) in function main
 in function __crt1_startup+174

 Enter Jump to source F5 Zoom F6 Next Alt+F7 Compile F10 Menu Alt+X Quit
```

The "Call frame traceback" sounds like a telephone wiretap and in a way it is. A traceback lists the address of each function that was called backward up to the very first function. In this case, you can see that something called `__crt1_startup` (how's that for a descriptive name?) called `main()`. The error actually occurred on Line 28 of the source file ErrorProgram.cpp within function `main()`. That's progress.

It turns out that Line 28 appears as follows:

```
cout << "\nAverage     // line 26
     << nSum/nNums     // line 27
     << "\n";          // line 28
```

I don't see a division on Line 28 at all. What's going on here?

C++ considers all of the expressions up to a semicolon to be a single command line. In this case, Lines 26 through 28 are all part of the same command line that terminates on Line 28. Thus, anything that happened on Line 26, 27, or 28 would be considered Line 28.

Armed with that knowledge, you know that the error actually occurred during the division on Line 27.

I know that at the time of the division, nNums must have been equal to zero. nNums is supposed to be a count of the number of values entered. I can see where nNums is initialized to 0, but where is it incremented? It isn't, and this is the bug. Clearly nNums should have been incremented during each loop of the input section. I edit the *for* loop as follows:

```
for (int nNums = 0; ;nNums++)
```

Catching bug #2

You have now found bug #1. Now execute the program using the same 1, 2, 3, –1 input that crashed the program earlier. This time, the program doesn't crash and it returns a return code of 0, but the program doesn't work either. The output shown below is ridiculous:

```
This program is designed to crash!

Enter another number:1

Enter another number:2

Enter another number:3

Enter another number:-1

Average is: -286331151
Press any key to continue
```

How can C++ tie an error message back to the source code?

The information I received when executing the program directly from Windows or from an MS-DOS window wasn't very informative. By comparison, both Visual C++ and rhide are able to direct me to the line from whence the problem originated. How did they do that?

C++ has two modes when building a program. By default, C++ builds the program in what is called debug mode. In debug mode, C++ adds line-number information that maps the lines of C++ code to the corresponding lines of machine code. For example, this map might say that line

200 of machine code in the executable code was created from the C++ source code on Line 16.

When the divide-by-zero error occurred, C++ was able to track the machine code address returned by MS-DOS to the source line number using this debug information.

As you may imagine, this debug information takes a lot of space. Before a program is "shipped," the program tells rhide to generate an executable without debug information.

Apparently, either nSum or nNums (or both) isn't being calculated properly. To get any further, you need to know the value of these variables. In fact, it would help if you knew the value of nValue as well, because nValue is used to calculate nSum.

To learn the values of the nSum, nNums, and nValue, modify the for loop as follows (this version of the program appears on the CD-ROM as ErrorProgram2.cpp):

```
for (int nNums = 0; ;nNums++)
{
    // enter another number to add
    int nValue;
    cout << "\nEnter another number:";
    cin  >> nValue;

    // if the input number is negative...
    if (nValue < 0)
    {
        // ...then output the average
        cout << "\nAverage is: "
            << nSum/nNums
            << "\n";
        break;

    }

    // output critical information
    cout << "nSum = " << nSum   << "\n";
    cout << "nNums= " << nNums  << "\n";
    cout << "nValue= "<< nValue << "\n";
    cout << "\n";

    // not negative, add the value to
    // the accumulator
    nSum += nValue;
}
```

Notice the addition of the output statements to display nSum, nNums, and nValue on each iteration through the loop.

The result of executing the program with the now standard 1, 2, 3, and –1 input is shown below. Even on the first loop, the value of nSum is unreasonable. In fact, at this point during the first loop, the program has yet to add a new value to nSum. You would think that the value of nSum should be 0.

```
This program is designed to crash!

Enter another number:1
nSum = -858993460
nNums= 0
nValue= 1
```

```
Enter another number:2
nSum = -858993459
nNums= 1
nValue= 2

Enter another number:3
nSum = -858993457
nNums= 2
nValue= 3

Enter another number:
```

On careful examination of the program, nSum is declared but it isn't initialized
to anything. The solution is to change the declaration of nSum to the following:

```
int nSum = 0;
```

Note: Until a variable has been initialized, the value of that variable is inde-
terminate.

Once you have convinced yourself that you have found the problem, "clean
up" the program as follows (this version is ErrorProgram3.cpp on the
enclosed CD-ROM):

```
// ErrorProgram - this program averages a series
//                of numbers
//                (This version has been fixed.)
#include <stdio.h>
#include <iostream.h>

int main(int argc, char* pszArgs[])
{
    cout << "This program works!\n";

    // accumulate input numbers until the
    // user enters a negative number, then
    // return the average
    int nSum = 0;
    for (int nNums = 0; ;nNums++)
    {
        // enter another number to add
        int nValue;
        cout << "\nEnter another number:";
        cin  >> nValue;

        // if the input number is negative...
        if (nValue < 0)
        {
            // ...then output the average
            cout << "\nAverage is: " << nSum/nNums << "\n";
            break;
        }
```

```
            // not negative, add the value to
            // the accumulator
            nSum += nValue;
    }
    return 0;
}
```

I rebuild the program and retest with the 1, 2, 3, and –1 sequence. This time I
see the expected average value of 2:

```
This program works!

Enter another number:1

Enter another number:2

Enter another number:3

Enter another number:-1

Average is: 2
```

After testing the program with a number of other inputs, I convince myself
that the program is now executing properly.

Calling for the Debugger

For small programs, the WRITE technique works reasonably well. Adding statements is simple enough and the programs rebuild quickly so the cycle time is
short enough. Problems with this approach don't really become obvious until
the size of the program grows beyond the simple programs you've seen so far.

In larger programs, the programmer often doesn't generally know where to
begin adding output statements. The constant cycle of adding write statements, executing the program, adding write statements, and on and on
becomes tedious. Further, in order to change an output statement, the programmer must rebuild the entire program. For a large program, this rebuild
time can itself be significant. (I have been on programs that took most of the
night to rebuild.)

Finally, finding pointer problems with the WRITE approach is almost impossible. A pointer written to the display in hex means nothing and as soon as you
attempt to dereference the pointer, the program blows.

A second, more sophisticated technique is based on a separate utility known
as a debugger. This approach avoids the disadvantages of the write statement
approach. Unfortunately, however, this approach involves learning to use a
new tool, the debugger.

Defining the debugger

A *debugger* is actually a tool built into the `rhide` and Microsoft Visual C++ environments (the debuggers are different between the two but work on the same principle).

The programmer controls the debugger through commands in the same way that the programmer might use the Edit commands when using the editor or the different build commands when creating the executable. These commands are available through menu items or by using hot keys.

The debugger allows the programmer to control the execution of her program. She can execute one step in the program at a time, she can stop the program at any point, and she can examine the value of variables.

To appreciate the power of the debugger you need to see it in action. This section introduces you to the use of the debugger by fixing a small program. (I use the `rhide` debugger, but Visual C++ can use your debugger by using the corresponding commands.)

Deciding which debugger to use

Unlike the C++ language, which is standardized across manufacturers, each debugger has its own command set. Fortunately, most debuggers offer the same basic commands. The commands you need are available in both the ubiquitous Microsoft Visual C++and the GNU C++`rhide` environments. In addition, both debuggers offer access to debugger commands by using either menu items or the function keys. Table 11-1 lists the command hot keys you use in both environments.

Throughout the rest of this chapter, I refer to the debug commands by name. Table 11-1 lists the corresponding keystrokes you use in your environment.

Table 11-1	Debugger Commands for Microsoft Visual C++ and GNU *rhide*	
Command	*Visual C++*	*GNU C++ (rhide)*
Build	Shift+F8	F9
Step in	F11	F7
Step over	F10	F8
View variable	menu only	Ctl+F4
Set breakpoint	F9	Ctl+F8

Command	Visual C++	GNU C++ (rhide)
Add watch	menu only	Ctl+F7
Go	F5	Ctl+F9
View User Screen	Click on Program Window	Alt+F5
Program reset	Shift+F5	Ctl+F2

Running a test program

The best way to learn how to fix a program using the debugger is to go through the steps to fix a buggy program. The following program has several problems that need to be discovered and fixed. This version is found on the CD-ROM as Concatenate1.cpp.

```cpp
// Concatenate - concatenate two strings
//                with a " - " in the middle
//                (this version crashes)
#include <stdio.h>
#include <iostream.h>

void concatString(char szTarget[], char szSource[]);

int main(int nArg, char* pszArgs[])
{
    cout << "This program concatenates two strings\n";
    cout << "(This version crashes.)\n\n";

    // read first string...
    char szString1[256];
    cout << "Enter string #1:";
    cin.getline(szString1, 128);

    // ...now the second string...
    char szString2[128];
    cout << "Enter string #2:";
    cin.getline(szString2, 128);

    // ...concatenate a " - " onto the first...
    concatString(szString1, " - ");

    // ...now add the second string...
    concatString(szString1, szString2);

    // ...and display the result
    cout << "\n" << szString1 << "\n";

    return 0;
}
```

```
// concatString - concatenate the string szSource
//                   to the end of szTarget
void concatString(char szTarget[], char szSource[])
{
    int nTargetIndex;
    int nSourceIndex;

    // find the end of the first string
    while(szTarget[++nTargetIndex])
    {
    }

    // tack the second to the end of the first
    while(szSource[nSourceIndex])
    {
        szTarget[nTargetIndex] =
            szSource[nSourceIndex];
        nTargetIndex++;
        nSourceIndex++;
    }
}
```

Build the program uneventfully. Execute the program. When it asks for string #1, enter **this is a string**. For string #2, enter **THIS IS A STRING** (you can use any two phrases that you want).

Rather than generate the proper output, the program terminates with the cursed 0xff return code. Click OK (I don't actually have any other choice). In an attempt to offer some solace, the debugger opens the Message Window containing the following:

```
Call frame traceback:
Concatenate.cpp(49) in function concatString__FPcTO
Concatenate.cpp(28) in function main
in function __crt1_startup+174
```

From this you can see that the error occurred on or about Line 49 of the module Concatenate.cpp, which is within the function concatString(). concateString() was called from Line 28 within the function main(). Finally, main() was invoked from some stupid function that we don't know anything about.

Line 49 appears as follows:

```
while(szTarget[++nTargetIndex])
```

while Line 28 contains the function call:

```
concatString(szString1, " - ");
```

Nothing appears to be wrong with the statement on Line 49 or the call on Line 28. You will need to use the rhide debugger.

Note: Actually, you may already see the problem based on the information that rhide provided, but work with me here.

Single-stepping through a program

The best first step when tracking down a program problem is to use a debugger feature known as single stepping. From within rhide, execute Program Reset.

Note: In Table 11-1 you can see that this is Ctrl+F2 within rhide and Shift+F5 within Visual C++, but I'm not going to give you hints anymore. For each debugger command, refer to Table 11-1. In addition, remember that each of these debugger commands is available from drop-down menu options.

The Program Reset command makes sure that everything within the debugger is reset back to the beginning in case you had been in the middle of debugging something already. It's always a good idea to reset the debugger before beginning.

Execute the Step Over command to begin debugging the program. rhide opens an MS-DOS window as if it were about to execute the program; however, the debugger immediately switches back the program edit window with the first executable line of the program highlighted.

An executable statement is a statement other than a declaration or a comment. An executable statement is one that generates machine code when compiled.

The debugger has actually executed the program up to the first line of the main() function and then snatched control. The debugger is waiting for you to decide what to do next.

Execute Step Over again — rhide repeats the process of displaying the user screen for just a second and returning to the edit window. This time the second line is highlighted. Click on View User Screen and you should see the output

```
This program concatenates two strings
```

from the previous C++ command line.

Execute through the program until it crashes by repeatedly executing Step Over. This should reveal a lot about what went wrong. Executing a program one line at a time is known as *single-stepping* the program.

When you try to Step Over the cin.getline() command, the debugger doesn't take control back from the MS-DOS window as it normally would. Instead, the program appears to be frozen at the prompt to enter the first string.

The reason for this apparent program crash is that the debugger doesn't take control back from the program until the C++ statement finishes executing — the statement containing the call to `getline()` cannot finish until you enter a string of text from the keyboard.

Enter **this is a string** and press Enter. The `rhide` debugger stops the program at the next statement, the `cout << "Enter string #2"`. Enter the single step command again and enter the second line of text in response to the second call to `getline()`.

If the debugger seems to halt without returning when single-stepping through a program, your program is waiting for something to happen. Most likely, the program is waiting for input, either from you or from an external device.

Eventually you will single-step down to the call to `concatString()`, as shown in Figure 11-4. When you try to Step Over the call, however, the program crashes as before.

Figure 11-4:
Something
in the
concat-
String()
function
causes the
program
to crash.

This doesn't tell reveal any more that the previous crash. What is needed is the ability to execute into the function rather than simply "stepping over" it.

Single-stepping into a function

A debugger allows the programmer to step into a function one instruction at a time. You will need this feature in order to ferret out the first bug in the test program.

You will need to start over. Execute Program Reset command in order to reset the debugger to the beginning of the program.

Single-step through the program using the Step Over command until you reach the call to concatString(). This time rather than step over the call, use the Step In command to move into the function. Immediately, the pointer moves to the first executable line in concatString() as shown in Figure 11-5.

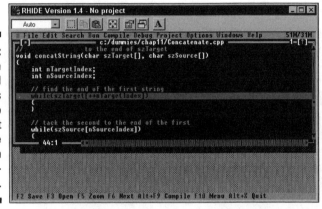

Figure 11-5: The Step In command moves control to the first executable line in concatString().

There's no difference between the Step Over and Step In commands when not executing a function call.

If you Step In to a function unintentionally, the debugger may ask you for the source code to some file that you've never heard of before. The function is probably within a library module. Execute the Cancel command to view a listing of machine instructions that aren't very useful even to the most hardened techies. To return to sanity, open the edit window, set a break point as described in the next section to the statement after the call, and execute the Go command.

Now use the Step Over command to execute the first statement in the function. The rhide debugger responds by reporting the same fatal error message as before.

Now you know for sure that something about the while loop is not correct and that executing it even the first time crashes the program. To find out what it is, you will need to stop the program right before it executes the offending line and take a look around.

Using breakpoints

Single-stepping a program is fine when you are just "sniffing around;" however, you can use a debugger command known as the breakpoint when you already know where you want to go.

To see this in action, execute the Program Reset command to move the debugger back to the beginning of the program. You could single-step back through the program to the `while` loop as you did before. With a large program, this could get laborious. You can employ the breakpoint shortcut instead. Place the cursor on the `while` statement and execute the Set breakpoint command. The editor highlights the statement, as shown in Figure 11-6.

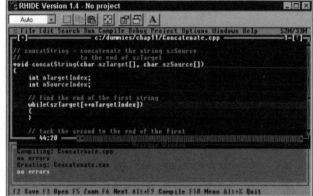

Figure 11-6: rhide highlights a breakpoint by turning the line red.

A *breakpoint* enables the program to execute normally up to the point where you want to take control A breakpoint tells the debugger to halt on that statement if control ever passes its way. Breakpoints are useful either when you know where to stop or when you want the program to execute normally until it's time to stop.

With the breakpoint set, execute the Go command. The program appears to execute normally up to the point of the `while` call. At that point, the program obediently hands the torch back to the debugger.

Now that you're here, you still probably don't know what's wrong.

Viewing and modifying variables

There isn't much point in executing the `while` statement again — you know that it will crash. You need more information about what the program is doing to determine why it crashed. For example, you might like to see the value of `nTargetIndex` immediately prior to the execution of the `while` loop.

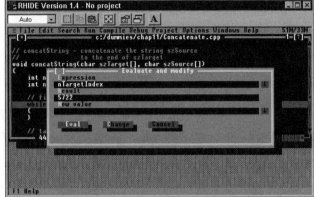

Figure 11-7:
A debugger
allows the
programmer
to view and
modify
program
variables.

First, double-click the variable name nTargetIndex. Next, execute the View
Variable command. A window appears with the name nTargetIndex in the
upper field. Click Eval to find the current value of the variable. The results,
shown in Figure 11-7, are obviously nonsensical.

Looking back at the C++ code, you will see that the program does not initialize either the nTargetIndex or nSourceIndex variables. To test this theory,
enter a **0** in the New Value window and click Change. Repeat the process for
nSourceIndex. Close the window and click Step Over to continue executing.

With the index variables initialized, single-step into the while loop. The program does not crash. Each Step Over or Step In command executes one iteration of the while loop. Because the cursor ends up right where it started,
there appears to be no change; however, after one loop, nTargetIndex has
incremented to 1.

It's too much work to reevaluate nTargetIndex on each iteration. Double-
click nTargetIndex and execute the Add Watch command. A window
appears with the variable nTargetIndex and the value 1 to the right. Execute
Step In a few more times. nTargetIndex increments on each iteration
through the loop. After several iterations, control eventually passes outside
of the loop.

Set a breakpoint on the closing brace of the concatString function and execute Go. The program stops immediately prior to returning from the function.

To check the string generated, double-click szTarget string and execute
View Variable. The results shown in Figure 11-8 are unexpected.

Figure 11-8:
Even after
solving the
initial prob-
lem, the
target string
resulting
from con-
catenation
isn't correct.

The 0xa73a8 is the address of the string in memory. This information can be useful when tracking pointers. For example, this information would be extremely helpful in debugging a linked-list application. It's of little use here.

The expected string "this is a string" is there, but it's immediately followed by a string of garbage. Apparently the target string is not being terminated after the source string has been appended onto the end.

Modifying a string after the terminating null or forgetting to terminate a string with a null are by far the two most common string-related errors.

You now know two errors — it would be prudent to go ahead and fix these errors in the source code before you forget them. Press Program Reset and fix the concatString() function. The updated concatString() function appears as follows:

```
void concatString(char szTarget[], char szSource[])
{
    int nTargetIndex = 0;
    int nSourceIndex = 0;

    // find the end of the first string
    while(szTarget[nTargetIndex])
    {
        nTargetIndex++;
    }

    // tack the second onto the end of the first
    while(szSource[nSourceIndex])
    {
        szTarget[nTargetIndex] =
            szSource[nSourceIndex];
        nTargetIndex++;
```

```
        nSourceIndex++;
    }

    // terminate the string properly
    szTarget[nTargetIndex] = '\0';
}
```

Just because you've fixed one problem does not mean that there aren't more
bugs. You should start the debug process again. Set a watch on szTarget
and nTargetIndex while executing the second loop. The source string
appears to be copied to the end of the target string properly.

You really need to execute this one yourself. It's the only way you can get a
feel for how neat it is to watch one string grow while the other string shrinks
on each iteration through the loop.

Convinced that all seems to be working well, clear any breakpoints left, and
execute Go to allow the program to continue to completion. The following
output seems correct:

```
This program concatenates two strings
(This version works.)

Enter string #1:this is a string
Enter string #2:THIS IS A STRING

this is a string - THIS IS A STRING
```

Congratulations! You're now a debugging expert.

Budget 1 Program

The chapters that make up Part I and II provide you the programming information necessary to write your own non-trivial programs. The following program, *BUDGET* is just such a program.

In actual fact, *BUDGET* appears multiple times in this book. Each version uses
the features introduced in earlier chapters. In this way, you can see the program advance in capability by incorporating more advanced features. This
version uses the functional (that is, function-based) programming techniques
of Parts I and II.

The BUDGET program is a simple bank account register program. Here's what
it does:

- ✔ Gives the user the ability to create one or more bank accounts.

- ✔ Assigns an account number to each account.

✔ Begins accepting transactions, consisting of deposits and withdrawals.

✔ After the user chooses to exit, the program displays the ending balance of all accounts and the total of all accounts.

This program mimics a few bank rules concerning transactions (we will add more rules as the program develops):

✔ Never let the balance become negative. (Your bank may be friendly, but I bet it's not that friendly.)

✔ Never charge for making a deposit.

The following budget program is explained below:

```
// BUDGET1.CPP - A "functional" Budget program
#include <iostream.h>
#include <stdio.h>

// the maximum number of accounts you can have
const int maxAccounts = 10;

// data describes accounts
unsigned accountNumber[maxAccounts];
double   balance[maxAccounts];


// prototype declarations
void process(unsigned& accountNumber,
             double&   balance);
void init(unsigned& accountNumber,
          double&   balance);

// main - accumulate the initial input and output totals
int main(int nArg, char* pszArgs[])
{
    // loop until someone enters
    int noAccounts = 0;            // the number of accounts

    // don't create more accounts than we have room for
    while (noAccounts < maxAccounts)
    {
        char transactionType;
        cout << "Enter C to continue or X to terminate:";
        cin  >> transactionType;

        // quit if the user enters an X; otherwise...
        if (transactionType == 'x' ||
            transactionType == 'X')
        {
            break;
        }
```

```
        // if the user enters a C...
        if (transactionType == 'c' ||
            transactionType == 'C')
        {
            // ...then initialize a new account...
            init(accountNumber[noAccounts],
                 balance[noAccounts]);

            // ...and input   transaction information
            process(accountNumber[noAccounts],
                    balance[noAccounts]);

            // move the index over to the next account
            noAccounts++;
        }
    }

    // now present totals
    // first for each account
    double total = 0;
    cout << "Account information:\n";
    for (int i = 0; i < noAccounts; i++)
    {
        cout << "Balance for account "
             << accountNumber[i]
             << " = "
             << balance[i]
             << "\n";

        // accumulate the total for all accounts
        total += balance[i];
    }


    // now display the accumulated value
    cout << "Balance for all accounts = "
         << total
         << "\n";

    return 0;
}

// init - initialize an account by reading
//        in the account number and zeroing out the
//        balance
void init(unsigned& accountNumber,
          double&   balance)
{
    cout << "Enter account number:";
    cin  >> accountNumber;
    balance = 0.0;
}
```

```
// process - update the account  balance by entering
//            the transactions from the user
void process(unsigned& accountNumber,
             double&   balance)
{
    cout << "Enter positive number for deposit,\n"
         << "negative for withdrawal,\n";

    double transaction;
    do
    {
        cout << ":";
        cin  >> transaction;

        // is it a deposit?
        if (transaction > 0)
        {
            balance += transaction;
        }

        // how about withdrawal?
        if (transaction < 0)
        {
            // withdrawal
            transaction = -transaction;
            if (balance < transaction)
            {
                cout << "Insufficient funds: balance "
                     << balance
                     << ", check "
                     << transaction
                     << "\n";
            }
            else
            {
                balance -= transaction;
            }
        }
    } while (transaction != 0);
}
```

To demonstrate the program in action, I entered the following sequence (output from the program in normal font, my input in **bold**):

```
Enter C to continue or X to terminate:c
Enter account number:1234
Enter positive number for deposit,
negative for withdrawal,
:200
:-100
:-200
Insufficient funds: balance 100, check 200
:0
Enter C to continue or X to terminate:c
Enter account number:2345
Enter positive number for deposit,
negative for withdrawal,
:200
:-50
:-50
:-50
:0
Enter C to continue or X to terminate:x
Account information:
Balance for account 1234 = 100
Balance for account 2345 = 50
Balance for all accounts = 150
```

Coding styles

You may notice that I try to be consistent in my indentation and in my naming of variables.

We humans have a limited amount of CPU power between our ears. We need to direct our CPU power toward getting programs working, not toward figuring out simple stuff like indentation.

This makes it important that you be consistent in how you name variables, where you place open and close braces, and so on. This is called your coding style. Once you have developed a style, stick to it — after a while, your coding style will become second nature. You'll find that you can code your programs with less time and read your programs with less effort.

When working on a project with several programmers, it's just as important that you all use the same style to avoid a Tower of Babel effect with conflicting and confusing styles. In addition, I strongly suggest that you enable every error and warning message that your compiler can produce. Even if you decide that a particular warning is not a problem, why would you want it suppressed? You can always ignore it. More often than not, even a warning represents a potential problem or programming style that needs to be corrected.

Some people don't like the compiler finding their slip-ups because they think it's embarrassing and they think that correcting things to get rid of the warnings wastes time. Just think how embarrassing and time-consuming it is to painstakingly search for a bug only to find that it's a problem your compiler told you about hours ago.

Here's how the BUDGET1.C program works. Two arrays are created, one to contain account numbers and the other their balances. These two arrays are kept in synch, that is, *balance[n]* contains the balance of the account *accountNumber[n]* no matter what the value of *n*. Due to the limitations of a fixed length array, the program can only accommodate *MAXACCOUNTS* number of bank accounts.

The main program is divided in two sections: the accumulation section, where the deposits and withdrawals are accumulated into accounts, and the display section. The accumulation section first enters a loop in which the accounts are handled separately. First, the program prompts the user for a C for continue or X for exit. If the user enters an X, the program breaks from the loop and enters the second section of *main()*.

The program exits the loop after *MAXACCOUNTS* number of accounts has been created, whether the user enters an X or not.

Notice that the program checks for both 'X' and 'x'. While C++ considers case to be important, people generally don't.

If the user enters C, control passes to the *init()* function which enters the account number information (creates an account) followed by the *process()* function which enters the transaction data into the account.

The arguments to *init()* and *process()* have been declared referential so that the functions can modify their values in the calling function as well. Otherwise, the new data might be lost when the function exits.

Once the program exits the account creation section, it enters the output second. Here, *main()* cycles through each account outputting the balance in each. The program ends with the total balance of all accounts.

The *init()* function creates a new account by prompting the user, inputting the account number and zeroing out the balance.

It is important to always create an element in a legal state. An initial balance of 0 makes sense - an initial balance containing random garbage does not.

The *process()* function enters a loop inputting transaction information. Positive values are taken to be deposits while negative values withdrawals. An entry of zero is assumed to be the last transaction for a given account.

The program is using an otherwise nonsensical value as a flag. This technique is common but not generally a good idea. I use the technique here only because it minimizes the size of the program.

Although other (even better) ways exist to implement this program, it serves nicely as the basis for our investigations. As you progress in your knowledge of C++, you will see this program morph into a full-blown, object-oriented C++ program.

Part III
Programming
with Class

"CAREFUL, SUNDANCE, THIS ONE'S BEEN LOCKED UP AND FORCED TO BETA-TEST POORLY DOCUMENTED SOFTWARE PRODUCTS ALLLL WEEK AND HE'S ITCHING FOR A FIGHT."

In this part . . .

The feature that differentiates C++ from other languages is C++'s support for object-oriented programming. *Object-oriented* is about the most hyped term in the computer world (okay, maybe *.com* has it beat). Computer languages, editors, and databases all claim to be object-oriented, sometimes with justification but most of the time without.

What is it about being object-oriented that makes it so desired around the world? Read on to find out.

Chapter 12

Examining Object-Oriented Programming

*W*hat, exactly, is object-oriented programming? Object-oriented programming, or OOP as those in the know prefer to call it, relies on two principles you learned before you ever got out of Pampers: abstraction and classification. To explain, let me tell you a little story.

Abstracting Microwave Ovens

Sometimes when my son and I are watching football, I whip up a terribly unhealthy batch of nachos. I dump some chips on a plate, throw on some beans, cheese, and lots of jalapeños, and nuke the whole mess in the microwave oven for five minutes.

To use my microwave, I open the door, throw the stuff in, and punch a few buttons on the front. After a few minutes, the nachos are done. (I try not to stand in front of the microwave while it's working lest my eyes start glowing in the dark.)

Now think for a minute about all the things I don't do to use my microwave:

> ✔ I don't rewire or change anything inside the microwave to get it to work. The microwave has an interface — the front panel with all the buttons and the little time display — that lets me do everything I need.

✔ I don't have to reprogram the software used to drive the little processor inside my microwave, even if I cooked a different dish the last time I used the microwave.

✔ I don't look inside my microwave's case.

✔ Even if I were a microwave designer and knew all about the inner workings of a microwave, including its software, I would still use it to heat my nachos without thinking about all that stuff.

These are not profound observations. You can deal with so much stress in your life. To reduce the number of things that you deal with, you work at a certain level of detail. In object-oriented (OO) computerese, the level of detail at which you are working is called the *level of abstraction*. To introduce another OO term while I have the chance, I *abstract away* the details of the microwave's innards.

When I'm working on nachos, I view my microwave oven as a box. (As I'm trying to knock out a snack, I can't worry about the innards of the microwave oven and still follow the Cowboys on the tube.) As long as I use the microwave only through its interface (the keypad), there should be nothing I can do to cause the microwave to enter an inconsistent state and crash or, worse, turn my nachos into a blackened, flaming mass.

Preparing functional nachos

Suppose I were to ask my son to write an algorithm for how Dad makes nachos. After he understood what I wanted, he would probably write "open a can of beans, grate some cheese, cut the jalapeños," and so on. When it came to the part about microwaving the concoction, he would write something like "cook in the microwave for five minutes" (on a good day).

That description is straightforward and complete. But it's not the way a functional programmer would code a program to make nachos. Functional programmers live in a world devoid of objects such as microwave ovens and other appliances. They tend to worry about flow charts with their myriad functional paths. In a functional solution to the nachos problem, the flow of control would pass through my finger to the front panel and then to the internals of the microwave. Pretty soon, flow would be wiggling around through complex logic paths about how long to turn on the microwave tube and whether to sound the "come and get it" tone.

In a world like this, it's difficult to think in terms of levels of abstraction. There are no objects, no abstractions behind which to hide inherent complexity.

Preparing object-oriented nachos

In an object-oriented approach to making nachos, I would first identify the types of objects in the problem: chips, beans, cheese, and an oven. Then I would begin the task of modeling these objects in software, without regard to the details of how they will be used in the final program.

While I am doing this, I'm said to be working (and thinking) at the level of the basic objects. I need to think about making a useful oven, but I don't have to think about the logical process of making nachos yet. After all, the microwave designers didn't think about the specific problem of my making a snack. Rather, they set about the problem of designing and building a useful microwave.

After the objects I need have been successfully coded and tested, I can ratchet up to the next level of abstraction. I can start thinking at the nacho-making level, rather than the microwave-making level. At this point, I can pretty much translate my son's instructions directly into C++ code.

Classifying Microwave Ovens

Critical to the concept of abstraction is that of classification. If I were to ask my son, "What's a microwave?" he would probably say, "It's an oven that. . . ." If I then asked, "What's an oven?" he might reply, "It's a kitchen appliance that. . . ." (If I then asked, "What's a kitchen appliance?" he would probably say, "Why are you asking so many stupid questions?")

The answers my son gave in my example questioning stem from his understanding of our particular microwave as an example of the type of things called microwave ovens. In addition, my son sees microwave ovens as just a special type of oven, which itself is just a special type of kitchen appliance.

In object-oriented computerese, my microwave is an *instance* of the class microwave. The class microwave is a subclass of the class oven, and the class oven is a subclass of the class kitchen appliances.

Humans classify. Everything about our world is ordered into taxonomies. We do this to reduce the number of things we have to remember. Take, for example, the first time you saw an SUV. The advertisement probably called the SUV "revolutionary, the likes of which have never been seen." But you and I know that that just isn't so. I like the looks of some SUVs (others need to go back to take another crack at it), but hey, an SUV is a car. As such, it shares all of (or at least most of) the properties of other cars. It has a steering wheel, seats, a motor, brakes, and so on. I bet I could even drive one without reading the user's manual first.

I don't have to clutter my limited storage with all the things that an SUV has in common with other cars. All I have to remember is "an SUV is a car that . . ." and tack on those few things that are unique to an SUV (like the price tag). I can go further. Cars are a subclass of wheeled vehicles along with other members, such as trucks and pickups. Maybe wheeled vehicles are a subclass of vehicles, which include boats and planes. And on and on and on.

Why Classify?

Why do we classify? It sounds like a lot of trouble. Besides, people have been using the functional approach for so long, why change now?

It may seem easier to design and build a microwave oven specifically for this one problem, rather than build a separate, more generic oven object. Suppose, for example, that I want to build a microwave to cook nachos and nachos only. There would be no need to put a front panel on it, other than a START button. I always cook nachos the same amount of time. I could dispense with all that DEFROST and TEMP COOK nonsense. It only needs to hold one flat little plate. Three cubic feet of space would be wasted on nachos.

For that matter, I can dispense with the concept of "microwave oven" altogether. All I really need is the guts of the oven. Then, in the recipe, I put the instructions to make it work: "Put nachos in the box. Connect the red wire to the black wire. Bring the radar tube up to about 3,000 volts. Notice a slight hum. Try not to stand too close if you intend to have children." Stuff like that.

But the functional approach has some problems:

- ✔ **Too complex.** I don't want the details of oven building mixed into the details of nacho building. If I can't define the objects and pull them out of the morass of details to deal with separately, I must deal with all the complexities of the problem at the same time.

- ✔ **Not flexible.** Someday I may need to replace the microwave oven with some other type of oven. I should be able to do so as long as its interface is the same. Without being clearly delineated and developed separately, it becomes impossible to cleanly remove an object type and replace it with another.

- ✔ **Not reusable.** Ovens are used to make lots of different dishes. I don't want to create a new oven every time I encounter a new recipe. Having solved a problem once, it would be nice to be able to reuse the solution in future programs.

Chapter 13

Adding Class to C++

. . . .

. . . .

*P*rograms often deal with groups of data: a person's name, rank, and serial number, stuff like that. Any one of these values is not sufficient to describe a person — only in the aggregate do the values make any sense. A simple structure such as an array is great for holding stand-alone values; however, it doesn't work very well for data groups. This makes good ol' arrays inadequate for storing complex data (such as personal credit records that the Web companies maintain so they can loose them to hackers).

For reasons that will become clear shortly, I'll call such a grouping of data an *object*. A microwave oven is an object. You are an object (me, I'm not so sure about). Your name, rank, and credit card number in a database is an object.

Introducing the Class

What we need is a structure that can hold all of the different types of data necessary to describe a single object. In our simple example, a single object would hold both the first name and last name along with the credit card number.

C++ calls the structure that combines multiples pieces of data into a single object a *Class*.

The format of a Class

A class used to describe a name and credit card grouping might appear as follows:

```
// the dataset class
class NameDataSet
{
    public:
        char firstName[128];
        char lastName [128];
        int  creditCard;
};

// a single instance of a dataset
NameDataSet nds;
```

A class definition starts with the keyword class followed by the name of the class and an open-closed brace pair.

The alternative keyword struct may be used. The keywords struct and class are completely identical except that the *public* declaration is assumed in the *struct*.

The statement after the open brace is the keyword public. (Hold off asking about the meaning of the public keyword. I'll make its meaning public a little later. Later chapters describe options to public, such as private. Thus, the *public* must stay private until I can make the *private* public.)

Following the public keyword are the entries it takes to describe the object. The NameDataSet class contains the first and last name entries along with the credit card number. As you would expect the first and last names are both character arrays — the credit card number is shown here as a simple integer ("the better to steal you with, my dear").

A class declaration includes the data necessary to describe a single object.

The last line of the snippet declares the variable nds to be a single entry of class NameDataSet. Thus, nds might be an entry that describes a single person.

We say that nds is an *instance* of the class NameDataSet. You *instantiate* the class NameDataSet to create nds. Finally, we say that firstName and the others are *members* or *properties* of the class. We say a whole lot of silly things.

Accessing the members of a Class

The following syntax is used to access the property of a particular object:

```
NameDataSet nds;
nds.creditCard = 10;
cin >> nds.firstName;
cin >> nds.lastName;
```

Here, nds is an instance of the class NameDataSet (for example, a particular NameDataSet object). The integer nds.creditCard is a property of the nds object. The type of nds.creditCard is int while that of nds.firstName is char[].

Okay, that's computerspeak. What has actually happened here? The program snippet declares an object nds, which it will use to describe a customer. For some reason, the program assigns the person the credit card number 10 (obviously bogus but it's not like I'm going to include one of my credit card numbers).

Next, the program reads the person's first and last names from the default input.

From now on, the program can refer to the single object nds without dealing with the separate parts (the first name, last name, and credit card number) until it needs to.

```
int getData(NameDataSet& nds)
{
    cout << "\nEnter first name:";
    cin  >> nds.firstName;

    if (stricmp(nds.firstName, "exit") == 0)
    {
        return 0;
    }

    cout << "Enter last name:";
    cin  >> nds.lastName;

    cout << "Enter credit card number:";
    cin  >> nds.creditCard;

    return 1;
}
```

```
// displayData - output the index'th data set
void displayData(NameDataSet& nds)
{
    cout << nds.firstName
         << " "
         << nds.lastName
         << "/"
         << nds.creditCard
         << "\n";
}

int main(int nArg, char* pszArgs[])
{
    const int MAX = 25;
    // allocate 25 name data sets
    NameDataSet nds[MAX];

    // load first names, last names and social
    // security numbers
    cout << "Read name/credit card information\n"
         << "Enter 'exit' for first name to exit\n";
    int index = 0;
    while (getData(nds[index]) && index < MAX)
    {
        index++;
    }

    cout << "\nEntries:\n";
    for (int i = 0; i < index; i++)
    {
        displayData(nds[i]);
    }
    return 0;
}
```

Example program

The following program demonstrates the `NameDataSet` class:

```
// DataSet - store associated data in
//           an array of objects
#include <stdio.h>
#include <iostream.h>
#include <string.h>

// NameDataSet - stores name and credit card
//               information
class NameDataSet
```

```
{
    public:
        char firstName[128];
        char lastName [128];
        int  creditCard;
};

// getData - read a name and credit card
//           number; return 0 if no more to
//           read
int getData(NameDataSet& nds)
{
    cout << "\nEnter first name:";
    cin  >> nds.firstName;

    if ((strcmp(nds.firstName, "exit") == 0)
         ||
        (strcmp(nds.firstName, "EXIT") == 0))
    {
        return 0;
    }

    cout << "Enter last name:";
    cin  >> nds.lastName;

    cout << "Enter credit card number:";
    cin  >> nds.creditCard;

    return 1;
}

// displayData - output the index'th data set
void displayData(NameDataSet& nds)
{
    cout << nds.firstName
         << " "
         << nds.lastName
         << "/"
         << nds.creditCard
         << "\n";
}

int main(int nArg, char* pszArgs[])
{
    // allocate 25 name data sets
    NameDataSet nds[25];
```

```
// load first names, last names  and social
// security numbers
cout << "Read name/credit card information\n"
     << "Enter 'exit' for first name to exit\n";
int index = 0;
while (getData(nds[index]))
{
    index++;
}

cout << "\nEntries:\n";
for (int i = 0; i < index; i++)
{
    displayData(nds[i]);
}
return 0;
}
```

The main() function allocates 25 objects of class NameDataSet. main(), prompts the user as to what is expected of her, and then enters a loop in which entries are read from the keyboard using the function getData(). The loop terminates when either getData() returns a 0 (FALSE) or when the maximum number of objects (25) have been created. The same objects read are next passed to displayData(NameDataSet) for display.

The getData() function accepts a NameDataSet object as its input argument which it assigns the name nds.

Ignore the ampersand for now — I explain it in Chapter 15.

getData() then reads a string from standard input into the entry firstName. If the stricmp() function can find no difference between the name entered and "exit," the function returns a 0 to main() indicating that it's time to quit. (The function *stricmp()* compares two strings without regards to their case. This function considers "exit" and "EXIT" plus any other combination of upper- and lowercase letters to be identical.) Otherwise the function pushes on reading the last name and the credit card number into the object nds.

The displayData() function outputs each of the members of the NameDataSet object nds separated by delimiters.

A simple run of this program appears as follows:

```
Read name/credit card information
Enter 'exit' for first name to exit

Enter first name:Stephen
Enter last name:Davis
Enter credit card number:123456
Enter first name:Marshall
Enter last name:Smith
Enter credit card number:567890

Enter first name:exit

Entries:
Stephen Davis/123456
Marshall Smith/567890
Press any key to continue
```

The program begins with an explanatory banner. I enter my own glorious name at the first prompt (I'm modest that way). Because the name entered does not rhyme with "exit," the program continues and I add a last name and a pretend credit card number. On the next pass, I tack onto that the name Marshall Smith and his real credit card number (have fun, Marshall). On the final path, I enter "exit" which terminated the input loop. The program does nothing more than spit the same names I just entered back at me.

Chapter 14

Making Classes Work

● ●

● ●

*P*rogrammers use classes to group related data elements into a single object. The following `Savings` class, associates an account balance with a unique account number:

```
class Savings
{
 public:
   unsigned accountNumber;
   float balance;
};
```

Every instance of `Savings` contains the same two data elements:

```
void fn(void)
{
   Savings a;
   Savings b;
   a.accountNumber = 1; // this is not the same as...
   b.accountNumber = 2; // ...this one
}
```

The variable `a.accountNumber` is different from the variable `b.accountNumber`. Just as the balance in my bank account is different from the balance in yours, even though they're both called balance (or, in the case of my account, lack of balance).

Activating Our Objects

We use classes to simulate real world objects. The closer C++ objects are to the real world, the easier it is to deal with them in programs. This sounds simple enough. However, the Savings class doesn't do a very good job of simulating a savings account.

Simulating real-world objects

Real-world objects certainly have data-type properties such as account numbers and balances. This makes the Savings class a good starting point for describing a real object. But real-world objects can also do things. Ovens cook. Savings accounts accumulate interest, CDs charge a substantial penalty for early withdrawal — stuff like that.

Functional programs "do things" via functions. A C++ program might call strcmp() to compare two strings or getLine() to input a string of characters. In fact, Chapter 26 explains that even stream I/O (cin >> and cout <<) are a special form of function call.

The Savings class needs active properties of its own:

```
class Savings
{
 public:
  unsigned accountNumber;
  float  balance;
  unsigned deposit(unsigned amount)
  {
   balance += amount;
   return balance;
  }
};
```

In addition to the account number and balance, this version of Savings includes a function deposit(). This gives Savings the ability to control its own future. A class MicrowaveOven has a function cook(), the class Savings has a function accumulateInterest(), and the class CD has a function penalizeForEarlyWithdrawal().

Functions defined in a class are called *member functions*.

Why bother with member functions?

Why should we bother with member functions? What's wrong with the good ol' days:

```
class Savings
{
 public:
  unsigned accountNumber;
  float  balance;
};
unsigned deposit(Savings& s, unsigned amount)
{
 s.balance += amount;
 return balance;
}
```

Ignore the ampersand for now — I explain it in Chapter 15.

Here deposit() implements the "deposit into savings account" function. This "support function" solution relies on an outside function, deposit(), to implement an activity which accounts do but Savings lacks. This gets the job done, but it does so by breaking our object-oriented rules.

The microwave oven has internal components which it "knows" how to use to cook, defrost, and burn to a crisp. Class data members are similar to the parts of a microwave — the member functions of class perform cook-like functions.

When I make nachos, I don't have to start hooking up the internal components of the oven in a certain way to make it work. I want my classes to work the same way. I want them to know how to manipulate their internals without outside intervention. Member functions of Savings such as deposit() can be written as external functions. I can put all of the functions necessary to make a savings account work in one place. Microwave ovens can be made to work by soldering and cutting wires. I don't want my classes or my microwave ovens to work that way. I want a Savings class that I can use in my banking program without considering how it might work on the inside.

Adding a Member Function

There are two aspects to adding a member function to a class: creating the member function and naming it (sounds silly, doesn't it?).

Creating a member function

To demonstrate member functions, start by defining a class `Student`. One possible representation of such a class follows:

```
class Student
{
 public:
  int   semesterHours;
  float gpa;

  // add a completed course to the record
  float addCourse(int hours, float grade)
  {
   // calculate the sum of all courses times
   // the average grade
   float weightedGPA;
   weightedGPA = semesterHours * gpa;

   // now add in the new course
   semesterHours += hours;
   weightedGPA += grade * hours;
   gpa = weightedGPA / semesterHours;

   // return the new gpa
   return gpa;
  }
};
```

The function `addCourse(int, float)` is called a member function of the class `Student`. In principle, it's a property of the class like the data members `semesterHours` and `gpa`.

There isn't a name for functions or data that are not members of a class, but I'll refer to them as *non-members*.

For historical reasons, member functions are also called *methods*. This term has an obtuse meaning in other object-oriented languages, but no meaning in C++. Nevertheless, it has gained some popularity in OO circles because it's easier to say than "member function." (The fact that it sounds more impressive probably doesn't hurt either.) So, if your friends start spouting off at a dinner party about "methods of the class," just replace methods with member functions and reparse anything they say. Because the term method has little relevance to C++, I won't use it here.

Naming class members

A member function is a lot like a member of a family. The full name of the function addCourse(int, float) is Student::addCourse(int, float) just as my full name is Stephen Davis. The short name of the function is addCourse(int, float) just as my short name is Stephen. The class name at the beginning of the full name indicates that the function is a member of the class Student. (The :: between the class name and the function name is simply a separator.) The name Davis on the end of my name indicates that I am a member of the Davis family.

Another name for a "full name" is extended name.

You can define an addCourse(int, float) function that has nothing to do with Student — there are Stephens out there who have nothing to do with my family. (I mean this literally: I know several Stephens who want *nothing* to do with my family.)

You could have a function Teacher::addCourse(int, float) or even Golf::addCourse(). A function addCourse(int, float) without any class name is just a plain ol' conventional non-member function.

Calling a Member Function

Before you look at how to call a member function, remember how to access a data member:

```
class Student
{
 public:
   int  semesterHours;
   float gpa;
};

Student s;
void fn(void)
{
   // access data members of s
   s.semesterHours = 10;
   s.gpa      = 3.0;
}
```

Notice that you have to specify an object along with the member name. In other words, the following makes no sense:

```
Student s;
void fn(void)
{
   // neither of these is legal
   semesterHours = 10;  // member of what object of what
              // class?
   Student::semesterHours = 10; // okay, I know the class
                                // but I still don't know
                                // the object
}
```

Accessing a member function

Remember that member functions function like data members functionally. This appears as follows:

```
Student s;
void fn()
{
   // all of the following reference an object
   s.semesterHours = 10;
   s.gpa        = 3.0;
   s.addCourse(3, 4.0); // call the member function
}
```

The syntax for calling a member function looks like a cross between the syntax for accessing a data member and that used for calling function. The right side of the dot looks like a conventional function call but an object is on the left of the dot.

Just as the phrase "half fast" makes sense if you sound it out: "*s* is the object on which addCourse() operates" or, said another way, *s* is the student to which the course is to be added. You can't fetch the number of semester hours without knowing from which student — you can't add a student to a course without knowing which student to add.

Calling a member function without an object makes no more sense than referencing a data member without an object.

Accessing other members from a member function

I can see it clearly: You repeat to yourself, "Accessing a member without an object makes no sense. Accessing a member without an object. Accessing. . . ." Just about the time you've accepted this, you look at the member function `Student::addCourse()` and *Wham!* It hits you: `addCourse()` accesses other class members without reference to an object. Just like the TV show: "How do they do that?"

Okay, which is it, can you or can't you? Believe me, you can't. When you reference a member of `Student` from `addCourse()`, that reference is against the `Student` object with which the call to `addCourse()` was made. Huh? Go back to the example:

```
#include "student.h"
float Student::addCourse(int hours, float grade)
{
  float weightedGPA;
  weightedGPA = semesterHours * gpa;

  // now add in the new course
  semesterHours += hours;
  weightedGPA += hours * grade;
  gpa = weightedGPA / semesterHours;
  return gpa;
}
int main(int argcs, char* pArgs[])
{
  Student s;
  Student t;

  s.addCourse(3, 4.0); // here's an A+
  t.addCourse(3, 2.5); // give this guy a C
  return 0;
}
```

When `addCourse()` is invoked with the object *s*, all of the otherwise unqualified member references in `addCourse()` refer to *s* as well. Thus, the reference to semesterHours in `addCourse()` refers to `s.semesterHours`, and gpa refers to `s.gpa`. But in the next line of `main()`, when `addCourse()` is invoked with the `Student` t, these same references are to `t.semesterHours` and `t.gpa` instead.

The object with which the member function was invoked is the "current" object, and all unqualified references to class members refer to this object. Put another way, unqualified references to class members made from a member function are always against the current object.

Naming the current object

How does the member function know what the current object is? It's not magic — the address of the object is passed to the member function as an implicit and hidden first argument. In other words, the following conversion is taking place:

```
s.addCourse(3, 2.5) is like
    Student::addCourse(&s, 3,
    2.5)
```

(Note that you can't actually use the syntax on the right; this is just the way that C++ sees it.)

Inside the function, this implicit pointer to the current object has a name, in case you need to refer to it. It is called this, as in "Which object? *This* object." Get it? The type of "this" is always a pointer to an object of the appropriate class.

Anytime a member function refers to another member of the same class without providing an object explicitly, C++ assumes "this." You also can refer to this explicitly, if you like. You could have written Student::addCourse() as follows:

```
float Student::addCourse(int
    hours, float grade)
{
    float weightedGPA;
    weightedGPA = this-
    >semesterHours * this->gpa;
    // now add in the new course
    this->semesterHours += hours;
    weightedGPA += hours * grade;
    this->gpa = weightedGPA /
    this->semesterHours;
    return this->gpa;
}
```

The effect is the same whether you explicitly include "this," as in the preceding example, or leave it implicit, as you did before.

Scope Resolution (And I Don't Mean How Well Your Microscope Works)

The :: in between a member and its class name is called the *scope resolution operator* because it indicates the scope to which class a member belongs. The class name before the colon is like the family last name while the function name after the colons is like the first name — the order is similar to an oriental name, family name first.

You can use the :: operator to describe a non-member function by using a null class name. The non-member function addCourse, for example, can be referred to as ::addCourse(int, float), if you prefer. This is like a function without a home.

Normally the *::* operator is optional, but there are a few occasions when this is not so. For example:

```
// addCourse - combine the hours and grade into
//               a weighted grade
float addCourse(int hours, float grade)
{
  return hours * grade;
}

class Student
{
 public:
  int   semesterHours;
  float gpa;

  // add a completed course to the record
  float addCourse(int hours, float grade)
  {
    // call some external function to calculate the
    // weighted grade
    float weightedGPA = addCourse(semesterHours, gpa);

    // now add in the new course
    semesterHours += hours;

    // use the same function to calculate the weighted
    // grade of this new course
    weightedGPA += addCourse(hours, grade);
    gpa = weightedGPA / semesterHours;

    // return the new gpa
    return gpa;
  }
};
```

Here, I want the member function Student::addCourse() to call the non-member function ::addCourse(). Without the *::* operator, however, a call to addCourse() from Student refers to Student::addCourse().

One member function can use the short name when referring to another member. The class name is understood.

Not indicating the class name in this case results in the function calling itself, generally not a good thing. Adding the *::* operator to the front directs the call to the global version, as desired:

```
class Student
{
 public:
  int  semesterHours;
  float gpa;

  // add a completed course to the record
  float addCourse(int hours, float grade)
  {
   // call some external function to calculate the
   // weighted grade
   float weightedGPA = ::addCourse(semesterHours, gpa);

   // now add in the new course
   semesterHours += hours;

   // use the same function to calculate the weighted
   // grade of this new course
   weightedGPA += ::addCourse(hours, grade);
   gpa = weightedGPA / semesterHours;

   // return the new gpa
   return gpa;
  }
};
```

This is just like when I call out Stephen in my own home, everyone assumes that I mean me — they default the Davis onto my name. If I mean some other Stephen out there outside of my family, I need to say "Stephen Smith" or "Stephen Jones" or whatever. That's what the scope resolution operator does.

The extended name of a function includes its arguments. Now we've added the class name to which the function belongs.

Defining a Member Function in the Class

A member function can be defined either in the class or separately. When defined in the class definition, the function looks like the following in student.h:

```
class Student
{
 public:
  int  semesterHours;
  float gpa;

  // add a completed course to the record
  float addCourse(int hours, float grade)
```

```
  {
    // calculate the sum of all courses times
    // the average grade
    float weightedGPA;
    weightedGPA = semesterHours * gpa;

    // now add in the new course
    semesterHours += hours;
    weightedGPA += grade * hours;
    gpa = weightedGPA / semesterHours;

    // return the new gpa
    return gpa;
  }
};
```

Using an include like this is pretty slick:

```
// MyProgram - mess around with students and courses
#include "Student.h"
#include "Course.h"

void updateRecord(Student s, Course c)
{
  // add the effects of taking the course to the student
  s.addCourse(c.hours, c.grade);
}
```

Inlining member functions

Member functions defined in the class default to inline (unless they have been specifically outlined by a compiler switch or because they contain a loop). Mostly, this is because a member function defined in the class is usually very small, and small functions are prime candidates for inlining.

The content of an inline function is inserted wherever it is invoked. An inline function executes faster because the processor doesn't have to jump over to where the function is defined — inline functions take up more memory because they get copied into every call rather than being defined just once.

There is another good, but more technical, reason to inline member functions defined within a class. Remember that C structures are normally defined in include files, which are then included in the .C source files that need them. Such include files should not contain data or functions because these files are compiled multiple times. Including an inline function is okay, however, because it (like a macro) expands in place in the source file. The same applies to C++ classes. By defaulting member functions defined in classes inline, the preceding problem is avoided.

This is cool because my function `updateRecord()` can concentrate on the act of updating students' records without worrying about the details of students or courses. The details of these classes have been neatly tucked away in their own include files.

Keeping a Member Function after Class

For larger functions, putting the code directly in the class definition can lead to some very large, unwieldy class definitions. To prevent this, C++ lets you define member functions outside the class.

When written outside the class declaration, the Student example looks like the following:

```
class Student
{
 public:
  int  semesterHours;
  float gpa;

  // add a completed course to the record
  float addCourse(int hours, float grade);
};

// Student::addCourse - add a completed course to a
//                      Student's record
float Student::addCourse(int hours, float grade)
{
  float weightedGPA;
  weightedGPA = semesterHours * gpa;

  // now add in the new course
  semesterHours += hours;
  weightedGPA += grade * hours;
  gpa = weightedGPA / semesterHours;
  return gpa;
}
```

This class declaration contains nothing more than a prototype declaration for the function `addCourse()`. The function definition appears separately.

The member function prototype declaration in the structure is analogous to any other prototype declaration and, like all prototype declarations, is required.

In this example, the class `Student` and the function `Student::addCourse()` are defined as if they were in the same file. This is possible, but not very common. Generally, the `Student` class is defined in a descriptively named include file, such as `Student.h` — can't get more descriptive than that. The function is then written in some separate source file `Student.cpp` or the like.

The file *Student.cpp* must be included in your project along with your own files. *Student.cpp* is compiled separately and the resulting *.obj* file is linked into your program during the build process. See Chapter 6 for details on how this is done.

Overloading Member Functions

Member functions can be overloaded in the same way that conventional functions are overloaded (see Chapter 6 if you don't remember what that means). Remember, however, that the class name is part of the extended name. Thus, the following functions are all legal:

```
class Student
{
 public:
  // grade - return the current grade point average
  float grade();
  // grade - set the grade and return previous value
  float grade(float newGPA);
  // ...data members and other stuff...
};
class Slope
{
 public:
  // grade -- return the percentage grade of the slope
  float grade();
  // ...stuff goes here too...
};

// grade - return the letter equivalent of a numerical grade
char grade(float value);

int main(int argcs, char* pArgs[])
{
  Student s;
  s.grade(3.5);     // Student::grade(float)
  float v = s.grade(); // Student::grade()

  char c = grade(v);   // ::grade(float)

  Slope o;
  float m = o.grade(); // Slope::grade()
  return 0;
}
```

Each call made from main() is noted in the comments with the extended name of the function called.

When calling overloaded functions, not only the arguments of the function but also the type of the object (if any) with which the function is invoked are used to disambiguate the call. (The term *disambiguate* is object-oriented talk for "decide at compile time which overloaded function to call.")

In the example, the first two calls to the member functions Student::grade(float) and Student::grade() are differentiated by their argument lists and the type of the object used. The call to s.grade() calls Student::grade() because s is of type Student.

The third call has no object, so it unambiguously denotes the non-member function ::grade(float).

The final call is made with an object of type Slope, it must refer to the member function Slope::grade().

Chapter 15

Creating Pointers to Objects

. . . .

. . . .

C++ programmers are forever generating arrays of things. Arrays of `int`s, arrays of floats, why not arrays of students? Students stand in line all the time — a lot more than they care to. The concept of `Student` objects all lined up quietly awaiting their name to jump into service is just too attractive to pass up.

Defining Arrays of and Pointers to Simple Things

An array is a sequence of identical objects much like the identical houses on a street that make up one of those starter neighborhoods. Each element in the array carries an index, which corresponds to the number of elements from the beginning of the array — the first element in the array carries an offset of 0.

C++ arrays are declared by using the bracket symbols containing the number of elements in the array:

```
int array[10];      // declare an array of 10 elements
```

The individual elements of the array may be accessed by counting the number of houses from the corner:

```
array[0] = 10;        // assign 10 to the first element
array[9] = 20;        // assign 20 to the last element
```

The program first assigns the value 10 to the first element in the array — the house zero houses from the house on the corner. The program then assigns 20 to the last element in the array — the ninth house from the intersection.

Always remember that C++ indices start at 0 and go through the size of the array minus 1.

To take the house analogy one step further, the array name represents the name of the street, and the house number in that street represents the array index. Similarly, variables can be identified by their unique address in computer memory. These addresses may be calculated and stored for later use.

```
int variable;          // declare an int object
int* pVariable =& variable; // store its address
                                        // in pVariable
*pVariable = 10;// assign 10 into the int
                        // pointed at by pVariable
```

The pointer pVariable is declared to contain the address of *variable*. The assignment stores 10 into the int pointed at by pVariable.

If we apply the house analogy one more time (I promise):

- *variable* is a house
- *pVariable* is like a piece of paper containing the address of the house
- the final assignment delivers the message 10 to the house whose address is written on pVariable just like a postman might (except unlike my postman, computers don't deliver mail to the wrong address)

Chapter 7 goes into the care and feeding of arrays of simple (intrinsic) variables while Chapters 8 and 9 describe simple pointers in detail.

Declaring Arrays of Objects

Arrays of objects work the same as arrays of simple variables. Take for example the following:

```
class Student
{
 public:
  int  semesterHours;
  float gpa;
  float addCourse(int hours, float grade);
};

void someFn()
{
  // declare an array of 10 students
  Student s[10];

  // assign the 5th student a gpa of 5.0 (lucky guy)
  s[4].gpa = 5.0;

  // add another course to the 5th student;
  // this time he failed - serves him right
  s[4].addCourse(3, 0.0);
}
```

Here *s* is an array of Student objects. s[4] refers to the 5th `Student` object in the array. By extension, s[4].gpa refers to the GPA of the 5th student. Further, s[4].addCourse( ) adds a course the 5th student object.

Declaring Pointers to Objects

Pointers to objects work like pointers to simple types:

```
#include <stdio.h>
#include <iostream.h>

class Student
{
 public:
  int  semesterHours;
  float gpa;
  float addCourse(int hours, float grade){return 0.0;};
};

int main(int argc, char* pArgs[])
{
  // create a Student object
  Student s;
```

```
// now create a pointer to a Student object
Student* pS;

// make the Student pointer point to our Student object
pS =& s;

return 0;
}
```

The type of pS is "pointer to a Student object" also written *Student**.

Dereferencing an object pointer

By analogy with pointers to simple variables, you might think that the following refers to the GPA of our student *s*:

```
int main(int argc, char* pArgs[])
{
    // the following is incorrect
    Student s;
    Student* pS =& s; // create a pointer to s

    // access the gpa member of the object pointed at by pS
    // (this doesn't work)
    *pS.gpa = 3.5;

    return 0;
}
```

As the comments indicate, this doesn't work. The problem is that the dot operator "." is evaluated before the pointer "*".

Note: The * operator is often referred to as the "splat" operator — not a popular term with insects.

C++ programmers use parentheses to override the order in which operations are performed. For example, the parentheses force addition to be performed before multiplication in the following expression:

```
int i = 2 * (1 + 3);   // addition performed
                       // before multiplication
```

Parentheses have the same effect when applied to pointer variables:

```
int main(int argc, char* pArgs[])
{
  Student s;
  Student* pS = &s; // create a pointer to s

  // access the gpa member of the object pointed at by pS
  // (this works as expected)
  (*pS).gpa = 3.5;

  return 0;
}
```

The *pS evaluates to the pointers object pointed at by pS. The ".gpa" refers to the gpa member of that object.

Shooting arrow pointers

Using the splat operator together with parentheses works just fine for dereferencing pointers to objects; however, even the most hardened techies would admit that this syntax is a bit tortured.

C++ offers a more convenient operator for accessing members of an object to avoid clumsy object pointer expressions. The -> operator is defined as follows:

```
ps->gpa is equivalent to(*pS).gpa
```

The arrow operator is used almost exclusively since it is easier to read; however, the two forms are completely equivalent.

Passing Objects to Functions

Passing pointers to functions is just one of the ways to entertain yourself with pointer variables.

Calling a function with an object value

As you know, C++ passes arguments to functions by value by default. (See Chapter 6 if you didn't know that.) Complex, user-defined class objects are passed by value as well:

```
#include "Student.h"

// pass a Student object by value
void someFn(Student valS)
{
    cout << "GPA = " << valS.gpa << "\n";
}

int main(int argcs, char* pArgs[])
{
    Student s;
    s.semesterHours = 10;
    s.gpa          = 3.0;

    // the following creates a copy of s for someFn()
    someFn(s);
    return 0;
}
```

The function `main()` creates an object *s* and then passes *s* to the function `someFn()`.

It is not the object *s* itself that is passed, but a copy of *s*.

The object `valS` in `someFn()` begins life as an exact copy of the variable *s* in `main()`. Any change to `valS` made within `someFn()` has no effect on *s* back in `main()`.

Calling a function with an object pointer

The C++ programmer can also pass the address of an object rather than the object itself:

```
#include <stdio.h>
#include <iostream.h>

class Student
{
  public:
    int   semesterHours;
    float gpa;
    float addCourse(int hours, float grade){return 0.0;};
};
```

```
void someFn(Student* pS)
{
  pS->semesterHours = 10;
  pS->gpa        = 3.0;
  pS->addCourse(3, 4.0); // call the member function
}

int main(int argc, char* pArgs[])
{
  Student s;

  // pass the address of s to someFn()
  someFn(&s);

  // pass the value of the pointer pS
  Student* pS;
  pS =& s;
  someFn(pS);
  return 0;
}
```

The type of the argument to someFn() is a pointer to a Student rather than a Student object itself. This is reflected in the way that the program calls someFn(), passing the address of *s* rather than the value of *s*. The fact that the pS argument is a pointer affects the way that someFn() accesses the members of the object — someFn() must use the arrow syntax for dereferencing pointer the pS pointer.

Conceptually, this is akin to writing down the address of the house *s* on the piece of paper pS and then passing a copy of that address to someFn().

Why pass pointers to functions when you can pass the object itself?

It's really cool that you can pass the address of an object as well as the object itself, but why bother? There are a number of reasons, but two jump out right away.

First, passing a pointer allows a function to modify the object passed to it. Consider the following variation of the earlier snippet:

```
#include <stdio.h>
#include <iostream.h>
```

```
class Student
{
 public:
  int  semesterHours;
  float gpa;
  float addCourse(int hours, float  grade){return 0.0;};
};

void someFn(Student copyS)
{
  copyS.semesterHours = 10;
  copyS.gpa           = 3.0;
  copyS.addCourse(3, 4.0); // call the member function
}

int main(int argc, char* pArgs[])
{
  Student s;
  s.gpa = 0.0;

  // display the value of s.gpa before calling someFn()
  cout << "The value of s.gpa = " << s.gpa << "\n";

  // pass the address of the existing object
  cout << "Calling someFn(Student)\n";
  someFn(s);

  // the value of s.gpa is now 3.0
  cout << "The value of s.gpa = " << s.gpa << "\n";
  return 0;
}
```

This example passes a copy of the object *s* to someFn() rather than the address of the existing object. The someFn() modifies the object passed to it; the problem is that its version of the Student object copyS is a copy of the original *s*. Thus, any changes made in someFn() are not retained back in main().

The output from the "pass copy of object" version of the program is as follows:

```
The value of s.gpa = 0
Calling someFn(Student)
The value of s.gpa = 0
Press any key to continue
```

Redefining someFn() to accept a pointer to the original object solves the problem:

```
#include <stdio.h>
#include <iostream.h>

class Student
{
 public:
   int  semesterHours;
   float gpa;
   float addCourse(int hours, float grade){return 0.0;};
};

void someFn(Student* pS)
{
   pS->semesterHours = 10;
   pS->gpa           = 3.0;
   pS->addCourse(3, 4.0); // call the member function
}

int main(int argc, char* pArgs[])
{
   Student s;
   s.gpa = 0.0;

   // display the value of s.gpa before calling someFn()
   cout << "The value of s.gpa = " << s.gpa << "\n";

   // pass the address of the existing object
   cout << "Calling someFn(Student*)\n";
   someFn(&s);

   // the value of s.gpa is now 3.0
   cout << "The value of s.gpa = " << s.gpa << "\n";
   return 0;
}
```

This call to someFn() passes the address of the existing object *s* rather than construct a new one.

You might say that C++ passes a copy of the address of an existing object rather than a copy of the object.

The output from this version of the program appears as follows:

```
The value of s.gpa = 0
Calling someFn(Student*)
The value of s.gpa = 3
Press any key to continue
```

Calling a function by using the reference operator

The reference operator described in Chapter 9 works for user-defined objects as well:

```
#include "Student.h"
// same as before, but this time using references
void someFn(Student& refS)
{
  refS.semesterHours = 10;
  refS.gpa          = 3.0;
  refS.addCourse(3, 4.0); // call the member function
}
Student s;
int main(int argcs, char* pArgs[])
{
  someFn(s);
  return 0;
}
```

In this example, C++ passes a reference to *s* rather than a copy. Changes made in someFn() are retained in main().

What's actually happening here is that C++ keeps track of the address of *s* passed to someFn(). C++ derefences the pointer on its own as necessary.

Returning to the Heap

The problems that exist for simple types of pointers plague class object pointers as well. In particular, you must make sure that the pointer you're using actually points to a valid object. For example, don't return a reference to an object defined local to the function:

```
MyClass* myFunc()
{
  // the following does not work
  MyClass  mc;
  MyClass* pMC =& mc;
  return pMC;
}
```

Upon return from myFunc(), the mc object goes out of scope. The pointer returned by myFunc() is not valid in the calling function.

Allocating the object off of the heap solves the problem:

```
MyClass* myFunc()
{
   MyClass* pMC = new MyClass;
   return pMC;
}
```

The heap is used to allocate objects in a number of different situations.

Linking up with Linked Lists

The second most common structure after thearray is the linked list. It is not necessary to declare the size of a linked list at compile times — linked lists can shrink and grow as necessary. The cost of such flexibility is access — it is much more difficult to access individual elements in a linked list.

The array data structure

As a container of objects, the array has a number of advantages including the ability to access a particular entry quickly and efficiently:

```
MyClass mc[100];        // allocate room for 100 entries
mc[n];                           // access the n+1'th ms
                                 entry
```

Weigh against that a number of disadvantages.

Arrays are of fixed length. You can calculate the number of array entries to allocate at run time, but once created, the size of the array can't be changed:

```
void fn(int nSize)
{
    // allocate an array to hold n number of
    // MyClass objects
    MyClass* pMC = new MyClass[n];

// size of the array is now fixed and cannot
// be changed

    // ...
}
```

In addition, each entry in the array must be of exactly the same type. It is not possible to mix objects of class MyClass and YourClass in the same array.

Finally, it is difficult to add an object into the middle of an array. To add or remove an object, the program must copy each of the adjoining elements up or down in order to make or remove a gap. (Image inserting a house in the middle of a block of existing houses and you get the idea.)

There are alternatives to arrays tat do not suffer from these limitations. The most well-known of these is the linked list.

The linked list

The linked list uses the same principle as the holding hands to cross the street exercise when you were a child. Each object contains a link to the next object in the chain. The teacher, otherwise known as the head pointer, points to the first element in the list.

Not every class can be used to create a linked list. A linkable class is declared as follows:

```
class LinkableClass
{
    public:
        LinkableClass* pNext;

        // other members of the class
};
```

The key is the pNext pointer to an object of class Linkable. At first blush, this seems odd indeed — a class contains a pointer to itself? Actually, this says that the class Linkable contains a pointer to another object also of class Linkable.

The pNext pointer is similar to the appendage used to form those chains of children. The list of children consists of a number of objects, all of type child. Each child points to another child.

The head pointer is simply a pointer of type LinkableClass*: To keep torturing the child chain analogy, the teacher points to an object of class child. (It's interesting to note that the teacher is not a child — the head pointer is not of type LinkableClass.)

```
LinkableClass* pHead = (LinkableClass*)0;
```

Always initialize any pointer to 0. Zero, generally known as null when used in the context of pointers, is universally known as the "non-pointer." In any case, referring to address 0 always causes the program to halt immediately.

The cast from the int 0 to LinkableClass* is not necessary. C++ understands 0 to be of all types, sort of the "universal pointer." However, I find it a good practice.

To see how linked lists work in practice, consider the following simple function, which adds the argument passed it to the beginning of the list:

```
void addHead(LinkableClass* pLC)
{
    pLC->pNext = pHead;
    pHead = pLC;
}
```

Performing other operations on a linked list

Adding an object to the head of a list is the simplest of the operations on a linked list. Adding an element to the end of the list is a bit trickier:

```
void addTail(LinkableClass* pLC)
{
    // start with a pointer to the beginning
    // of the linked list
    LinkableClass* pCurrent = pHead;

    // iterate through the list until we find
    // the last object in the list - this will
    // be the one with the null next pointer
    while(pCurrent->pNext != (LinkableClass*)0)
    {
        // move pCurrent over to the next entry
        pCurrent = pCurrent->pNext;
    }

    // now make that object point to LC
    pCurrent->pNext = pLC;

    // make sure that LC's next pointer is null
    // thereby marking it as the last element in
    // the list
    pLC->pNext = (LinkableClass*)0;
}
```

The addTail() function begins by iterating through the loop looking for the entry who's pNext pointer is null — this is the last entry in the list. With that in hand, addTail() links the *pLC object onto the end.

(Actually, as written addTail() has a bug. A special test must be added for pHead itself being null indicating that the list was previously empty.)

A remove() function is similar. This function removes the specified object from the list and returns a 1 if successful or a 0 if not.

```
int remove(LinkableClass* pLC)
{
    LinkableClass* pCurrent = pHead;

    // if the list is empty, then obviously
    // we couldn't find *pLC in the list
    if (pCurrent == (LinkableClass*)0)
    {
        return 0;
    }

    // iterate through the loop looking for the
    // specified entry rather than the end of
    // the list
    while(pCurrent->pNext)
    {
        // if the next entry is the *pLC object...
        if (pLC == pCurrent->pNext)
        {
            // ...then point the current entry at
            // the next entry instead
            pCurrent->pNext = pLC->pNext;

            // not absolutely necessary, but remove
            // the next object from *pLC so as not
            // to get confused
            pLC->pNext = (LinkableClass*)0;
            return 1;
        }
    }
    return 0;
}
```

The remove() function first checks to make sure that the list is not empty. If it is, remove() returns a fail indicator because obviously the *pLC object is not present if the list is empty. If the list is not empty, remove() iterates through each member until it finds the object which points to *pLC. If it finds that object, remove() moves the pCurrent->pNext pointer around *pLC.

Properties of linked lists

Linked lists are everything that arrays are not. Linked lists can expand and contract at will as entries are added and removed. Inserting an object in the middle of a linked list is quick and simple — existing members do not need to be copied about. Similarly, sorting elements in a linked list is much quicker than the same process on the elements of an array.

On the negative side of the ledger, finding a member in a linked list is not nearly as quick as referencing an element in an array. Array elements are directly accessible via the index — no similar feature is available for the linked list. Programs must search sometimes the entire list to find any given entry.

Hooking Up with a LinkedListData Program

The *LinkedListData* program shown here implements a linked list of objects containing students' name and social security number.

```
// LinkedListData - store name data in
//                  a linked list of objects
#include <stdio.h>
#include <iostream.h>
#include <string.h>

// NameDataSet - stores name and social security
//               information
class NameDataSet
{
    public:
        char szFirstName[128];
        char szLastName [128];
        int  nSocialSecurity;

        // the link to the next entry in the list
        NameDataSet* pNext;
};

// the pointer to the first entry
// in the list
NameDataSet* pHead = 0;

// addTail - add a new member to the linked list
```

```
void addTail(NameDataSet* pNDS)
{
    // make sure that our list pointer is NULL
    // since we are now the last element in the list
    pNDS->pNext = 0;

    // if the list is empty,
    // then just point the head pointer to the
    // current entry and quit
    if (pHead == 0)
    {
        pHead = pNDS;
        return;
    }

    // otherwise find the last element in the list
    NameDataSet* pCurrent = pHead;
    while(pCurrent->pNext)
    {
        pCurrent = pCurrent->pNext;
    }

    // now add the current  entry onto the end of that
    pCurrent->pNext = pNDS;
}

// getData - read a name and social security
//           number; return null if no more to
//           read
NameDataSet* getData()
{
    // get a new entry to fill
    NameDataSet* pNDS = new NameDataSet;

    // read the first name
    cout << "\nEnter first name:";
    cin  >> pNDS->szFirstName;

    // if the name entered is 'exit'...
    if ((stricmp(pNDS->szFirstName, "exit") == 0))
    {
        // ...delete the still  empty object...
        delete pNDS;

        // ...return a null to terminate input
        return 0;
    }

    // read the remaining members
    cout << "Enter last name:";
    cin  >> pNDS->szLastName;
```

```
        cout << "Enter social security number:";
        cin  >> pNDS->nSocialSecurity;

        // zero the pointer to the next entry
        pNDS->pNext = 0;

        // return the address of the object created
        return pNDS;
}

// displayData - output the index'th data set
void displayData(NameDataSet* pNDS)
{
        cout << pNDS->szFirstName
             << " "
             << pNDS->szLastName
             << "/"
             << pNDS->nSocialSecurity
             << "\n";
}

int main(int argc, char* pArgs[])
{
        cout << "Read name/social security information\n"
             << "Enter 'exit' for first name to exit\n";

        // create (another) NameDataSet object
        NameDataSet* pNDS;
        while (pNDS = getData())
        {
            // add it onto the end of  the list of
            // NameDataSet objects
            addTail(pNDS);
        }

        // to display the objects, iterate  through the
        // list (stop when the next address is NULL)
        cout << "Entries:\n";
        pNDS = pHead;
        while(pNDS)
        {
            // display current entry
            displayData(pNDS);

            // get the next entry
            pNDS = pNDS->pNext;
        }
        return 0;
}
```

Although somewhat lengthy, the LinkedListData program is relatively simple. The main() function begins by calling getData() to fetch another NameDataSet entry from the user. If the user enters "exit," then getData() returns a null. main() calls addTail() to add the entry returned from getData() to the end of the linked list.

When there are no more NameDataSet objects forthcoming from the user, main() iterates through the list, displaying each using the displayData() function.

The getData() function first allocates an empty NameDataSet object from the heap. getData() continues by reading the first name of the entry to add. If the user enters a first name of "exit" or "EXIT," the function deletes the object and returns a null to the caller. getData() continues by reading the last name and social security number. Finally, getData() zeroes out the pNext pointer before returning.

Never leave link pointers uninitialized. Use the old programmer's wives' tale: "Zero them out when in doubt." (Wives of old programmers say that.)

The addTail() function appearing here is similar to the addTail() function demonstrated earlier in the chapter. Unlike that earlier version, this addTail() checks to see if the list is empty before starting. If pHead is null, then addTail() points it at the current entry and terminates.

The displayData() function is a pointer based version of the earlier displayData() functions.

Chapter 16

Protecting Members: Do Not Disturb

C hapter 13 introduced the concept of the class. That chapter described the `public` keyword as if it were part of the class declaration — just something that you do. In this chapter, you find out about an alternative to *public*.

Protecting Members

The members of a class can be marked protected, which makes them inaccessible outside the class. The alternative is to make the members public. Public members are accessible to all.

Why you need protected members

To understand the role of protected, think about the goals of object-oriented programming:

> ✔ Protect the internals of the class from outside functions. Suppose, for example, that you have a plan to build a software microwave (or whatever), provide it with a simple interface to the outside world, and then put a box around it to keep others from messing with the insides. The protected keyword is that box.

✔ Make the class responsible for maintaining its internal state. It's not fair to ask the class to be responsible if others can reach in and manipulate its internals (any more than it's fair to ask a microwave designer to be responsible for the consequences of my mucking with a microwave's internal wiring).

✔ Limit the interface of the class to the outside world. It's easier to learn and use a class that has a limited interface (the public members). Protected members are hidden from the user and need not be learned. The interface becomes the class; this is called *abstraction* (see Chapter 8).

✔ Reduce the level of interconnection between the class and other code. By limiting interconnection, you can more easily replace one class with another, or use the class in other programs.

Now I know what you functional types out there are saying: "You don't need some fancy feature to do all that. Just make a rule that says certain members are publicly accessible and others are not."

Although that is true in theory, it doesn't work. People start out with all kinds of good intentions, but as long as the language doesn't at least discourage direct access of protected members, these good intentions get crushed under the pressure to get the product out the door.

Discovering how protected members work

Adding the keyword `public` to a class makes subsequent members public, which means that they are accessible by non-member functions. Adding the keyword `protected` makes subsequent members of the class protected, which means they are not accessible by non-members of the class. You can switch between public and protected as often as you like.

Suppose you have a class named `Student`. In this example, the following capabilities are all that a fully functional, upstanding `Student` needs (notice the absence of `spendMoney()` and `drinkBeer()` — this is a highly stylized student):

`addCourse (inthours, float grade)` — add a course

`grade()` — return the current grade point average

`hours()` — return the number of hours earned toward graduation

The remaining members of `Student` can be declared protected to keep other functions' prying expressions out of `Student`'s business.

```
class Student
{
 public:
  // grade - return the current grade point average
  float grade()
  {
   return gpa;
  }
  // hours - return the number of semester hours
  int hours()
  {
   return semesterHours;
  }
  // addCourse - add another course to the student's record
  float addCourse(int hours, float grade);

  // the following members are off-limits to others
 protected:
  int  semesterHours; // hours earned toward graduation
  float gpa;           // grade point average
};
```

Now the members semester hours and gpa are accessible only to other
members of Student. Thus, the following doesn't work:

```
Student s;
int main(int argcs, char* pArgs[])
{
  // raise my grade (don't make it too high; otherwise, no
  // one would believe it)
  s.gpa = 3.5;   // <- generates compiler error
  float gpa = s.grade(); // <- this public function reads
         // a copy of the value, but you can't
         // change it from here
  return 0;
}
```

The application's attempt to change the value of gpa is flagged with a
compiler error.

It's considered good form not to rely on the default and specify either public
or private at the beginning of the class. Most of the time, people start with
the public members, because these make up the interface of the class.
Protected members are saved until later.

Class members can be protected from access by non-member functions also by declaring them private. In fact, private is the default for classes (that is, classes start out in private mode). The difference between protected and private first becomes apparent in the presence of inheritance, which is covered in Chapter 21.

Making an Argument for Using Protected Members

Now that you know a little more about how to use protected members in an actual class, I replay the arguments for using protected members.

Protecting the internal state of the class

Making the gpa member protected precludes the application from setting the grade point average to some arbitrary value. The application can add courses, but it can't change the grade point average.

If the application has a legitimate need to set the grade point average directly, the class can provide a member function for that purpose, as follows:

```
class Student
{
 public:
  // same as before
  float grade()
  {
   return gpa;
  }
  // here we allow the grade to be changed
  float grade(float newGPA)
  {
   float oldGPA = gpa;
   // only if the new value is valid
   if (newGPA > 0& & newGPA <= 4.0)
   {
     gpa = newGPA;
   }
   return oldGPA;
  }
  // ...other stuff is the same including the data members:
 protected:
  int   semesterHours; // hours earned toward graduation
  float gpa;
};
```

The addition of the member function grade (float allows the application to set the gpa). Notice, however, that the class still hasn't given up control completely. The application can't set `gpa` to any old value; only a `gpa` in the legal range of values (from 0 through 4.0) is accepted.

Thus, Student has provided access to an internal data member without abdicating its responsibility to make sure that the internal state of the class is valid.

Using a class with a limited interface

A class provides a limited interface. To use a class, all you need (or want) to know are its public members, what they do, and what their arguments are. This can drastically reduce the number of things you need to learn — and remember — to use the class.

As conditions change or as bugs are found, you want to be able to change the internal workings of a class. When you have hidden the internal workings of the class, changes to those details are less likely to require changes in the external application code.

Giving Non-Member Functions Access to Protected Members

Occasionally, you want a non-member function to have access to the protected members of a class. You can do this by naming that function a friend of the class using the keyword `friend`.

Why do I need friends? (I am a rock, I am an island)

Sometimes an external function requires direct access to a data member. Without some type of friend mechanism, the programmer would be forced to declare the member public. This would give everyone else access to the one function as well.

It's like having a neighbor check on your house during your vacation. Giving non-family members the key to your house is not normally a good idea, but it beats the alternative of leaving the house unlocked.

The friend declaration appears in the class that contains the protected member. The friend declaration is like a prototype declaration in that it includes the extended name and the return type. In the following example, the function `initialize()` can now access anything it wants in Student:

```
class Student
{
   friend void initialize(Student*);
 public:
   // same public members as before...
 protected:
   int  semesterHours; // hours earned toward graduation
   float gpa;
};
// the following function is a friend of Student
// so it can access the protected members
void initialize(Student *pS)
{
   pS->gpa = 0;         // this is now legal...
   pS->semesterHours = 0;  // ...when it wasn't before
}
```

A single function can be declared to be a friend of two classes at the same time. Although this can be convenient, it tends to bind the two classes together. This binding of classes is normally considered bad because it makes one class dependent on the other. If the two classes naturally belong together, however, it's not all bad. For example:

```
class Student;   // forward declaration
class Teacher
{
   friend void registration();
 protected:
   int    noStudents;
   Student *pList[100];
 public:
   void assignGrades();
};
class Student
{
   friend void registration();
 public:
   // same public members as before...
 protected:
   Teacher *pT;
   int  semesterHours; // hours earned toward graduation
   float gpa;
};
```

In this example, the `registration()` function can reach into both the Student and Teacher classes to tie them together at registration time, without being a member function of either one.

Notice that the first line in the example declares the class Student but none of its members. Remember, this is called a forward declaration and just defines the name of the class so that other classes, such as Teacher, can refer to it. Forward references are necessary when two classes refer to each other.

A member function of one class may be declared a friend of another class. For example:

```
class Teacher
{
  // ...other members as well...
 public:
  void assignGrades();
};
class Student
{
  friend void Teacher::assignGrades();
 public:
  // same public members as before...
 protected:
  int  semesterHours; // hours earned toward graduation
  float gpa;
};
void Teacher::assignGrades()
{
  // can access protected members of Teacher from here
}
```

Unlike in the non-member example, the member function assignGrades() must be declared before the class Student can declare it to be a friend.

An entire class can be named a friend of another. This has the effect of making every member function of the class a friend. For example:

```
class Student;    // forward declaration
class Teacher
{
 protected:
  int   noStudents;
  Student *pList[100];
 public:
  void assignGrades();
};
class Student
{
```

```
   friend class Teacher; // make entire class a friend
  public:
   // same public members as before...
  protected:
   int  semesterHours; // hours earned toward graduation
   float gpa;
};
```

Now any member function of Teacher has access to the protected members of Student. Declaring one class a friend of the other inseparably binds the two classes together.

Chapter 17

Building and Tearing Down Objects: The Constructor and Destructor

• •

• •

*O*bjects in programs are built and scrapped just like objects in the real world. If the class is to be responsible for its well-being, it must have some control over this process. As luck would have it (I suppose some pre-planning was involved as well), C++ provides just the right mechanism. But first, a discussion of what it means to create an object.

Creating Objects

Some people get a little sloppy in using the terms *class* and *object*. What's the difference? What's the relationship?

I can create a class Dog that describes the relevant properties of man's best friend. At my house, we have two dogs. Thus, my class Dog has two instances, Trudie and Scooter (well, I think there are two instances — I haven't seen Scooter in a few days).

A *class* describes a type of thing. An *object* is an instance of a class. The class is Dog, and the objects are Trudie and Scooter. Each dog has a separate object, but there is only one class Dog, no matter how many dogs I may have.

Objects are created and destroyed, but classes simply exist. My pets Trudie and Scooter come and go, but the class Dog (evolution aside) is perpetual.

Different types of objects are created at different times. Global objects are created when the program first begins execution. Local objects are created when the program encounters their declaration.

A global object is one that is declared outside of any function. A local object is one that is declared within a function and is, therefore, local to the function. In the following example, the variable me is global and the variable noMe is local to the function pickOne():

```
int me;
void pickOne()
{
   int noMe;
}
```

Under C rules, global objects are initialized to all zeros. Objects declared local to a function have no particular initial value. This is generally not acceptable to classes.

C++ allows the class to define a special member function that is invoked automatically when an object of that class is created. This member function, called the constructor, must initialize the object to some valid initial state. In addition, the class may define a destructor to handle the destruction of the object. These two functions are the topics of this chapter.

Using Constructors

The constructor is a member function that is called automatically when an object of a certain class is created. Its primary job is to initialize the object to a legal initial value for the class.

Explaining the need for constructors

You could initialize an object as part of the declaration — that's the way the C programmer would do it. For example:

```
struct Student
{
  int  semesterHours;
  float gpa;
};
void fn()
{
  Student s = {0, 0};
  // ...function continues...
}
```

This doesn't work for a true C++ class because the application doesn't have access to the protected members of the class. The following snippet is invalid:

```
class Student
{
 public:
  // ...public members...
 protected:
  int  semesterHours;
  float gpa;
};
void fn()
{
  Student s = {0, 0};  // illegal; data members not
                       // accessible
  // ...function continues...
}
```

In this example, the non-member fn() can't write to the protected members semesterHours and gpa.

You could outfit the class with an initialization function that the application calls as soon as the object is created. Because this initialization function is a member of the class, it would have access to the protected members. This solution appears as follows:

```
class Student
{
 public:
  void init()
  {
    semesterHours = 0;
    gpa = 0.0;
  }
  // ...other public members...
 protected:  int  semesterHours;
  float gpa;
};
void fn()
{
```

```
    Student s;      // create the object...
    s.init();       // ...then initialize it
    // ...function continues...
  }
```

The only problem with this solution is that it abrogates the responsibility of the class to look after its own data members. In other words, the class must rely on the application to call the init() function. If it does not, the object is full of garbage and who knows what might happen.

What is needed is a way to take the responsibility for calling the init() function away from the application code and give it to the compiler. Every time an object is created, the compiler can insert a call to the special init function to initialize it. That's a constructor!

Making constructors work

The constructor is a special member function that's called automatically when an object is created. It carries the same name as the class. That way, the compiler knows which member function is the constructor. (The designers of C++ could have made up a different rule, such as: "The constructor must be called init()." It wouldn't have made any difference, as long as the compiler could recognize the constructor.) In addition, the constructor has no return type since it is called automatically (if the constructor did return something there would be no place to put it).

With a constructor, the class Student appears as follows:

```
#include <iostream.h>
class Student
{
  public:
    Student()
    {
      cout << "constructing student\n";
      semesterHours = 0;
      gpa = 0.0;
    }
    // ...other public members...
  protected:
    int   semesterHours;
    float gpa;
};
void fn()
{
    Student s;      // create the object and initialize it
    // ...function continues...
}
```

At the point of the declaration of s, the compiler inserts a call to the constructor Student::Student().

This simple constructor was written as an inline member function. Constructors can be written also as outline functions. For example:

```
#include <iostream.h>

class Student
{
  public:
    Student();
    // ...other public members...
  protected:
    int   semesterHours;
    float gpa;
};
Student::Student()
{
    cout << "constructing student\n";
    semesterHours = 0;
    gpa = 0.0;
}
void fn()
{
    Student s;      // create the object and initialize it
    // ...function continues...
}
int main(int argcs, char* pArgs[])
{
    fn();
    return 0;
}
```

I added a small main() function here so that you can execute this program. You really should single-step this simple program in your debugger before going any further.

Explanations for the care and feeding of the GNU C++ debugger are contained in Chapter 29.

As you single-step through this example, control eventually comes to rest at the Student s declaration. Select Step Into or Trace one more time and control magically jumps to Student::Student(). (If you are using the inline version, be sure to compile with the "Outline inline functions" compiler switch enabled; otherwise the entire constructor is executed as a single statement, and you won't notice the call.) Continue single-stepping through the constructor. When the function has finished, control returns to the statement after the declaration.

Multiple objects can be declared on a single line. Rerun the single-step experiment with `fn()` declared as follows:

```
void fn()
{
  Student s[5];  // create an array of objects
  // ...function continues...
}
```

You should see the constructor invoked five times, one time for each element in the array.

The output statement has been added so that you can see output to the screen whenever the constructor is invoked in case you can't get the debugger to work (or you just don't want to bother). The effect is not as dramatic, but it is convincing.

The constructor can be invoked only automatically. It can't be called like a normal member function. That is, you can't use something like the following to reinitialize a `Student` object:

```
void fn()
{
  Student s;     // initialize the object
  // ...other stuff...
  s.Student();   // reinitialize it; this doesn't work
}
```

The constructor has no return type, not even `void`.

If a class contains a data member that is an object of another class, the constructor for that class is called automatically as well. Consider the following example. Output statements have been added so that you can see the order in which the objects are invoked.

```
#include <iostream.h>
class Student
{
 public:
  Student()
  {
   cout << "constructing student\n";
   semesterHours = 0;
   gpa = 0.0;
  }
  // ...other public members...
 protected:
  int  semesterHours;
```

```
    float gpa;
};
class Teacher
{
  public:
    Teacher()
    {
      cout << "constructing teacher\n";
    }
};
class TutorPair
{
  public:
    TutorPair()
    {
      cout << "constructing tutor pair\n";
      noMeetings = 0;
    }
  protected:
    Student student;
    Teacher teacher;
    int    noMeetings;
};
int main(int argcs, char* pArgs[])
{
    TutorPair tp;
    cout << "back in main\n";
    return 0;
}
```

Executing this program generates the following output:

```
constructing student
constructing teacher
constructing tutor pair
back in main
```

Creating the object tp in main invokes the constructor for TutorPair automatically. Before control passes into the body of the TutorPair constructor, however, the constructors for the two-member objects student and teacher are invoked.

The constructor for Student is called first because it is declared first. Then the constructor for Teacher is called. After these objects have been constructed, control returns to the open brace and the constructor for TutorPair is allowed to construct the remainder of the object.

It would not do for `TutorPair` to be responsible for initializing student and teacher. Each class is responsible for initializing its own objects.

Understanding the Destructor

Just as objects are created, so are they destroyed (ashes to ashes, dust to dust). If a class can have a constructor to set things up, it should also have a special member function to take the object apart. This member is called the destructor.

Why you need the destructor

A class may allocate resources in the constructor; these resources need to be deallocated before the object ceases to exist. For example, if the constructor opens a file, the file needs to be closed before leaving that class or the program itself. Or if the constructor allocates memory from the heap, this memory must be freed before the object goes away. The destructor allows the class to do these cleanup tasks automatically without relying on the application to call the proper member functions.

Working with destructors

The destructor member has the same name as the class but with a tilde (~) added to the front. (C++ is being cute again — the tilde is the symbol for the logical NOT operator. Get it? A destructor is a "not constructor." Tres clever.) Like a constructor, the destructor has no return type. For example, the class `Student` with a destructor added appears as follows:

```
class Student
{
  public:
   Student()
   {
     semesterHours = 0;
     gpa = 0.0;
   }
   ~Student()
   {
     // ...whatever assets are returned here...
   }
   // ...other public members...
  protected:
   int  semesterHours;
   float gpa;
};
```

The destructor is invoked automatically when an object is destroyed, or in C++ parlance, when an object is *destructed*. That sounds sort of circular ("the destructor is invoked when an object is destructed"), so I've avoided the term until now. You can also say, "when the object goes out of scope." A local object goes out of scope when the function returns. A global or static object goes out of scope when the program terminates.

If more than one object is being destructed, the destructors are invoked in the reverse order in which the constructors were called. This is also true when destructing objects that have class objects as data members. For example, here's the example Tutor Pair program with destructors added:

```cpp
#include <iostream.h>
class Student
{
 public:
  Student()
   {
    cout << "constructing student\n";
    semesterHours = 0;
    gpa = 0.0;
   }
  ~Student()
   {
    cout << "destructing student\n";  }
  // ...other public members...
 protected:
  int  semesterHours;
  float gpa;
};
class Teacher
{
 public:
  Teacher()
   {
    cout << "constructing teacher\n";
   }
  ~Teacher()
   {
    cout << "destructing teacher\n";
   }
};
class TutorPair
{
   public:
   TutorPair()
    {
     cout << "constructing tutor pair\n";
```

```
      noMeetings = 0;
   }
  ~TutorPair()
   {
     cout << "destructing tutor pair\n";
   }
 protected:
  Student s;
  Teacher t;
  int    noMeetings;
};
int main(int argcs, char* pArgs[])
{
   TutorPair tp;
   cout << "back in main\n";
   return 0;
}
```

If you execute this program, it generates the following output:

```
constructing student
constructing teacher
constructing tutor pair
back in main
destructing tutor pair
destructing teacher
destructing student
```

The constructor for TutorPair is invoked at the declaration of tp. The destructor is invoked at the closing brace of main().

Chapter 18

Making Constructive Arguments

• •

In This Chapter

▶ Making argumentative constructors

▶ Overloading the constructor

▶ Creating objects by using constructors

▶ Invoking member constructors

▶ Order of construction and destruction

• •

A class represents a type of object in the real world. For example, we have used the class Student to represent the properties of a student complete with name and Social Security Number.

Just like students, classes think that they are self-reliant. Unlike a student, a class is responsible for its own care and feeding — a class must keep itself in a valid state at all times. For example, a Student ID of 0 is probably not valid. It's up to the class to make sure that the ID is initialized to a legal value when the object is created.

C++ allows the programmer to define a special member function called the constructor that's called automatically when the object is created. The constructor allows the class to initialize the object properly when it's created.

The constructors shown in Chapter 17 have no arguments — they have no choice but to initialize the object to some default state This chapter examines constructors with arguments.

Outfitting Constructors with Arguments

C++ allows the programmer to define a constructor with arguments. For example:

```
#include <iostream.h>
#include <string.h>
class Student
{
    Student(char *pName)
    {
        cout << "constructing student " << pName << "\n";
        strncpy(name, pName, sizeof(name));
        name[sizeof(name) - 1]  = '\0';
    }
            // ...other public members go here
    protected:
     char   name[40];
     int    semesterHours;
     float  gpa;
};
```

Justifying constructors

Something as straightforward as adding arguments to the constructor shouldn't require much justification, but let me take a shot at it anyway. First, allowing arguments to constructors is convenient. It's a bit silly to make the programmer construct a default object and then immediately call an initialization function to store data in it. A constructor with arguments is like one-stop shopping — sort of a full-service constructor.

Another more important reason to provide arguments to constructors is that it may not be possible to construct a reasonable default object. Remember that a constructor's job is to construct a legal object (legal as defined by the class). If some default object is not legal, the constructor isn't doing its job.

For example, a bank account without an account number is probably not legal. (C++ doesn't care one way or the other, but the bank might get snitty.) We could construct a numberless BankAccount object and then require that the application use some other member function to initialize the account number before it's used. This breaks our rules, however, because it forces the class to rely on the application for initialization.

Using a constructor?

Conceptually, the idea of adding an argument is simple. A constructor is a member function and member functions can have arguments. Therefore, constructors can have arguments.

Remember, though, that you don't call the constructor like a normal function. Therefore, the only way to pass arguments to the constructor is when the object is created. For example, the following program creates an object s of class Student by calling the Student(char*) constructor. The object s is destructed when the function main() returns.

```cpp
#include <iostream.h>
#include <string.h>
class Student
{
  public:
   Student(char *pName)
   {
      cout << "constructing student " << pName << "\n";
      strncpy(name, pName, sizeof(name));
      name[sizeof(name) - 1] = '\0';
      semesterHours = 0;
      gpa = 0.0;
   }
   ~Student()
   {
      cout << "destructing " << name << "\n";

      // it's a good idea to wipe out the student name
      // since the object is no longer valid
      name[0] = '\0';
   }

   // ...other public members...
  protected:
   char  name[40];
   int   semesterHours;
   float gpa;
};

int main(int argcs, char* pArgs[])
{
   Student s("Danny");          // construct little Danny
   return 0;
}                               // now, get rid of him
```

The constructor looks like the constructors shown in Chapter 17 except for the addition of the char* argument pName. The constructor initializes the data members to their empty start-up values, except for the data member name, which gets its initial value from pName.

The object s is created in main(). The argument to be passed to the constructor appears in the declaration of s, right next to the name of the object. Thus, the student s is given the name Danny in this declaration. The closed brace invokes the destructor on poor little Danny.

Executing the program generates the following output:

```
constructing student Danny
destructing Danny
```

Many of the constructors in this chapter violate the "functions with more than three lines shouldn't be inlined" rule. I decided to make them inline anyway because I think they're easier for you to read that way. Aren't I a nice guy?

When outlined, constructors and destructors appear as follows:

```
#include <iostream.h>
#include <string.h>
class Student
{
  public:
    // declarations only
    Student(char *pName);
    ~Student();

    // ...other public members...
  protected:
    char   name[40];
    int    semesterHours;
    float  gpa;
};

// definitions (notice no return type)
Student::Student(char *pName)
{
    cout << "constructing student " << pName << "\n";
    strncpy(name, pName, sizeof(name));
    name[sizeof(name) - 1]  = '\0';
    semesterHours = 0;
    gpa = 0.0;
}

// check out this destructor declaration
//      - does this look bizarre or what?
Student::~Student()
{
    cout << "destructing " << name << "\n";
}
```

As your experience in C++ grows, you should have no trouble mentally converting from one form to the other.

Overloading the Constructor (Is That Like Placing Too Many Demands on the Carpenter?)

While I'm drawing parallels between constructors and other, more normal member functions in this chapter, I can draw one more: Constructors can be overloaded.

Overloading a function means to define two functions with the same short name but with different types of arguments. See Chapter 6 for the latest news in function overloading.

C++ chooses the proper constructor based on the arguments in the declaration of the object. For example, the class Student can have all three constructors shown in the following snippet at the same time:

```cpp
#include <iostream.h>
#include <string.h>
class Student
{
  public:
    Student()
    {
        cout << "constructing student no name\n";
        semesterHours = 0;
        gpa = 0.0;
        name[0] = '\0';
    }
    Student(char *pName)
    {
        cout << "constructing student " << pName << "\n";
        strncpy(name, pName, sizeof(name));
        name[sizeof(name) - 1] = '\0';
        semesterHours = 0;
        gpa = 0;
    }
    Student(char *pName, int xfrHours, float xfrGPA)
    {
        cout << "constructing student " << pName << "\n";
        strncpy(name, pName, sizeof(name));
        name[sizeof(name) - 1] = '\0';
        semesterHours = xfrHours;
        gpa = xfrGPA;
    }
    ~Student()
    {
```

```
        cout << "destructing student\n";
    }
    // ...other public members...
  protected:
    char  name[40];
    int   semesterHours;
    float gpa;
};

// the following invokes each constructor in turn
int main(int argcs, char* pArgs[])
{
    Student noName;
    Student freshMan("Smell E. Fish");
    Student xfer("Upp R. Classman", 80, 2.5);
    return 0;
}
```

Because the object noName appears with no arguments, it's constructed using the constructor Student::Student(). This constructor is called the default, or *void,* constructor. (I prefer the latter name, but the former is more common, so I use it in this book — I'm a slave to fashion.) The freshMan is constructed using the constructor that has only a char* argument and the xfer Student uses the constructor with three arguments.

Notice how similar all three constructors are, particularly the last two. By adding defaults to the last constructor, all three constructors can be combined into one. For example, the following class combines all three constructors into a single, clever constructor:

```
#include <iostream.h>
#include <string.h>
class Student

{
  public:
    Student(char *pName  = "no name",
            int xfrHours = 0,
            float xfrGPA = 0.0)
    {
        cout << "constructing student " << pName << "\n";
        strncpy(name, pName, sizeof(name));
        name[sizeof(name) - 1] = '\0';
        semesterHours = xfrHours;
        gpa = xfrGPA;
    }
    ~Student()
    {
```

```
        cout << "destructing student\n";
    }

    // ...other public members...
    protected:
    char   name[40];
    int    semesterHours;
    float  gpa;
};

int main(int argcs, char* pArgs[])
{
    Student noName;
    Student freshMan("Smell E. Fish");
    Student xfer("Upp R. Classman", 80, 2.5);
    return 0;
}
```

Now all three objects are constructed using the same constructor; defaults are provided for nonexistent arguments in `noName` and `freshMan`.

 In earlier versions of C++, you couldn't create a default constructor by providing defaults for all the arguments. The default constructor had to be a separate explicit constructor. Although this restriction was lifted in the standard (it seems to have had no good basis), some older compilers may still impose it.

Defaulting Default Constructors

As far as C++ is concerned, every class must have a constructor; otherwise, you can't create any objects of that class. If you don't provide a constructor for your class, C++ should probably just generate an error, but it doesn't. To provide compatibility with existing C code, which knows nothing about constructors, C++ automatically provides a default constructor (sort of a default default constructor) that sets all the data members of the object to binary zero. Sometimes I call this a Miranda constructor — you know, "if you cannot afford a constructor, a constructor will be provided for you."

If your class already has a constructor, C++ doesn't provide the automatic default constructor. (Having tipped your hand that this isn't a C program, C++ doesn't feel obliged to do any extra work to ensure compatibility.)

 The result is: If you define a constructor for your class but you also want a default constructor, you must define it yourself.

Some code snippets help demonstrate this. The following is legal:

```
class Student
{
   // ...all the same stuff as before but no constructors
};

int main(int argcs, char* pArgs[])
{
   Student noName;
   return 0;
}
```

noName is declared with no arguments, so C++ invokes the default constructor to construct it. Because the programmer has not already defined any constructors for class Student, C++ provides a default constructor that zeros
out any data members that Student may have.

The following code snippet does not compile properly:

```
class Student
{
  public:
     Student(char *pName);
};

int main(int argcs, char* pArgs[])
{
   Student noName;
   return 0;
}
```

The seemingly innocuous addition of the Student(char*) constructor precludes C++ from automatically providing a Student() constructor with
which to build object noName. This example generates the following error
message from the GNU C++ compiler which comes on the enclosed CD-ROM.
(The error message from any other compiler would be similar.)

```
Error: no matching function for call to 'Student::Student ()'
```

The compiler is telling you that it can't find the Student::Student() constructor. Adding a default constructor solves the problem:

```
class Student
{
  public:
    Student(char *pName);
    Student();                    // manually provided default
            constructor
};
int main(int argcs, char* pArgs[])
```

```
{
   Student noName;              // used to build this object
   return 0;
}
```

It's just this type of illogic that explains why C++ programmers get the really big bucks!

Constructing Class Members

In the preceding examples, all data members have been of simple types, such as `int` and `float`. With simple types, it's sufficient to assign a value to the variable within the constructor. But what if the class contains data members of a user-defined class? Consider the following example:

```
#include <iostream.h>
#include <string.h>

int nextStudentId = 0;
class StudentId
{
  public:
   StudentId()
   {
      value = ++nextStudentId;
      cout << "Assigning student id " << value << "\n";
   }
  protected:
   int value;
};

class Student
{
  public:
   Student(char *pName  = "no name")
   {
      cout << "Constructing student " << pName << "\n";
      strncpy(name, pName, sizeof(name));
      name[sizeof(name) - 1]  = '\0';
   }
  protected:
   char  name[40];
   StudentId id;
};

int main(int argcs, char* pArgs[])
{
   Student s("Randy");
   return 0;
}
```

A student ID is assigned to each student as the student object is constructed. In this example, IDs are handed out sequentially using the global variable nextStudentId.

This Student class contains a member id of class StudentId. The constructor for Student can't assign a value to this id member because Student does not have access to the protected members of StudentId. You could make Student a friend of StudentId, but that violates the "you take care of your business, I'll take care of mine" philosophy. Somehow you need to invoke the constructor for StudentId when Student is constructed.

C++ does this for you automatically in this case, invoking the default constructor StudentId::StudentId() on id. This occurs after the Student constructor is called but before control passes to the first statement in the constructor. (Single step the preceding program in the debugger to see what I mean. As always, be sure that inline functions are forced outline.) The output from executing this simple program follows:

```
Assigning student id 1
Constructing student Randy
```

Notice that the message from the StudentId constructor appears before the output from the Student constructor.

(By the way, with all these constructors performing output, you may think that constructors must output something. Most constructors don't output a bloody thing.)

If the programmer does not provide a constructor, the default constructor provided by C++ automatically invokes the default constructors for any data members. The same is true come harvesting time. The destructor for the class automatically invokes the destructor for any data members that have destructors. The C++-provided destructor does the same.

Okay, this is all great for the default constructor. But what if we wanted to invoke a constructor other than the default? Where do we put the object? To demonstrate, assume that instead of calculating the student ID, it is provided to the Student constructor, which passes the ID to the constructor for class StudentId.

Let me first show you what doesn't work. Consider the following program:

```
#include <iostream.h>
#include <string.h>

class StudentId
{
  public:
    StudentId(int id = 0)
    {
```

```
        value = id;
        cout << "Assigning student id " << value << "\n";
    }

  protected:
    int value;
};

class Student
{
  public:
    Student(char *pName  = "no name", int ssId = 0)
    {
        cout << "Constructing student " << pName << "\n";
        strncpy(name, pName, sizeof(name));
        name[sizeof(name) - 1] = '\0';
        // don't try this at home kids. It doesn't work
        StudentId id(ssId);    // construct a student id
    }
  protected:
    char  name[40];
    StudentId id;
};

int main(int argcs, char* pArgs[])
{
    Student s("Randy", 1234);
    cout << "This message from main\n";
    return 0;
}
```

The constructor for StudentId has been changed to accept a value exter-
nally (the default value is necessary to get the example to compile, for reasons that will become clear shortly). Within the constructor for Student, the
programmer (that's me) has (cleverly) attempted to construct a StudentId
object named id.

If you look at the output from this program, you notice a problem:

```
Assigning student id 0
Constructing student Randy
Assigning student id 1234
Destructing id 1234
This message from main
Destructing id 0
```

The first problem is that the constructor for StudentId appears to be
invoked twice, once with zero and a second time with the expected 1234.
Then we notice that the 1234 object is destructed before the output string in
main(). Apparently the StudentId object is destructed within the Student
constructor itself.

The explanation for this rather bizarre behavior is clear. The data member id already exists by the time the body of the constructor is entered. Rather than constructing the existing data member id, the declaration provided in the constructor creates a local object of the same name. This local object is destructed upon returning from the constructor.

Somehow we need a different mechanism to indicate "construct the existing member; don't create a new one." This mechanism needs to appear before the open brace, before the data members are declared. For this, C++ defined a new construct, as follows:

```
class Student
{
  public:
    Student(char *pName = "no name", int ssId = 0) : id(ssId)
    {
        cout << "Constructing student " << pName << "\n";
        strncpy(name, pName, sizeof(name));
        name[sizeof(name) - 1] = '\0';
    }
  protected:
    char  name[40];
    StudentId id;
};
```

Notice in particular the first line of the constructor. Here's something you may not have seen before. The : means that what follows are calls to the constructors of data members of the current class. To the C++ compiler, this line reads: "Construct the member id using the argument ssId of the Student constructor. Whatever data members are not called out in this fashion are constructed using the default constructor."

This new program generates the expected result:

```
Assigning student id 1234
Constructing student Randy
This message from main
Destructing id 1234
```

The : syntax must also be used to assign values to const or reference type members. Consider the following silly class:

```
class SillyClass
{
  public:
    SillyClass(int& i) : ten(10), refI(i)
    {
    }
```

```
   protected:
     const int ten;
     int& refI;
};

int main(int argcs, char* pArgs[])
{
    int i;
    SillyClass sc(i);
    return 0;
}
```

After the constructor for `SillyClass` has been entered, the data members `ten` and `refI` have already been created. This is analogous to declaring a const or reference variable in a function. Such variables must be assigned a value when declared.

In fact, any data member can be declared using the preceding syntax, but const and reference variables must be declared in this way.

Avoiding the "object declaration trap"

Look again at the way the `Student` objects were declared in the earlier example:

```
Student noName;

Student freshMan("Smell E.
  Fish");

Student xfer("Upp R. Classman",
  80, 2.5);
```

All `Student` objects except `noName` are declared with parentheses surrounding the arguments to the constructor. Why is `noName` declared without parentheses?

To be neat and consistent, you may think you could have declared `noName` as follows:

```
Student noName();
```

Unfortunately, this is allowed, but it doesn't have the intended effect. Instead of declaring an object `noName` of class `Student` to be constructed with the default constructor, this declares a function that returns an object of class `Student` by value. Surprise! (I think I need a raise.)

The following two declarations demonstrate how similar the new C++ format for declaring an object is to that of declaring a function. (I think this was a mistake, but what do I know?) The only difference is that the function declaration contains types in the parentheses, whereas the object declaration contains objects:

```
Student thisIsAFunc(int);

Student thisIsAnObject(10);
```

If the parentheses are empty, nothing can differentiate between an object and a function. To retain compatibility with C, C++ chose to make a declaration with empty parentheses a function. (A safer alternative would have been to force the keyword `void` in the function case, but that would not have been compatible with existing C programs.)

Constructing the Order of Construction

When there are multiple objects, all with constructors, the programmer usually doesn't care about the order in which things are built. If one or more of the constructors has side effects, however, the order can make a difference.

The rules for the order of construction are as follows:

- ✔ Local and static objects are constructed in the order in which their declarations are invoked.
- ✔ Static objects are constructed only once.
- ✔ All global objects are constructed before main().
- ✔ Global objects are constructed in no particular order.
- ✔ Members are constructed in the order in which they are declared in the class.
- ✔ Destructors are invoked in the reverse order from constructors.

A static variable is a variable that is local to a function but retains its value from one function invocation to the next. A global is a variable declared outside of any function.

Consider each of the above rules in turn.

Local objects construct in order

Local objects are constructed in the order in which the program encounters their declaration. Normally this is the same as the order in which the objects appear in the function, unless your function jumps around particular declarations. (By the way, jumping around declarations is a bad thing to do. It confuses the reader and the compiler.)

Static objects construct only once

Static objects are similar to other local variables, except that they are constructed only once. This is to be expected because statics retain their value from one invocation of the function to the next. However, unlike C, which is free to initialize statics when the program begins, C++ must wait until the first time control passes through the static's declaration to perform the construction. Consider the following trivial program:

```
#include <iostream.h>
#include <string.h>
class DoNothing
{
  public:
   DoNothing(int initial)
   {
      cout << "DoNothing constructed with a value of "
           << initial
           << "\n";
   }
};
void fn(int i)
{
   static DoNothing dn(i);
   cout << "In function fn with i = " << i << "\n";
}

int main(int argcs, char* pArgs[])
{
   fn(10);
   fn(20);
   return 0;
}
```

Executing this program generates the following results:

```
DoNothing constructed with a value of 10
In function fn with i = 10
In function fn with i = 20
```

Notice that the message from the function fn() appears twice, but the message from the constructor for DoNothing appears only the first time fn() is called.

All global objects construct before main ()

All global variables go into scope as soon as the program starts. Thus, all global objects are constructed before control is passed to main().

This can cause a real debugging headache. Some debuggers try to execute up to main() as soon as the program is loaded and before they hand over control to the user. This makes perfect sense for C because no user code is ready to execute until main() is entered. For C++, however, this can be a problem because the constructor code for all global objects has already been executed by the time you get control. If one of them has a fatal bug, you never even get control. In this case, the program appears to die before it even starts!

You can approach this problem in several ways. One is to test each constructor on local objects before using them on globals. If that doesn't solve the problem, you can try adding output statements to the beginning of all suspected constructors. The last output statement you see probably came from the flawed constructor.

Global objects construct in no particular order

Figuring out the order of construction of local objects is easy. An order is implied by the flow of control. With globals, no such flow is available to give order. All globals go into scope simultaneously, remember? Okay, you argue, why can't the compiler just start at the top of the file and work its way down the list of global objects? That would work fine for a single file (and I presume that's what most compilers do).

Unfortunately, most programs in the real world consist of several files that are compiled separately and then linked. Because the compiler has no control over the order in which these files are linked, it cannot affect the order in which global objects are constructed from file to file.

Most of the time this is pretty ho-hum stuff. Once in a while, though, it can generate bugs that are extremely difficult to track down. (It happens just often enough to make it worth mentioning in a book.)

Consider the following example:

```
// in Student.H:
class Student
{
  public:
    Student (unsigned id) : studentId(id)
    {
    }
  const unsigned studentId;
};class Tutor
{
  public:
    Tutor(Student& s)
    {
        tutoredId = s.studentId;
    }
  protected:
    unsigned tutoredId;
};
```

```
// in FILE1.CPP
// set up a student
Student randy(1234);


// in FILE2.CPP
// assign that student a tutor
Tutor   jenny(randy);
```

Here the constructor for Student assigns a student ID. The , constructor for Tutor records the ID of the student to help. The program declares a student randy and then assigns that student a tutor jenny.

The problem is that you're making the implicit assumption that randy gets constructed before jenny. Suppose that it was the other way around. Then jenny would get constructed with a block of memory that had not yet been turned into a Student object and, therefore, had garbage for a student ID.

The preceding example is not too difficult to figure out and more than a little contrived. Nevertheless, problems deriving from global objects being constructed in no particular order can appear in subtle ways. To avoid this problem, don't allow the constructor for one global object to refer to the contents of another global object.

Members construct in the order in which they are declared

Members of a class are constructed according to the order in which they're declared within the class. This isn't quite as obvious as it may sound. Consider the following example:

```
class Student
{
  public:
    Student (unsigned id, unsigned age) : sAge(age), sId(id)
    {
    }
    const unsigned sId;
    const unsigned sAge;
};
```

In this example, sId is constructed before sAge even though it appears second in the constructor's initialization list. The only time you could probably detect any difference in the construction order is if both of these were members of classes that had constructors and these constructors had some mutual side effect.

Destructors destruct in the reverse order of the constructors

Finally, no matter in what order the constructors kick off, you can be assured that the destructors are invoked in the reverse order. (It's nice to know that at least one rule in C++ has no ifs, ands, or buts.)

Chapter 19

Copying the Copy Copy Copy Constructor

●　●

In This Chapter

▶ Introducing the copy constructor

▶ Making copies

▶ Having copies made for you automatically

▶ Shallow copies versus deep copies

▶ Avoiding all those copies

●　●

*T*he constructor is a special function that C++ invokes automatically when an object is created to allow the object to initialize itself. Chapter 17 introduces the concept of the constructor whereas Chapter 18 describes other types of constructors. This chapter examines a particular variation of the constructor known as the copy constructor.

Copying an Object

A copy constructor is the constructor that C++ uses to make copies of objects. It carries the name X::X(X&), where X is the name of the class. That is, it's the constructor of class X, which takes as its argument a reference to an object of class X. Now I know that this sounds really useless, but just give me a chance to explain why C++ needs such a beastie.

Why do I need it?

Think for a moment about what happens when you call a function like the following:

```
void fn(Student fs)
{
   // ...same scenario; different argument...
}
int main(int argcs, char* pArgs[])
{
   Student ms;
   fn(ms);
   return 0;
}
```

In the call to fn(), C++ passes a copy of the object ms and not the object itself.

C++ passes arguments to functions by value.

Consider for a minute what it means to create a copy of an object. First, it takes a constructor to create an object, even a copy of an existing object. C++ could copy the existing object into the new object one byte at a time, but what if we don't want a simple copy of the object? What if something else is required? (Ignore the "why?" of this for a little while.) You need to be able to specify how the copy should be constructed.

Thus, the copy constructor is necessary in the preceding example to create a copy of the object ms on the stack during the call of function fn(). This particular copy constructor would be Student::Student(Student&) — say that three times quickly.

Using the copy constructor

The best way to understand how the copy constructor works is to see one in action. Consider the following Student class:

```
#include <iostream.h>
#include <string.h>
class Student
{
 public:
   // conventional constructor
   Student(char *pName = "no name", int ssId = 0)
   {
     cout << "Constructing new student "
          << pName
          << "\n";
```

```
      strncpy(name, pName, sizeof(name));
      name[sizeof(name) - 1] = '\0';
      id = ssId;
    }
   // copy constructor
   Student(Student& s)
   {
     cout << "Constructing Copy of "
          << s.name
          << "\n";
     strcpy(name, "Copy of ");
     strcat(name, s.name);
     id = s.id;
   }

  ~Student()
   {
     cout << "Destructing " << name << "\n";
   }

   protected:
   char name[40];
   int  id;
};

// fn - receives its argument by value
void fn(Student s)
{
   cout << "In function fn()\n";
}

int main(int argcs, char* pArgs[])
{
   Student randy("Randy", 1234);
   cout << "Calling fn()\n";
   fn(randy);
   cout << "Returned from fn()\n";
   return 0;
}
```

The output from executing this program follows:

```
Constructing new student Randy
Calling fn()
Constructing Copy of Randy
In function fn()
Destructing Copy of Randy
Returned from fn()
Destructing Randy
```

Starting with `main()`, you can see how this program works. The normal constructor generates the first message. `main()` generates the `calling...` message. C++ calls the copy constructor to make a copy of `randy` to pass to `fn()`, which generates the next line of output. The copy is destructed at the return from `fn()`. The original object, `randy`, is destructed at the end of `main()`.

The copy constructor here is flagged with comments. It looks like a normal constructor except that it takes its input from another object rather than from several separate arguments.

(Notice that this copy constructor does a little bit more than just make a copy of the object; it tacks the phrase *Copy of* to the front of the name. That was for your benefit. Normally, copy constructors should restrict themselves to just making copies. But, if the truth be known, they can do anything they want.)

The Automatic Copy Constructor

Like the default constructor, the copy constructor is important. Important enough that C++ thinks no class should be without one. If you don't provide your own copy constructor, C++ generates one for you. (This is different from the default constructor that C++ provides unless your class has any constructors defined for it.)

The copy constructor provided by C++ performs a member-by-member copy of each data member. Originally, the copy constructor that C++ provided performed a bit-wise copy. The difference is that a member-by-member copy invokes any copy constructors that might exist for the members of the class, whereas a bit-wise copy does not. You can see the effects of this difference in the following example:

```
#include <iostream.h>
#include <string.h>

class Student
{
 public:
  Student(char *pName = "no name")
  {
   cout << "Constructing new student " << pName << "\n";
   strncpy(name, pName, sizeof(name));
   name[sizeof(name) - 1] = '\0';
  }

  Student(Student& s)
  {
```

```
    cout << "Constructing Copy of " << s.name << "\n";
    strcpy(name, "Copy of ");
    strcat(name, s.name);
  }

  ~Student()
  {
    cout << "Destructing " << name << "\n";
  }

protected:
  char name[40];
};

class Tutor
{
 public:
  Tutor(Student& s) : student(s) // invoke copy
                 // constructor
  {              // on member student
    cout << "Constructing tutor\n";
  }
 protected:
  Student student;
};

void fn(Tutor tutor)
{
  cout << "In function fn()\n";
}

int main(int argcs, char* pArgs[])
{
  Student randy("Randy");
  Tutor tutor(randy);
  cout << "Calling fn()\n";
  fn(tutor);
  cout << "Returned from fn()\n";
  return 0;
}
```

Executing this program generates the following output:

```
Constructing new student Randy
Constructing Copy of Randy
Constructing tutor
Calling fn()
Constructing Copy of Copy of Randy
In function fn()
Destructing Copy of Copy of Randy
Returned from fn()
Destructing Copy of Randy
Destructing Randy
```

Constructing the object `randy` invokes the `Student` constructor, which outputs the first line.

The object `tutor` is created by invoking the constructor `Tutor(Student&)`. This constructor initializes the data member `Tutor::student` by invoking the copy constructor for `Student` explicitly. This generates the next line of output.

The call to function `fn()` requires a copy of `tutor` to be created. Because I didn't provide a copy constructor for `Tutor`, the default copy constructor (provided by C++) copies each member. This invokes the copy constructor for class `Student` to copy the data member `tutor.student`.

Creating Shallow Copies versus Deep Copies

Performing a member-by-member copy seems the obvious thing to do in a copy constructor. Other than adding the capability to tack silly things such as Copy of to the front of students' names, when would you ever want to do anything but a member-by-member copy?

Consider what happens if the constructor allocates an asset, such as memory off the heap. If the copy constructor simply makes a copy of that asset without allocating its own, you end up with a troublesome situation: two objects thinking they have exclusive access to the same asset. This becomes nastier when the destructor is invoked for both objects and they both try to put the same asset back. To make this more concrete, consider the following example class:

```
#include <iostream.h>
#include <string.h>
class Person
{
  public:
   Person(char *pN)
   {
     cout << "Constructing " << pN << "\n";
     pName = new char[strlen(pN) + 1];
     if (pName != 0)
     {
                 strcpy(pName, pN);
            }
   }
  ~Person()
   {
```

```
      cout << "Destructing " << pName << "\n";
      // let's wipe out the name just for the heck of it
      pName[0] = '\0';
      delete pName;
      }
  protected:
    char *pName;
};
int main(int argcs, char* pArgs[])
{
    Person p1("Randy");
    Person p2 = p1;     // invoke the copy constructor...
    return 0;           // ...equivalent to Person p2(p1);
}
```

Here, the constructor for `Person` allocates memory off the heap to store the person's name, rather than put up with some arbitrary limit imposed by a fixed-length array. The destructor dutifully puts this heap memory back as it should. The main program simply creates one person, p1, and then makes a copy of that person, p2.

When you execute this program, you get only one constructor output message. That's not too surprising, because C++ provided the copy constructor used to build p2 and it performs no output. As p1 and p2 go out of scope, you don't receive the two output messages that you might have expected.

If you are single-stepping the program under a debugger such as Visual C++, you should see the expected `Destructing Randy` message when the first object is destructed. Instead of a second destructor message, however, you get some type of error message. In the case of Microsoft Visual C++, you get a window like the one shown in Figure 19-1.

Figure 19-1:
An error
window
opened
by the
Visual C++
debugger.

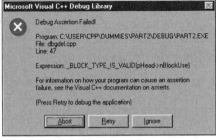

The constructor is called once and allocates a block of memory off the heap to hold the person's name. The copy constructor provided by C++ copies that address into the new object without allocating a new block.

When the objects are destructed, the destructor for p2 gets at the block first. This destructor clears out the name and then releases the block. When p1 comes along, the memory has been released and the name has been wiped out already. This explains the error message (the message is a bit obscure, but if you look into dbgdel.cpp, one of the functions that makes up the Visual C++ standard C++ library, you see that this function is making sure that the pointer you handed it refers to a block of heap memory that is still in use). The problem is shown in Figure 19-2. The object p1 is copied into the new object p2, but the assets are not. Thus, p1 and p2 end up pointing to the same assets (in this case, heap memory). This is known as a shallow copy because it just "skims the surface," copying the members themselves.

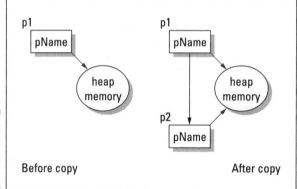

Figure 19-2:
Shallow copy of p1 to p2.

What you need to fix the problem shown in Figure 19-2 is a copy constructor that allocates its own assets to the new object. Add one of these to Person and see how it looks. The following shows an appropriate copy constructor for class Person:

```
class Person
{
  public:
    // copy constructor allocates a new block
    // from the heap
    Person(Person& p)
    {
      cout << "Copying " << p.pName << " into its ownÆ block\n";
      pName = new char[strlen(p.pName) + 1];
      if (pName != 0)
      {
        strcpy(pName, p.pName);
      }
    }
    // ...everything else the same...
}
// ...same here as well...
```

Here you see that the copy constructor allocates its own memory block for the name and then copies the contents of the source object name into this new name block. See Figure 19-3. Deep copy is so named because it reaches down and copies all the assets. (Okay, the analogy is pretty strained, but that's what they call it.)

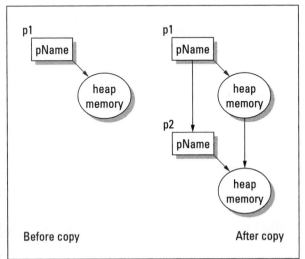

Figure 19-3:
Deep copy
of p1 to p2.

Before copy   After copy

The output from this program is as follows:

```
Constructing Randy
Copying Randy into its own block
Destructing Randy
Destructing Randy
```

Heap memory is not the only asset that requires a deep copy constructor, but it is the most common. Open files, ports, and allocated hardware (such as printers) also require deep copies. These are the same types of assets that destructors must return. Thus, a general rule is that if your class requires a destructor to deallocate assets, it also requires a copy constructor.

It's a Long Way to Temporaries

Copies are generated when objects are passed by value. Copies are created under other conditions as well, such as when objects are returned by value. Consider the following example:

```
Student fn();          // returns object by value
int main(int argcs, char* pArgs[])
{
    Student s;
    s = fn();              // call to fn() creates temporary

    // how long does the temporary returned by fn()last?
    return 0;
}
```

The function fn() returns an object by value. Eventually, the returned object is copied to s, but where does it reside until then?

C++ creates a temporary object into which it stuffs the returned object. (Temporaries are created in other ways, as well.) "Okay," you say. "C++ creates the temporary, but how does it know when to destruct the temporary?" (How clever you are for asking just the right question!) In this example, it doesn't make much difference because you'll be through with the temporary when the copy constructor copies it into s. But what if s were defined as a reference:

```
int main(int argcs, char* pArgs[])
{
    Student& refS = fn();
    // ...now what?...
    return 0;
}
```

Now it makes a big difference how long temporaries live because refS exists for the entire function. Temporaries created by the compiler are valid through-out the extended expression in which they were created and no further. In the following function, I mark the point at which the temporary is no longer valid:

```
Student fn1();
int fn2(Student&);
int main(int argcs, char* pArgs[])
{
    int x;
    // create a Student object by calling fn1().
    // Pass that object to the function fn2().
    // fn2() returns an integer that is used in some
    // silly calculation.
    // All this time the temporary returned from fn1()
    // remains valid.
    x = 3 * fn2(fn1()) + 10;
    // the temporary returned from fn1() is now no longer valid
    // ...other stuff...
    return 0;
}
```

The comments seem to wrap in example above. I've retained the text but broke them up differently.

This makes the reference example invalid, because the object may go away before refS does, leaving refS referring to a non-object.

It may have occurred to you that all this copying of objects hither and yon can be a bit time-consuming. What if you don't want to make copies of everything? The most straightforward solution is to pass objects to functions and return objects from functions by reference. This knocks out the majority of cases.

But what if you're still not convinced that C++ isn't out there craftily constructing temporaries that you know nothing about? Or what if your class allocates unique assets that you don't want copied? What do you do then?

You can simply add an output statement to your copy constructor. The presence of this message warns you that a copy has just been made. Another approach is to declare the copy constructor protected, as follows:

```
class Student
{
 protected:
  Student(Student&s){}

 public:
  // ...everything else normal...
};
```

This precludes any external functions, including C++, from constructing a copy of your Student objects. (This does not affect the capability of member functions to create copies.)

The fact that the copy constructor is used to create temporaries and copies on the stack answers one pesky detail that may have occurred to you. Namely, consider the following program:

```
class Student
{
 public:
            Student()
            {
          // ...whatever...
            }

            Student(Student s)
            {
          // ...whatever...
            }
};
```

```
void fn(Student fs)
{
}

int main(int argcs, char* pArgs[])
{
        Student ms;
        fn(ms);
        return 0;
}
```

Why is it that the copy constructor for the class Student isn't declared Student::Student(Student)? In fact, such a declaration isn't even legal. The GNU C++ compiler complains with the following helpful error message

```
Error: invalid constructor; you probably meant `Student
       (const Student&)'
```

Why must the argument to the constructor be referential? Consider carefully the program. When main() calls the function fn(), the C++ compiler uses the copy constructor to create a copy of the Student object on the stack. However, the copy constructor itself requires an object of class Student. No problem, the compiler can invoke the copy constructor to create a Student object for the copy constructor. But, of course, that requires another call to the copy constructor, and so it goes until eventually the compiler collapses in a confused heap of exhaustion.

Chapter 20

Static Members: Can Fabric Softener Help?

*B*y default, data members are allocated on a "per object" basis. For example, each student has his or her own name.

You can also declare a member to be shared by all objects of a class by declaring that member static. The term *static* applies to both data members and member functions, although the meaning is slightly different. This chapter describes these differences, beginning with static data members.

Defining a Static Member

Data members are made common to all objects of a class by declaring them *static*. Such members are called *static data members* (I would be a little upset if they were called something else).

Why do I need them?

Most properties are properties of the object. Using the well-worn (one might say, threadbare) student example, properties such as name, ID number, and courses are specific to the individual student. However, some properties are shared by all students — for example, the number of students currently enrolled, the highest grade of all students or a pointer to the first student in a linked list.

It's easy enough to store this type of information in a common, ordinary, garden-variety global variable. For example, we could use a lowly *int* variable to keep track of the number of *Student* objects. The problem with this solution is that global variables are "outside" the class. It's like putting the voltage regulator for my microwave outside of the enclosure. Sure, it could be done, and it would probably work — the only problem is that when my dog got across the wires and I had to peel him off the ceiling, I might get angry (the dog wouldn't like it too much, either).

If the class is going to be held responsible for its own state, global variables such as that have to be brought inside the class, just as the voltage regulator has to be inside the microwave lid, away from prying paws. This is the idea behind static members.

You may hear static members referred to as *class members* because they are shared by all objects in the class. By comparison, normal members are referred to as *instance members,* or *object members,* because each object gets its own copy of these members.

Using static members

A static data member is one that has been declared with the `static` storage class. For example:

```
class Student
{
 public:
  Student(char *pName = "no name")
  {
    strcpy(name, pName);
    noOfStudents++;
  }

  ~Student()
  {
    noOfStudents--;
  }

  int number()
  {
    return noOfStudents;
  }

 protected:
  static int noOfStudents;
  char name[40];
};

Student s1;
Student s2;
```

The data member noOfStudents is part of the class Student but is not part of either s1 or s2. That is, for every object of class Student, there is a separate name, but there is only one noOfStudents, which all Students must share.

"Well then," you ask, "if the space for noOfStudents is not allocated in any of the objects of class Student, where is it allocated?" The answer is, "It isn't." You have to specifically allocate space for it, as follows:

```
int Student::noOfStudents = 0;
```

This somewhat peculiar-looking syntax allocates space for the static data member and initializes it to zero. Static data members must be global — a static variable cannot be local to a function.

The name of the class is required for any member when it appears outside its class boundaries.

Referencing static data members

The access rules for static members are the same as the access rules for normal members. From within the class, static members are referenced like any other class member. Public static members can be referenced from outside the class as well-protected static members can't. Both types of reference are shown in the following code snippet:

```
class Student
{
 public:
  Student()
  {
   noOfStudents++;    // reference from inside the class
   // ...other stuff...
  }

  static int noOfStudents;
  // ...other stuff like before...
};

void fn(Student& s1, Student& s2)
{
   // reference public static
   cout << "No of students "
        << s1.noOfStudents // reference from outside
                           // of the class
        << "\n";
}
```

In `fn()`, `noOfStudents` is referenced using the object `s1`. But `s1` and `s2` share the same member `noOfStudents` — how did I know to choose `s1`? Why didn't I use `s2` instead? It doesn't make any difference. You can reference a static member using any object of that class. For example:

```
// ...class defined the same as before...
void fn(Student& s1, Student& s2)
{
   // the following produce identical results
   cout << "No of students " << s1.noOfStudents << "\n";
   cout << "No of students " << s2.noOfStudents << "\n";
}
```

In fact, you don't need an object at all. You can use the class name directly instead, if you prefer, as in the following:

```
// ...class defined the same as before...
void fn(Student& s1, Student& s2)
{
   // the following produce identical results
   cout << "No of students "
        << Student::noOfStudents
        << "\n";
}
```

If you use an object name, C++ uses only the class of the object.

This is a minor technicality, but in the interest of full disclosure: The object used to reference a static member is not evaluated even if it's an expression. For example, consider the following case:

```
class Student
{
 public:
   static int noOfStudents;
   Student& nextStudent();
   // ...other stuff the same...
};

void fn(Student& s)
{
   cout << s.nextStudent().noOfStudents << "\n"
}
```

The member function `nextStudent()` is not actually called. All C++ needs to access `noOfStudents` is the return type, and it can get that without bothering to evaluate the expression. This is true even if `nextStudent()` should do other things, such as wash windows or shine your shoes. None of those things will get done. Although the example is obscure, it does happen. That's what you get for trying to cram too much stuff into one expression.

Uses for static data members

There are umpteen uses for static data members, but let me touch on a few here. First, you can use static members to keep count of the number of objects floating about. In the Student class, for example, the count is initialized to zero, the constructor increments it, and the destructor decrements it. At any given instant, the static member contains the count of the number of existing Student objects. Remember, however, that this count reflects the number of Student objects (including any temporaries) and not necessarily the number of students.

A closely related use for a static member is as a flag to indicate whether a particular action has occurred. For example, a class Radio may need to initialize hardware before sending the first tune command but not before subsequent tunes. A flag indicating that this is the first tune is just the ticket. This includes flagging when an error has occurred.

Another common use is to contain the pointer to the first member of a linked list. Static members can allocate bits of "common data" that all objects in all functions share (overuse of this common memory is a really bad idea since it makes tracking errors difficult).

Declaring Static Member Functions

Member functions can be declared static as well. Like static data members, static member functions are associated with a class and not with any particular object of that class. This means that like a reference to a static data member, a reference to a static member function does not require an object. If an object is present, only its type is used.

Thus, both calls to the static member function number() in the following example are legal:

```
#include <iostream.h>
#include <string.h>
class Student
{
 public:
   static int number()
   {
     return noOfStudents;
   }

   // ...other stuff the same...
 protected:
   char name[40];
```

```
    static int noOfStudents;
};

int Student::noOfStudents = 0;

int main(int argcs, char* pArgs[])
{
  Student s;
  cout << s.number() << "\n";
  cout << Student::number() << "\n";
  return 0;
}
```

Notice how the static member function can access the static data member. A static member function is not directly associated with any object, however, so it does not have default access to any non-static members. Thus, the following would not be legal:

```
class Student
{
 public:
  // the following is not legal
  static char *sName()
  {
    return name;     // which name? there is no object
  }

  // ...other stuff the same...
 protected:
  char name[40];
  static int noOfStudents;
};
```

That's not to say that static member functions have no access to non-static data members. Consider the following useful function:

```
#include <iostream.h>
#include <string.h>

class Student
{
 public:
  // same constructor and destructor as earlier
  Student(char *pName);
 ~Student();

  // findName - return student w/specified name
  static Student *findName(char *pName);

 protected:
  static Student *pFirst;
```

```
   Student *pNext;
   char name[40];
};

Student* Student::pFirst = 0;

// findName - return the Student with the
//            specified name.
//            Return zero if no match.
Student* Student::findName(char *pName)
{
   // loop thru the linked list...
   for (Student *pS = pFirst; pS; pS = pS->pNext)
   {
     // ...if we find the specified name...
     if (strcmp(pS->name, pName) == 0)
     {
        // ...then return the object's address
        return pS;
     }
   }
   // ...otherwise, return a zero (item not found)
   return (Student*)0;
}

int main(int argcs, char* pArgs[])
{
   Student s1("Randy");

   Student s2("Jenny");
   Student s3("Kinsey");
   Student *pS = Student::findName("Jenny");
   return 0;
}
```

The function findName() has access to pFirst because it's shared by all
objects. Being a member of class Student, findName() has access also to
name, but the call must specify the object to use (that is, whose name). No
default object is associated with a static member function. Calling the static
member function with an object doesn't help. For example:

```
// ...same as before...
int main(int argcs, char* pArgs[])
{
   Student s1("Randy");
   Student s2("Jenny");
   Student s3("Kinsey");
   Student *pS = s1.findName("Jenny");
   return 0;
}
```

The s1 is not evaluated and not passed to findName(). Only its class is used to decide which findName() to call.

Static member functions are useful when you want to associate an action to a class but you don't need to associate that action with any particular object. For example, the member function Duck::fly() is associated with a particular duck() while the rather more drastic member function Duck::goExtinct() is not.

What is this about, anyway?

I mention this a few times throughout this book, but let's look at it again just for grins. this is a pointer to the "current" object within a member function. It's used when no other object name is specified. In a normal member function, this is the implied first argument to the function. For example:

```
class SC
{
 public:
    void nFn(int a); // like
  SC::nFn(SC *this, int a)
    static void sFn(int a); //
  like SC::sFn(int a)
};

void fn(SC& s)
{
```

```
    s.nFn(10); // -converts to->
    SC::nFn(&s, 10);

    s.sFn(10); // -converts to->
    SC::sFn(10);
}
```

That is, the function nFn() is interpreted almost as if it were declared void SC::nFn(SC *this, int a). The call to nFn() is converted by the compiler as shown, with the address of s passed as the first argument. (You can't actually write the call this way; this is only what the compiler is doing.)

References to other non-static members within SC::nFn() automatically use the this argument as the pointer to the current object. When SC::sFn() was called, no object address was passed. Thus, it has no this pointer to use when referencing non-static functions. This is why we say that a static member function is not associated with any current object.

A Budget with Class — BUDGET2.CPP

In this section, we will look over a version of the BUDGET program first addressed at the end of Part II. Rather than the function-based solution presented back then, this is an object-based solution based on active classes.

The "budget problem" is to setup accounts like you would see in a bank. These simple accounts provide for deposits (that's good) and withdrawals (that's even better). (The earlier version of BUDGET introduced back at the end of Part II handled only a single type of bank account.) This version handles two types of accounts each with its own slightly different rules.

Checking accounts:

- ✔ Charge a fee of 20 cents per check if the balance drops below $500
- ✔ Do not charge a fee when the balance is above $500

Savings accounts:

- ✔ Do not charge a fee for the first withdrawal of the month
- ✔ Charge a fee of $5.00 for each withdrawal thereafter

Looking at the BUDGET problem, it's easy to see that the class candidates are Checking and Savings. We know that it's a good idea to make data members protected, so a few access functions are necessary in case a non-member function needs the account number or balance.

Like all classes, Checking and Savings need a constructor to initialize objects to legal values (mostly to a balance of zero). Two additional member functions are also necessary: deposit() and withdrawal().

Finally, I added one other member function called display() to display the current object. This is not a requirement, but it is common to let the object display itself rather than rely on an external function to do it. (Those other functions would need knowledge of the class's internals to know how to display it properly, and that's something you want to avoid.)

Here is the resulting program:

```
// BUDGET2.CPP - Budget program with active classes.

#include <iostream.h>
#include <stdio.h>
```

```
// the maximum number of accounts one can have
const int maxAccounts = 10;

// Checking - this describes checking accounts
class Checking
{
 public:
  Checking(int initializeAN = 0)
  {
   accountNumber = initializeAN;
   balance = 0.0;
  }

  // access functions
  int accountNo()
  {
   return accountNumber;
  }
  double acntBalance()
  {
   return balance;
  }
  // transaction functions
  void deposit(double amount)
  {
   balance += amount;
  }
  void withdrawal(double amount);

  // display function for displaying self on 'cout'
  void display()
  {
   cout << "Account " << accountNumber
        << " = "   << balance
        << "\n";
  }

 protected:
  unsigned accountNumber;
  double  balance;
};
// withdrawal - this member function is too big to
//              be defined inline
void Checking::withdrawal(double amount)
{
  if (balance < amount)
  {
   cout << "Insufficient funds: balance " << balance
        << ", check "              << amount
```

```
            << "\n";
    }
  else
  {
   balance -= amount;

   // if balance falls too low,...
   if (balance < 500.00)
   {
     // ...charge a service fee
     balance -= 0.20;
   }
  }
}

// Savings - you can probably figure this one out
class Savings
{
 public:
  Savings(int initialAN = 0)
  {
   accountNumber = initialAN;
   balance = 0.0;
   noWithdrawals = 0;
  }

  // access functions
  int accountNo()
  {
   return accountNumber;
  }
  double acntBalance()
  {
   return balance;
  }

  // transaction functions
  void deposit(double amount)
  {
   balance += amount;
  }
  void withdrawal(double amount);

  // display function - display self to cout
  void display()
  {
   cout << "Account "          << accountNumber
      << " = "               << balance
      << " (no. withdrawals = " << noWithdrawals
      << ")\n";
  }
```

```cpp
protected:
  unsigned accountNumber;
  double  balance;
  int     noWithdrawals;
};
void Savings::withdrawal(double amount)
{
  if (balance < amount)
  {
    cout << "Insufficient funds: balance " << balance
         << ", withdrawal "          << amount
         << "\n";
  }
  else
  {
    // after more than one withdrawal in a month...
    if (++noWithdrawals > 1)
    {
      // ...charge a $5 fee
      balance -= 5.00;
    }

    // now make the withdrawal
    balance -= amount;
  }
}

// prototype declarations
void process(Checking* pChecking);
void process(Savings*  pSavings);

// checking and savings account objects
Checking* chkAcnts[maxAccounts];
Savings*  svgAcnts[maxAccounts];

// main - accumulate the initial input and output totals
int main(int argcs, char* pArgs[])
{
  // loop until someone enters an 'X' or 'x'
  int noChkAccounts = 0;  // count the number of accounts
  int noSvgAccounts = 0;
  char   accountType;   // S or C
  while (1)
  {
    cout << "Enter S for Savings, "
         << "C for Checking, "
         << "X for exit:";
    cin >> accountType;

    // exit the loop when the user enters an X
    if (accountType == 'x' || accountType == 'X')
    {
        break;
```

```
  }

  // otherwise, handle according to the account type
  switch (accountType)
  {
    // checking account
    case 'c':
    case 'C':
     if (noChkAccounts < maxAccounts)
     {
       int acnt;
       cout << "Enter account number:";
       cin  >> acnt;
       chkAcnts[noChkAccounts] = new Checking(acnt);
       process(chkAcnts[noChkAccounts]);
       noChkAccounts++;
     }
     else
     {
       cout << "No more room for checking accounts\n";
     }
     break;

    // savings account
    case 's':
    case 'S':
     if (noSvgAccounts < maxAccounts)
     {
       int acnt;
       cout << "Enter account number:";
       cin  >> acnt;
       svgAcnts[noSvgAccounts] = new Savings(acnt);
       process(svgAcnts[noSvgAccounts]);
       noSvgAccounts++;
     }
     else
     {
       cout << "No more room for savings accounts\n";
     }
     break;

    default:
     cout << "I didn't get that.\n";
  }
}

// now present totals
double chkTotal = 0;    // total of all checking accounts
cout << "Checking accounts:\n";
for (int i = 0; i < noChkAccounts; i++)
{
```

```
      chkAcnts[i]->display();          // Note 10
      chkTotal += chkAcnts[i]->acntBalance();
    }

    double svgTotal = 0;      // total of all savings accounts
    cout << "Savings accounts:\n";
    for (int j = 0; j < noSvgAccounts; j++)
    {
      svgAcnts[j]->display();
      svgTotal += svgAcnts[j]->acntBalance();
    }

    double total = chkTotal + svgTotal;
    cout << "Total for checking accounts = "
         << chkTotal
         << "\n";

    cout << "Total for savings accounts = "
         << svgTotal
         << "\n";

    cout << "Total worth             = "
         << total
         << "\n";
    return 0;
}

// process(Checking) - input the data for a checking account
void process(Checking* pChecking)
{
    cout << "Enter positive number for deposit,\n"
         << "negative for check, 0 to terminate\n";
    double transaction;
    do
    {
      cout << ":";
      cin >> transaction;

      // deposit
      if (transaction > 0)
      {
        pChecking->deposit(transaction);
      }

      // withdrawal
      if (transaction < 0)
      {
        pChecking->withdrawal(-transaction);
      }
    } while (transaction != 0);
}
```

```
// process(Savings) - input the data for a savings account
void process(Savings* pSavings)
{
  cout << "Enter positive number for deposit,\n"
       << "negative for withdrawal, 0 to terminate\n";
  double transaction;
  do
  {
   cout << ":";
   cin >> transaction;

   // deposit
   if (transaction > 0)
   {
     pSavings->deposit(transaction);
   }

   // withdrawal
   if (transaction < 0)
   {
     pSavings->withdrawal(-transaction);
   }
  } while (transaction != 0);
}
```

I executed the program with the following data in order to demonstrate how the program works (or, as is so often the case with my programs, doesn't work). **Bold** characters indicate user input, while non-bold characters indicate output from the program.

```
Enter S for Savings, C for Checking, X for exit:S
Enter account number:123
Enter positive number for deposit,
negative for withdrawal, 0 to terminate
:200
:-20
:0
Enter S for Savings, C for Checking, X for exit:s
Enter account number:234
Enter positive number for deposit,
negative for withdrawal, 0 to terminate
:200
:-10
:-10
:0
Enter S for Savings, C for Checking, X for exit:c
Enter account number:345
Enter positive number for deposit,
negative for check, 0 to terminate
:200
:-20
```

```
:0
Enter S for Savings, C for Checking, X for exit:C
Enter account number:456
Enter positive number for deposit,
negative for check, 0 to terminate
:600
:-20
:0
Enter S for Savings, C for Checking, X for exit:x
Checking accounts:
Account 345 = 179.8
Account 456 = 580
Savings accounts:
Account 123 = 180 (no. withdrawals = 1)
Account 234 = 175 (no. withdrawals = 2)
Total for checking accounts = 359.6
Total for savings accounts = 355
Total worth           = 1114.8
Press any key to continue
```

Starting with class `Checking`, you can see each of the member functions mentioned earlier. The constructor assigns the account number. The "= 0" allows the program to construct an object with a default account number of 0:

```
Checking c1 = new Checking(124);
Checking c2 = new Checking();
```

In this case, the `Checking` object c1 is created with account number 123 while the object c2 is created with the default account number of 0.

The functions `accountNo()` and `acntBalance()` give the outside world access to the protected members `accountNumber` and `balance`. The point of such a function is to allow non-class functions to read these values but not modify them. In addition, these access functions would shield outside functions from any future changes in the way that the account number or the balance is stored.

The `deposit()` and `withdrawal()` functions either deposit or withdraw amount. Since the `deposit()` function is simple, it is defined directly inline within the class. The `withdrawal()` function, being a bit more complicated, is declared here but defined later.

The `display()` function outputs the important data members to the standard output.

The class `Savings` is virtually identical to the class `Checking` except for the addition of the member `noWithdrawals`, which is used to track the number of withdrawals made.

Room for the savings account and checking account objects is allocated in the arrays svgAcnts and chkAcnts, respectively. The maximum number of accounts is maxAccounts.

The main() function is slightly more complicated that its Budget1 cousin since it must deal with two different types of accounts. After the check for 'X', main() uses the switch construct to decide between 'C' checking and 'S' savings accounts. The switch construct is used here since it is a) easier to extend by adding more cases and b) it provides a default case to handle erroneous input.

Just as before, the second section of main() actually displays the account data accumulated in the initial section.

Notice how the internals of the Checking and Savings objects are hidden from main(). For example, main() asks the objects to display themselves (meaning display the internal components) - main() has no idea how the classes may choose to do this nor does it care.

The process() function which handles the actual deposits and withdrawals relies on the deposit() and withdrawal() member functions to do the dirty work. Although you know how these actions are performed, remember that process() does not — again, nor does it care. However, how a savings account may choose to withdraw cash is up to the class.

I encourage you to type this program and single step through it. Nothing else will give you a feel for what's going on faster than seeing the program in action.

Believe it or not, from a programming standpoint Budget2 is actually easier to program than Budget1. When writing Savings, I didn't have to worry about how the main program might use the class. The same applied to Checking. In addition, while working on the main functions, I didn't concern myself with class internals. "Render unto the class that which is the class's" or something like that.

On the negative side, it is clear that there are a lot of similarities between the Savings and Account classes. Somehow, there should be a way to reduce the duplications. In fact, this is exactly the topic of Part IV. You can see this implemented in Budget3 at the end of that part.

Part IV
Class Inheritance

The 5th Wave   By Rich Tennant

WITH OBJECT-ORIENTED PROGRAMMING, I UNDERSTAND THE "ENCAPSULATION" AND "INHERITANCE" PART PRETTY WELL. IT'S THAT DARN "CLUTTERMORPHISM" THAT STUMPS ME.

In this part . . .

In the discussions of object-oriented philosophy in Part III, two main features of real-world solutions are seemingly not shared by functional programming solutions.

The first is the capability of treating objects separately. I present the example of using a microwave oven to whip up a snack. The microwave oven provides an interface (the front panel) that I use to control the oven, without worrying about its internal workings. This is true even if I know all about how the darn thing works (which I don't).

A second aspect of real-world solutions is the capability of categorizing like objects — recognizing and exploiting their similarities. If my recipe calls for an oven of any type, I should be okay because a microwave is an oven.

I already presented the mechanism that C++ uses to implement the first feature, the class. To support the second aspect of object-oriented programming, C++ uses a concept known as inheritance, which extends classes.

Inheritance is the central topic of this part.

Chapter 21

Inheriting a Class

• •

• •

*T*his chapter discusses *inheritance,* the ability of one class to inherit capabilities or properties from another class.

Inheritance is a common concept. I am a human (except when I first wake up in the morning). I inherit certain properties from the class `Human`, such as my ability to converse (more or less) intelligently and my dependence on air, water, and carbohydrate-based nourishment (a little too dependent on the latter, I'm afraid). These properties are not unique to humans. The class `Human` inherits the dependencies on air, water, and nourishment from the class `Mammal`, which inherited it from the class `Animal`.

The capability of passing down properties is a powerful one. It enables you to describe things in an economical way. For example, if my son asks, "What's a duck?" I can say, "It's a bird that goes quack." Despite what you may think, that answer conveys a considerable amount of information. He knows what a bird is, and now he knows all those same things about a duck plus the duck's additional property of "quackness." (Refer to Chapter 12 for a further discussion of this and other profound observations.)

Object-oriented languages express this inheritance relationship by allowing one class to inherit from another. Thus, OO languages can generate a model that's closer to the real world (remember that real-world stuff!) than the model generated by languages that don't support inheritance.

C++ allows one class to inherit another class as follows:

```
class Student
{
};

class GraduateStudent : public Student
{
};
```

Here, a GraduateStudent inherits all the members of Student. Thus, a GraduateStudent IS a Student. Of course, GraduateStudent may also contain members unique to a GraduateStudent.

Do I Need Inheritance?

Inheritance was introduced into C++ for several reasons. Of course, the major reason is the capability of expressing the inheritance relationship. (I'll return to that in a moment.) A minor reason is to reduce the amount of typing. Suppose that you have a class Student, and you're asked to add a new class called GraduateStudent. Inheritance can drastically reduce the number of things you have to put in the class. All you really need in the class GraduateStudent are things that describe the differences between students and graduate students.

A more important, related issue is that major buzzword reuse. Software scientists have known for some time that it doesn't make much sense to start from scratch with each new project, rebuilding the same software components.

Compare the situation in software to that of other industries. How many car manufacturers that you know of start by building their own wrenches and screwdrivers before they construct a car? And even if they did, how many would start over completely, building all new tools for the next model? Practitioners in other industries have found that it makes more sense to start from existing screws, bolts, nuts, and even larger off-the-shelf components, such as motors and compressors.

Unfortunately, this same philosophy doesn't seem to exist in the software industry. Except for very small functions like those found in the Standard C library, it's rare to find much reuse of software components. One problem is that it's virtually impossible to find a component from an earlier program that does exactly what you want. Generally, all existing components require "tweaking" before they can be used in the current application.

There's a rule in software: "If you open it, you've broken it." In other words, if you have to modify a function or class to adapt it to a new application, you need to retest everything, not just the parts you add. Changes can introduce bugs anywhere in existing code. ("The one who last touched it is the one who gets to fix it" in software is just as true as the ancient principle "he who drinks the last cup has to make a new pot.")

Inheritance allows existing classes to be adapted to new applications without the need for internal modifications. The existing class is inherited into a new subclass that contains the necessary additions and modifications.

This carries with it a third benefit of inheritance. Suppose you inherit from some existing class. Later you find that the base class has a bug that must be corrected. If you've modified the class to reuse it, you must manually check for, correct, and retest the bug in each application separately. If you've inherited the class without changes, you can generally stick the updated class into the other application without much hassle.

This is amazing

To make sense out of our surroundings, humans build extensive taxonomies. Fido is a special case of dog, which is a special case of canine, which is a special case of mammal, and so it goes. This shapes our understanding of the world.

To use another example, a student is a (special type of) person. Having said this, I already know a lot of things about students (American students, anyway). I know they have Social Security Numbers, they watch too much TV, and they daydream about about the opposite sex (the male ones, anyway). I know all these things because these are properties of all people.

In C++, we say that the class Student inherits from the class Person. Also, we say that Person is a *base class* of Student, and Student is a *subclass* of Person. Finally, we say that a Student IS_A Person (using all caps is a common way of expressing this unique relationship — I didn't make it up). C++ shares this terminology with other object-oriented languages.

Notice that although Student IS_A Person, the reverse is not true. A Person IS not A Student. (A statement like this always refers to the general case. It could be that a particular Person is, in fact, a Student.) A lot of people who are members of class Person are not members of class Student. In addition, class Student has properties it does not share with class Person. For example, Student has a grade point average, but Person does not.

The inheritance property is transitive. For example, if I define a new class GraduateStudent as a subclass of Student, GraduateStudent must also be Person. It has to be that way: If a GraduateStudent IS_A Student and a Student IS_A Person, then a GraduateStudent IS_A Person.

How Does a Class Inherit?

Here's the `GraduateStudent` example again. Fill it out with a few example members:

```
#include <string.h>
class Advisor
{
};

class Student
{
 public:
  Student(char *pName = "no name")
  {
   strncpy(name, pName, sizeof(name));
    average = 0.0;
   semesterHours = 0;
  }

  void addCourse(int hours, float grade)
  {
   average = (semesterHours * average + grade);
   semesterHours += hours;
   average = average / semesterHours;
  }

  int hours( ) { return semesterHours;}
  float gpa( ) { return average;}

 protected:
  char name[40];
  int  semesterHours;
  float average;
};

class GraduateStudent : public Student
{
 public:
  int qualifier( ) { return qualifierGrade;};

 protected:
  Advisor advisor;
  int qualifierGrade;
};

int main( )
{
```

```
    Student llu("Lo Lee Undergrad");
    GraduateStudent gs;
    llu.addCourse(3, 2.5);
    gs.addCourse(3, 3.0);
    return 0;
}
```

The class Student has been defined in the conventional fashion. The object llu is just like other Student objects. The class GraduateStudent is a bit different, however; the colon followed by the phrase public Student declares GraduateStudent to be a subclass of Student.

The appearance of the keyword public implies that there is probably protected inheritance as well. All right, it's true, but *protected* inheritance is beyond the scope of this book.

The object gs, as a member of a subclass of Student, can do anything that llu can do. It has the data members name, semesterHours, and average and the member function addCourse( ). GraduateStudent adds the members qualifier(), advisor, and qualifierGrade. After all, gs quite literally IS_A Student plus a little bit more than a Student.

Consider the following scenario:

```
void fn(Student& s)
{
    // whatever fn it wants to have
}

int main( )
{
    GraduateStudent gs;
    fn(gs);
    return 0;
}
```

Notice that the function fn( ) expects to receive as its argument an object of class Student. The call from main( ) passes it an object of class GraduateStudent. However, this is fine because once again (all together now) "a GraduateStudent IS_A Student."

Basically, the same condition arises when invoking a member function of Student with a GraduateStudent object. For example:

```
int main( )
{
    GraduateStudent gs;
    gs.addCourse(3, 2.5); // calls Student::addCourse( )
    return 0;
}
```

Constructing a Subclass

Even though a subclass has access to the protected members of the base class and could initialize them, it would be nice if the base class constructed itself. In fact, this is exactly what happens.

Before control passes beyond the open brace of the constructor for GraduateStudent, control passes to the default constructor of Student (because no other constructor was indicated). If Student were based on another class, such as Person, the constructor for that class would be invoked before the Student constructor got control. Like a skyscraper, the object is constructed starting at the "base"-ment class and working its way up the class structure one story at a time.

Just as with member objects, you sometimes need to be able to pass arguments to the base class constructor. You handle this in almost the same way as with member objects, as the following example shows:

```
class GraduateStudent : public Student
{
 public:
   GraduateStudent(char *pName = "no name",
          Advisor& adv) : Student(pName),
                 advisor(adv)
   {
    qualifierGrade = 0;
   }

   // ...remainder as before...
};

void fn(Advisor& advisor)
{
   GraduateStudent gs("Yen Kay Doodle", advisor);
   // ...whatever this function does...
}
```

Here the constructor for GraduateStudent invokes the Student constructor, passing it the argument pName. The base class is constructed before any member objects; thus, the constructor for Student is called before the constructor for Advisor. After the constructor for Advisor is called for advisor, the constructor for GraduateStudent gets a shot at it.

Following the rule that destructors are invoked in the reverse order of the constructors, the destructor for GraduateStudent is given control first. After it's given its last full measure of devotion, control passes to the destructor for Advisor and then to the destructor for Student. If Student were based on a class Person, the destructor for Person would get control after Student.

This is logical. The blob of memory is first converted to a Student object. Only then is it the job of the GraduateStudent constructor to transform this simple Student into a GraduateStudent. The destructor simply reverses the process.

Having a HAS_A Relationship

Notice that the class GraduateStudent includes the members of class Student and Advisor, but in a different way. By defining a data member of class Advisor, you know that a Student has all the data members of an Advisor within it; however you can't say that a GraduateStudent is an Advisor — instead you say that a GraduateStudent HAS_A Advisor. What's the difference between this and inheritance?

Use a car as an example. You could logically define a car as being a subclass of vehicle, and so it inherits the properties of other vehicles. At the same time, a car has a motor. If you buy a car, you can logically assume that you are buying a motor as well. (Unless you went to the used-car lot where I got my last junk heap.)

If some friends asked you to show up at a rally on Saturday with your vehicle of choice and you came in your car, they couldn't complain (even if someone else showed up on a bicycle) because a car IS_A vehicle. But if you appeared on foot carrying a motor, your friends would have reason to laugh at you because a motor is not a vehicle. A motor is missing certain critical properties that vehicles share — such as electric clocks that don't work.

From a programming standpoint, the HAS_A relationship is just as straightforward. Consider the following:

```
class Vehicle
{
};
class Motor
{
};
class Car : public Vehicle
{
 public:
   Motor motor;
};

void VehicleFn(Vehicle& v);
void motorFn(Motor& m);

int main( )
{
```

```
Car c;
VehicleFn(c);     // this is allowed
motorFn(c);       // this is not allowed
motorFn(c.motor);// this is, however
return 0;
}
```

The call VehicleFn(c) is allowed because c IS_A Vehicle. The call motorFn(c) is not because c is not a Motor, even though it contains a Motor. If what was intended was to pass the motor portion of c to the function, this must be expressed explicitly, as in the call motorFn(c.motor).

Chapter 22

Examining Virtual Member Functions: Are They for Real?

. . . .

. . . .

*T*he number and type of a function's arguments are included in its full, or extended, name. This enables you to give two functions the same name as long as the extended name is different:

```
void someFn(int);
void someFn(char*);
void someFn(char*, double);
```

In all three cases the short name for these functions is someFn() (hey! this is some fun). The extended names for all three differ: someFn(int) versus someFn(char*) and so on. C++ is left to figure out which function is meant by the arguments during the call.

The return type is not part of the extended name so you can't have two functions with the same extended name that differ only in type of object they return.

Member functions can be overloaded. Not only are the number and type of arguments part of the extended name, but the class name as well.

Inheritance introduces a whole new wrinkle, however. What if a function in a base class has the same name as a function in the subclass? Consider, for example, the following simple code snippet:

```
class Student
{
 public:
   // ...all as it was before...
   float calcTuition();
};

class GraduateStudent : public Student
{
 public:
   float calcTuition();
};

int main(int argcs, char* pArgs[])
{
   Student s;
   GraduateStudent gs;
   s.calcTuition();    // calls Student::calcTuition()
   gs.calcTuition();   // calls...
                       // GraduateStudent::calcTuition()
   return 0;
}
```

As with any overloading situation, when the programmer refers to
`calcTuition()`, C++ has to decide which `calcTuition()` is intended.
Obviously, if the two functions differed in the type of arguments, there's no
problem. Even if the arguments were the same, the class name should be sufficient to resolve the call, and this example is no different. The call
`s.calcTuition()` **refers to** `Student::calcTuition()` **because** s is
declared locally as a `Student`, **whereas** `gs.calcTuition()` **refers to**
`GraduateStudent::calcTuition()`.

But what if the exact class of the object can't be determined at compile time?
To demonstrate how this can occur, change the preceding program in a seemingly trivial way:

```
class Student
{
 public:
   // ...all as it was before...
   float calcTuition()
   {
     return 0;
   }
};

class GraduateStudent : public Student
{
 public:
   float calcTuition()
   {
```

```
    return 0;
  }
};

void fn(Student& x)
{
  x.calcTuition();    // to which calcTuition() does
                      // this refer?
}

int main(int argcs, char* pArgs[])
{
  Student s;
  GraduateStudent gs;
  fn(s);
  fn(gs);
  return 0;
}
```

Instead of calling `calcTuition()` directly, the call is now made through an intermediate function, `fn()`. Depending on how `fn()` is called, x can be a `Student` or a `GraduateStudent`. A `GraduateStudent` IS_A `Student`.

If you didn't know that, it isn't because anyone IS_A dummy — you just need to look over Chapter 21.

The argument x passed to `fn()` is declared to be a reference to `Student` in order to save time and space. C++ would have to construct a whole new `Student` object on every call to `fn()` were it to be passed by value. Depending upon the class `Student` and the number of times `fn()` is called, this could add up. Only the address of the existing `Student` object is passed when calling `fn(Student&)` or `fn(Student*)`. See Chapter 15 if this doesn't make sense.

We would like `x.calcTuition()` to call `Student::calcTuition()` when x is a `Student` but call `GraduateStudent::calcTuition()` when x is a `GraduateStudent`. It would be really cool if C++ were that smart for really cool reasons that you'll see later in this chapter.

Normally, the compiler decides which function a call refers to at compile time. When you click the button to tell the C++ compiler (be it GNU C++, Visual C++ or whatever) to rebuild your executable program, the compiler has to snoop around in your program and decide which function you meant every time an overloaded function is called based on the arguments used.

In the case described here, the declared type of the argument to `fn()` is not completely descriptive. Although the argument is declared to be a Student, it may actually be a GraduateStudent. A decision can't be made until you're actually executing the program (this is known as run time). Only when the function is actually called can C++ look at the type of the argument and decide whether it's plain old Student or a GraduateStudent.

The type that you've been accustomed to until now is called the declared or compile-time type. The declared type of x is Student in both cases because that's what the declaration in fn() says. The other type, you might say the actual type, is the run-time type. In the case of the example function fn(), the run-time type of x is Student when fn() is called with s and GraduateStudent when fn() is called with gs. Aren't we having fun?

The capability of deciding at run time, which of several overloaded member functions to call based on the run-time type is called *polymorphism,* or late binding. The term *polymorphism* comes from *poly* (meaning multiple), *morph* (meaning form), and *ism* (meaning unintelligible Greek word). C++ supports polymorphism. (This is not very surprising by now; I wouldn't be spending all this time talking about polymorphism if C++ didn't support it.) Deciding which overloaded member functions to call at compile time is called early binding because that sounds like the opposite of late binding.

Polymorphism and late binding are not quite identical terms. Polymorphism refers to the capability of the call to decide between possible actions at run time. Late binding is the mechanism C++ uses to implement polymorphism. The difference is subtle, however.

Overloading a base class function is called overriding the base class function. This new name is used in order to differentiate this more complicated case from the normal overload case.

Why Do I Need Polymorphism?

Polymorphism is key to the power of object-oriented programming. It's so important that languages that don't support polymorphism can't advertise themselves as OO languages. (I think it's a FDA regulation - you can't label a language that doesn't support OO unless you add a disclaimer from the Surgeon General, or something like that.)

Languages that support classes but not polymorphism are called object-based languages. Ada is an example of such a language.

Without polymorphism, inheritance has little meaning. Let me spring yet another example on you to show why. Suppose that I had written a really boffo program that used some class called, just to pick a name out of the air, Student. After months of design, coding, and testing, I release this application to rave reviews from colleagues and critics alike. (There's even talk of starting a new Nobel Prize category for software, but I modestly brush such talk aside.)

Time passes and my boss asks me to add to this program the capability of handling graduate students who are similar but not identical to normal students. (The graduate students probably claim that they're not similar at all.) Now, my boss doesn't know or care that deep within the program, someFunction() calls the member function calcTuition(). (There's a lot that he doesn't know or care about, by the way.)

```
void someFunction(Student& s)
{
  // ...whatever it might do...
  s.calcTuition();
  // ...continues on...
}
```

If C++ didn't support late binding, I would need to edit someFunction() to something like the following to add class GraduateStudent:

```
#define STUDENT 1
#define GRADUATESTUDENT 2
void someFunction(Student& s)
{
  // ...whatever it might do...
  // add some member type that indicates
  // the actual type of the object
  switch (s.type)
  {
   STUDENT:
     s.Student::calcTuition();
     break;

   GRADUATESTUDENT:
     s.GraduateStudent::calcTuition();
     break;
  }
  // ...continues on...
}
```

I would have to add the variable type to the class. I would then add the assignment type = STUDENT to the constructor for Student and type = GRADUATESTUDENT to the constructor for GraduateStudent. The value of type would then indicate the run-time type of s. I would then add the test shown in the preceding code snippet to every place where an overridden member function is called.

That doesn't seem so bad, except for three things. First, this is only one function. Suppose that calcTuition() is called from a lot of places and suppose that calcTuition() is not the only difference between the two classes. The chances are not good that I will find all the places that need to be changed.

Second, I must edit (read "break") code that was debugged and working, introducing opportunities for screwing up. Edits can be time-consuming and boring, which usually makes my attention drift. Any one of my edits may be wrong or may not fit in with the existing code. Who knows?

Finally, after I've finished editing, redebugging, and retesting everything, I now have two versions to keep track of (unless I can drop support for the original version). This means two sources to edit when bugs are found (perish the thought) and some type of accounting system to keep them straight.

Then what happens when my boss wants yet another class added? (My boss is like that.) Not only do I get to repeat the process, but I'll have three copies to keep track of.

With polymorphism, there's a good chance that all I need to do is add the new subclass and recompile. I may need to modify the base class itself, but at least it's all in one place. Modifications to the application code should be minimal to none.

At some philosophical level, there's an even more important reason for polymorphism. Remember how I made nachos in the oven? In this sense, I was acting as the late binder. The recipe read: Heat the nachos in the oven. It didn't read: If the type of oven is microwave, do this; if the type of oven is conventional, do that; if the type of oven is convection, do this other thing. The recipe (the code) relied on me (the late binder) to decide what the action (member function) heat means when applied to the oven (the particular instance of class Oven) or any of its variations (subclasses), such as a microwave oven (Microwave). This is the way people think, and designing a language along lines of the way people think allows the programming model to more accurately describe the real world.

How Does Polymorphism Work?

Any given language could support early or late binding upon its whim. C++ supports both forms; however, you may be surprised that the default for C++ is early binding. The reason is simple if a little dated. Polymorphism adds a small amount of overhead to each and every function call both in terms of data storage and code needed to perform the call. The founders of C++ were concerned that any additional overhead they introduced over and above its predecessor C would be used as a reason not to adopt C++ as the system's language of choice, so they made the more efficient early binding the default.

To make a member function polymorphic, the programmer must flag the function with the C++ keyword virtual, as follows:

```
#include <iostream.h>
class Base
{
 public:
  virtual void fn()
   {
    cout << "In Base class\n";
   }
};

class SubClass : public Base
{
 public:
  virtual void fn()
   {
    cout << "In SubClass\n";
   }
};

void test(Base& b)
{
   b.fn();      // this call bound late
}

int main(int argcs, char* pArgs[])
{
   Base bc;
   SubClass sc;
   cout << "Calling test(bc)\n";
   test(bc);
   cout << "Calling test(sc)\n";
   test(sc);
   return 0;
}
```

It is the keyword virtual that tells C++ fn() is a polymorphic member function. That is to say, declaring fn() virtual means that calls to it will be bound late if there is any doubt as to the run-time type of the object with which fn() is called.

In the example snippet, fn() is called through the intermediate function test(). When test() is passed a Base class object, b.fn() calls Base::fn(). But when test() is passed a SubClass object, the same call invokes SubClass::fn().

Executing the program generates the following output:

```
Calling test(bc)
In Base class
Calling test(sc)
In SubClass
```

If you're comfortable with the debugger that comes with your C++ environment, you really should single step through this example.

You only need to declare the function virtual in the base class. The "virtualness" is carried down to the subclass automatically. In this book, however, I follow the coding standard of declaring the function virtual everywhere (virtually).

Making Nachos the Polymorphic Way

Okay, now that you've seen some of the nitty-gritty details of declaring a virtual function, return to the nacho example and see what it looks like in code. Consider the following code snippet:

```
#include <dos.h>          // needed for sleep() function
class Stuff{};

class Nachos : public Stuff{};// nachos are a type
                             // of stuff

//Oven - implements a conventional oven
class Oven
{
  public:
    virtual void cook(Nachos& nachos);
    // support functions that we need
    void turnOn();        // apply current
    void turnOff();       // turn off current
    void insert(Stuff& s);  // put stuff in oven
    void remove(Stuff& s);  // pull stuff out

  protected:
    float temp;
};
void Oven::cook(Nachos& nachos)
{
    // preheat oven (turn oven on and sit in a loop
    // waiting for the temperature to reach 350 degrees)
    turnOn();
```

```
   while (temp < 350)
   {
   }
   // now put nachos in for 15 minutes
   insert(nachos);
   sleep(15 * 60);

   // get them out and turn the oven off
   remove(nachos);
   turnOff();
}

class Microwave : public Oven
{
 public:
   virtual void cook(Nachos& nachos);
   void rotateStuff(Stuff& s);
};
void Microwave::cook(Nachos& nachos)
{
   // no preheating necessary - temperature irrelevant
   // put nachos in first
   insert(nachos);
   turnOn();

   // only cook for a minute (rotate in the middle)
   sleep(30);    // wait 30 seconds
   rotateStuff(nachos);
   sleep(30);    // wait 30 seconds

   // turn the oven off first (lest your hair fall out)
   turnOff();
   remove(nachos);
}

Nachos makeNachos(Oven& oven)
{
   // get all the stuff together
   // and assemble the parts
   Nachos n;

   // now (here comes the critical part), cook it
   // (given whatever kind of oven you have)
   oven.cook(n);

   // return the results
   return n;
}
```

Here you see the class Nachos, which is declared as a subclass of Stuff (meaning cookable stuff). The class Oven is outfitted with the common functions turnOn(), turnOff(), insert(), and remove(). (The last two refer to the insertion and extraction of stuff from the oven.) In addition, the class Oven has a member function cook(Nachos&), which has been declared virtual.

The function cook(Nachos&) has been declared virtual because it is implemented differently in the subclass Microwave, which inherits from the class Oven. The implementation of Oven::cook(Nachos&) preheats the oven to a temperature of 350 degrees, puts the nachos in, and cooks them for 15 minutes. It then removes said nachos before turning off the oven. The implementation of Microwave::cook(Nachos&), by comparison, puts the nachos in, turns the power on for 30 seconds, rotates the nachos, and then waits another 30 seconds before turning the oven off and removing the nachos.

This is fine and dandy, but it's all just a buildup for the really interesting part. The function makeNachos() is passed an Oven of some type. Given that oven, it assembles all the parts into an object n and then cooks them by calling oven.cook(). Exactly which function is used, function Oven::cook() or function Microwave::cook(), depends on the real-time type of oven. The function makeNachos() has no idea — and doesn't want to know — what the run-time type of oven is.

Why is polymorphism such a good idea? First, it allows the maker of ovens — and not the cooker of nachos — to worry about the details of how ovens work. Our division of labor lays such details at the oven programmer's feet.

Second, polymorphism can greatly simplify the code. Look how simple makeNachos() appears without any of the oven details. (I realize that it wouldn't be too complicated even with the details, but remember that polymorphism works for real-world problems with their attendant complexity.) The nacho functions can concentrate on nacho details. Finally, the result is extensible. When a new subclass ConvectionOven comes along with a new member function ConvectionOven::cook(Nachos&), we don't need to change one iota of makeNachos() to incorporate the new function. Polymorphism automatically includes the new function and calls it when necessary.

This is heady stuff. Reflect on what this means. Polymorphism is the key that unlocks the power of inheritance.

When Is a Virtual Function Not?

Just because you think that a particular function call is bound late doesn't mean that it is.

C++ generates no indication at compile time of which calls it thinks are bound early and late.

The most critical thing to watch for is that all the member functions in question are declared identically, including the return type. If not declared with the same arguments in the subclasses, the member functions are not overridden polymorphically, whether or not they are declared virtual. For example, change the previous function so that the arguments don't match exactly, and then rerun the program:

```cpp
#include <iostream.h>
class Base
{
 public:
  virtual void fn(int x)
  {
   cout << "In Base class, int x = " << x << "\n";
  }
};

class SubClass : public Base
{
 public:
  virtual void fn(float x)
  {
   cout << "In SubClass, float x = " << x << "\n";
  }
};

void test(Base& b)
{
  int i = 1;
  b.fn(i);     // this call not bound late
  float f = 2.0F;
  b.fn(f);     // neither is this one
}

int main(int argcs, char* pArgs[])
{
  Base bc;
  SubClass sc;
  cout << "Calling test(bc)\n";
  test(bc);
  cout << "Calling test(sc)\n";
  test(sc);
  return 0;
}
```

The only difference between this program and the one before it is that fn() in Base is declared as fn(int), whereas the SubClass version is declared fn(float). No error is generated because this program is legal. The results, however, show no sign of polymorphism:

```
Calling test(bc)
In Base class, int x = 1
In Base class, int x = 2
Calling test(sc)
In Base class, int x = 1
In Base class, int x = 2
```

Because the first call passes an int, it's not surprising that the compiler calls fn(int) with both bc and sc. It is a little surprising that the float in the second call is converted to an int and that the same Base::fn(int) is called the second time in test(). This happens because the object b passed to test() is declared as an object of class Base. Without polymorphism, calls to b.fn() in test() refer to Base::fn(int).

If the arguments don't match exactly, there is no late binding.

One exception to the preceding identical declaration rule is that if the member function in the base class returns a pointer or reference to a base class object, an overridden member function in a subclass may return a pointer or reference to an object of the subclass. In other words, the following is allowed:

```
class Base
{
  public:
    // return a copy of the current object
    Base* makeACopy()
    {
      // ...do whatever it takes to make a copy
    }
};

class SubClass : public Base
{
  public:
    // return a copy of the current object
    SubClass* makeACopy()
    {
      // ...do whatever it takes to make a copy
    };
};
```

```
void fn(BaseClass& bc)
{
   BaseClass* pCopy = bc.makeACopy();

   // proceed on...
}
```

In practice, this is quite natural. A makeACopy() function should return an object of type SubClass even though it might override BaseClass::makeACopy().

Considering Virtual Considerations

There are a few things to keep in mind when using virtual functions.

First, static member functions cannot be declared virtual. Because static member functions are not called with an object, there is no run-time object to have a type.

Second, specifying the class name in the call forces a call to bind early whether the function is virtual or not. For example, the following call is to Base::fn() because that's what the programmer indicated, even if fn() is declared virtual:

```
void test(Base& b)
{
   b.Base::fn();      // this call is not bound late
}
```

Next, a virtual function cannot be inlined. To expand a function inline, the compiler must know which function is intended at compile time. Thus, although the example member functions so far have been declared in the class, all of them have been outline functions.

Finally, constructors cannot be virtual because there is no (completed) object to use to determine the type. At the time the constructor is called, the memory that the object occupies is just an amorphous mass. It's only after the constructor has finished that the object is a member of the class in good standing.

By comparison, the destructor should be declared virtual. If not, you run the risk of improperly destructing the object, as in the following circumstance:

```
class Base
{
 public:
  ~Base();
};

class SubClass : public Base
{
 public:
  ~SubClass();
};

void finishWithObject(Base* pHeapObject)
{
   // ...work with object...
   // now return it to the heap
   delete pHeapObject; // this calls ~Base() no matter
                       // the run-time type of
                       // pHeapObject
}
```

If the pointer passed to finishWithObject() really points to a SubClass, the SubClass destructor is not invoked properly — because the destructor has been not been declared virtual, it's always bound early. Declaring the destructor virtual solves the problem.

So when would you not want to declare the destructor virtual? There's only one case. Virtual functions introduce a "little" overhead. Let me be more specific. When the programmer defines the first virtual function in a class, C++ adds an additional, hidden pointer — not one pointer per virtual function, just one pointer if the class has any virtual functions. A class that has no virtual functions (and does not inherit any virtual functions from base classes) does not have this pointer.

Now, one pointer doesn't sound like much, and it isn't unless the following two conditions are true:

- ✔ The class doesn't have many data members (so that one pointer represents a lot compared to what's there already).
- ✔ You intend to create a lot of objects of this class (otherwise, the overhead doesn't make any difference).

If these two conditions are met and your class doesn't already have any virtual member functions, you may not want to declare the destructor virtual.

Except for this one case, always declare destructors to be virtual even if a class is not subclassed (yet) — you never know when someone will come along and use your class as the base class for her own. If you don't declare the destructor virtual, document it!

Chapter 23

Factoring Classes

· ·

In This Chapter

▶ Factoring common properties into a base class

▶ Using abstract classes to hold factored information

▶ Declaring abstract classes

▶ Using dynamic typing

· ·

*T*he concept of inheritance allows one class to inherit the properties of a base class. Inheritance has a number of purposes, including paying for my son's college. It can save programming time by avoiding needless code repetition. Inheritance allows the program to reuse existing classes in new applications by overriding functions.

The main benefit of inheritance is the ability to point out the relationship between classes. This is the so-called IS_A relationship — a MicrowaveOven IS_A Oven and stuff like that.

Factoring is great stuff if you make the correct correlations. For example, the microwave versus conventional oven relationship seems natural. Claim that microwave is a special kind of toaster and you're headed for trouble. True, they both make things hot, they both use electricity, and they're both found in the kitchen but the similarity ends there — a microwave can't make toast.

Identifying the classes inherent in a problem and drawing the correct relationships between these classes is a process known as *factoring*. (The word is related to the arithmetic that you were forced to do in grade school: factoring out the Least Common Denominators; for example, 12 is equal to 2 times 2 times 3.)

Factoring

To see how factoring works, look back at the two classes used in the BUDGET examples appearing at the end of each Part, Checking and Savings. I can talk until I'm blue in the face about these classes; however, object-oriented programmers have come up with a concise way to describe the salient points of a class in a drawing. The Checking and Savings classes are shown in Figure 23-1.

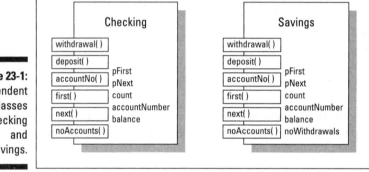

Figure 23-1: Independent classes Checking and Savings.

To read this figure and the other figures, remember the following:

- The big box is the class, with the class name at the top.
- The names in boxes are member functions.
- The names not in boxes are data members.
- The names that extend partway out of the boxes are publicly accessible members; that is, these members can be accessed by functions which are not part of the class or any of its decendents. Those members that are completely within the box are not accessible from outside the class.
- A thick arrow represents the IS_A relationship.
- A thin arrow represents the HAS_A relationship.

A Car IS_A Vehicle but a Car HAS_A Motor.

You can see in Figure 23-1 that the Checking and Savings classes have a lot in common. For example, both classes have a withdrawal() and deposit() member function. Because the two classes aren't identical, however, they must remain as separate classes. (In a real-life bank application, the two classes would be a good deal more different than in this example.) Still, there should be a way to avoid this repetition.

We could have one of these classes inherit from the other. Savings has more members than Checking, so we could let Savings inherit from Checking. This arrangement is shown in Figure 23-2. The Savings class inherits all of the members. The class is completed with the addition of the data member noWithdrawals and by overriding the function withdrawal(). We have to override withdrawal() because the rules for withdrawing money from a savings account are different than those for a checking account. (These rules don't apply to me because I don't have any money to withdraw anyway.)

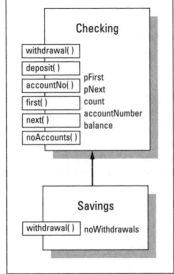

Figure 23-2:
Savings
implemented
as a
subclass of
checking.

Although letting Savings inherit from Checking is labor-saving, it's not completely satisfying. The main problem is that it, like the weight listed on my driver's license, misrepresents the truth. This inheritance relationship implies that a Savings account is a special type of Checking account, which it is.

"So what?" you say. "Inheriting works and it saves effort." True, but my reservations are more than stylistic trivialities — my reservations are at some of the best restaurants in town, at least that's what all the truckers say. Such misrepresentations are confusing to the programmer, both today's and tomorrow's. Someday, a programmer unfamiliar with our programming tricks will have to read and understand what our code does. Misleading representations are difficult to reconcile and understand.

In addition, such misrepresentations can lead to problems down the road. Suppose, for example, that the bank changes its policies with respect to checking accounts. Say it decides to charge a service fee on checking accounts only if the minimum balance dips below a given value during the month.

A change like this can be easily handled with minimal changes to the class Checking. You'll have to add a new data member to the class Checking to keep track of the minimum balance during the month. Let's go out on a limb and call it minimumBalance.

But now we have a problem. Because Savings inherits from Checking, Savings gets this new data member as well. It has no use for this member because the minimum balance does not affect savings accounts, so it just sits there. Remember that every Checking account object has this extra minimumBalance member. One extra data member may not be a big deal, but it adds further confusion.

Changes like this accumulate. Today it's an extra data member, tomorrow it's a changed member function. Eventually, the Savings account class is carrying a lot of extra baggage that is applicable only to Checking accounts.

Now the bank comes back and decides to change some savings account policy. This requires us to modify some function in Checking. Changes like this in the base class automatically propagate down to the subclass unless the function is already overridden in the subclass Savings. For example, suppose that the bank decides to give away toasters for every deposit into the checking account. (Hey — it could happen!) Without the bank (or its programmers) knowing it, deposits to checking accounts would automatically result in toaster donations. Unless you're very careful, changes to Checking may unexpectedly appear in Savings.

How can we avoid these problems? Claiming that Checking is a special case of Savings changes but doesn't remove our problems. What we need is some third class (call it Account just for grins) that embodies the things that are common between Checking and Savings. This relationship is shown in Figure 23-3.

How does building a new account solve the problems? First, creating a new account is a more accurate description of the real world (whatever that is). In our concept of things (or at least in mine), there really is something known as an account. Savings accounts and checking accounts are special cases of this more fundamental concept.

In addition, the class Savings is insulated from changes to the class Checking (and vice versa). If the bank institutes a fundamental change to all accounts, we can modify Account and all subclasses will automatically inherit the change. But if the bank changes its policy only for checking accounts, we can modify just the Checking account class without modifying Savings.

This process of culling out common properties from similar classes is called *factoring*. This is an important feature of object-oriented languages for the reasons described so far, plus one more: reduction in redundancy. Let me repeat, redundancy is bad, there is no place for redundancy; said another way. . . .

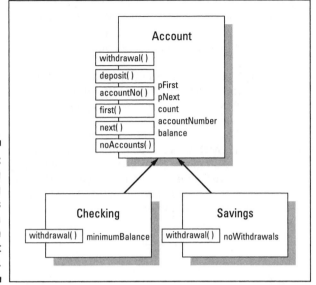

Figure 23-3: Basing Checking and Savings on a common Account class.

Factoring is legitimate only if the inheritance relationship corresponds to reality. Factoring together a class Mouse and Joystick because they're both hardware pointing devices is legitimate. Factoring together a class Mouse and Display because they both make low-level operating system calls is not.

Factoring can and usually does result in multiple levels of abstraction. For example, a program written for a more developed bank may have a class structure such as that shown in Figure 23-4.

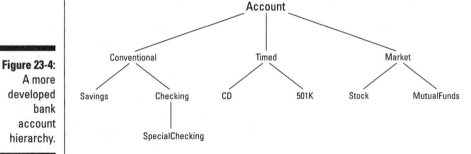

Figure 23-4: A more developed bank account hierarchy.

Here you see that another class has been inserted between Checking and Savings and the most general class Account. This class, called Conventional, incorporates features common to conventional accounts. Other account types, such as stock market accounts, are also foreseen.

Such multitiered class structures are common and desirable as long as the relationships they express correspond to reality. Note, however, that no one correct class hierarchy exists for any given set of classes.

Suppose that the bank allows account holders to access checking and stock market accounts remotely. Withdrawals from other account types can be made only at the bank. Although the class structure in Figure 23-4 seems natural, the one shown in Figure 23-5 is also justifiable given this information. The programmer must decide which class structure best fits the data and leads to the cleanest, most natural implementation.

Figure 23-5:
An alternate class hierarchy to the one in Figure 23-4.

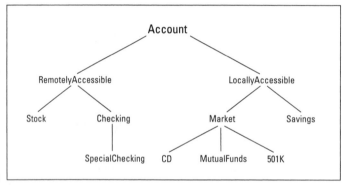

Implementing Abstract Classes

As intellectually satisfying as factoring is, it introduces a problem of its own. Return one more time to the bank account classes, specifically the common base class Account. Think for a minute about how you might go about defining the different member functions defined in Account.

Most Account member functions are no problem because both account types implement them in the same way. Implementing those common functions with Account.withdrawal() is different, however. The rules for withdrawing from a Savings account are different than those for withdrawing from a Checking account. We'll have to implement Savings::withdrawal() differently than Checking::withdrawal(). But how are we supposed to implement Account::withdrawal()?

Let's ask the bank manager for help. I imagine the conversation going something like the following:

"What are the rules for making a withdrawal from an account?" you ask expectantly.

"What type of account? Savings or checking?" comes the reply.

"From an account," you say. "Just an account."

Blank look. (One might say a "blank bank look" . . . then again, maybe not.)

The problem is that the question doesn't make sense. There's no such thing as "just an account." All accounts (in this example) are either checking accounts or savings accounts. The concept of an account is an abstract one that factors out properties common to the two concrete classes. It is incomplete, because it lacks the critical property `withdrawal()`. (After you get further into the details, you may find other properties that a simple account lacks.)

An abstract class is one that only exists in subclasses. A concrete class is a class that is not abstract.

Let me borrow an example from the animal kingdom. You can observe the different species of warm-blooded, baby-bearing animals and conclude that there is a concept called mammal. You can derive classes from mammal, such as canine, feline, and hominid. It is impossible, however, to find anywhere on earth a pure mammal, that is, a mammal that isn't a member of some subspecies of mammal. Mammal is a high-level concept that man has created — no instances of mammal exist.

Note that I can make this assertion confidently although time has passed since I wrote this. Scientists discover new animals all the time. One scientist even discovered a new phylum. Not once has a scientist come back and said, "This new thing is a mammal and nothing more . . . just a mammal." The problem with a statement like this is that this animal surely has properties that other mammals don't share and, even if doesn't, there's a distinct possibility that someone will find such a property in the future.

In order to reflect this situation, C++ provides the capability of defining abstract classes incompletely.

Describing the abstract class concept

An *abstract class* is a class with one or more pure virtual functions. Oh, great! That helps a lot. . . .

Okay, a *pure virtual* function is a virtual member function that is marked as having no implementation probably because no one knows how to implement it.

It doesn't make sense to ask exactly how to implement the withdrawal() function in the class Account. However, the concept of a withdrawal from an account does make sense. The C++ programmer can write a function withdrawal() that represents the concept of withdrawing money but has no function body because we don't know how to implement this feature. Such a function is called a pure virtual function. (Don't ask me where they came up with that name.)

The syntax for declaring a function pure virtual is demonstrated in the following class Account:

```
// Account - this class is an abstract class
class Account
{
  protected:
   Account(Account& c);
  public:
   Account(unsigned accNo, float initialBalance = 0.0F);

   // access functions
   unsigned int accountNo( );
   float acntBalance( );
   static Account *first( );
   Account *next( );
   static int noAccounts( );

   // transaction functions
   void deposit(float amount);

   // the following is a pure virtual function
   virtual void withdrawal(float amount) = 0;

  protected:
   // keep accounts in a linked list so there's no limit
   // to the number of accounts
   static Account *pFirst;
   Account *pNext;
   static int count;      // number of accounts
   unsigned  accountNumber;
   float   balance;
};
```

The = 0 after the declaration of withdrawal() indicates that the programmer does not intend to define this function. The declaration is a placeholder for the subclasses. The subclasses of Account are expected to override this function with a concrete function.

I think this notation is silly, and I don't like it any more than you do. But it's here to stay, so you just have to learn to live with it. There is a reason, if not exactly a justification, for this notation. Every virtual function must have an entry in a special table. This entry contains the address of the function. The entry for a pure virtual function is zero.

An abstract class cannot be instanced with an object; that is, you can't make an object out of an abstract class. For example, the following declaration is not legal:

```
void fn( )
{
    // declare an account with 100 dollars
    Account acnt(1234, 100.00);// this is not legal
    acnt.withdrawal(50);        // what would you expect
                                // this call to do?
}
```

If the declaration were allowed, the resulting object would be incomplete, lacking in some capability. For example, what should the preceding call do? Remember, there is no Account::withdrawal().

Abstract classes serve as base classes for other classes. An Account contains all the properties associated with a generic bank account. You can create other types of bank accounts by inheriting from Account, but they can't be instanced with an object.

Making an honest class out of an abstract class

The subclass of an abstract class remains abstract until all pure virtual functions have been overridden. The class Savings is not abstract because it overrides the pure virtual function withdrawal() with a perfectly good definition. An object of class Savings knows how to perform withdrawal() when called on to do so. The same is true of class Checking: The class is not virtual, because the function withdrawal() overrides the pure virtual function in the base class.

A subclass of an abstract class can remain abstract, however. Consider the following classes:

```
class Display
{
 public:
  virtual void initialize( ) = 0;
  virtual void write(char *pString) = 0;
};

class SVGA : public Display
{
  // override both member functions with "real" functions
  virtual void initialize( );
  virtual void write(char *pString);
};

class HWVGA : public Display
{
  // override the only function we know how to up until now
  virtual void write(char *pString);
};

class ThreedVGA : public HWVGA
{
  virtual void initialize( );
};

void fn( )
{
  SVGA mc;
  VGA vga;
  // ...what the function chooses to do from here...
}
```

The class Display, intended to represent video PC displays, has two pure virtual functions: initialize() and write(). You can't implement either function for adapters in general. The different types of video cards do not initialize or write in the same way.

One of the subclasses, SVGA, is not abstract. This is a particular type of video adapter that the programmer knows how to program. Therefore, the class SVGA has overridden both initialize() and write() appropriately for this adapter.

HWVGA, another one of the subclasses, is also not abstract. Here again, the programmer knows how to program the accelerated VGA adapter hardware. In this case, however, a level of abstraction is between the generic Display and the specific case of the ThreedVGA display, which represents the special 3-D hardware display cards.

For this discussion, assume that all hardware accelerated VGA cards are written to in the same way, but that each must be initialized in its own way. (This isn't necessarily true, but assume that it is.) To express the common write property, introduce the class HWVGA to implement the write() function (along with any other properties that all HWVGA have in common). Don't override the member function initialize(), however, because the different HWVGAs do not have this property in common.

Therefore, although the function write() has been overridden, the class HWVGA is still abstract because the initialize() function has yet to be overridden.

Because ThreedVGA inherits from HWVGA, it has to override only the one missing member function, initialize(), to complete the definition of Display adapter. The function fn() is therefore free to instance and use a ThreedVGA object.

Overriding the last pure virtual function with a normal member function makes the class complete (that is, non-abstract). Only non-abstract classes can be instanced with an object.

Originally, every pure virtual function in a subclass had to be overridden, even if the function was overridden with another pure virtual function. Eventually, the people who count realized that this was as silly as it sounds and dropped the requirement. Older compilers may still require it, though.

Passing abstract classes

Because you can't instance an abstract class, it may sound odd that it's possible to declare a pointer or a reference to an abstract class. With polymorphism, however, this isn't as crazy as it sounds. Consider the following code snippet:

```
void fn(Account *pAccount);  // this is legal
void otherFn( )
{
   Savings s;
   Checking c;

   // this is legitimate because Savings IS_A Account
   fn(&s);
   // same here
   fn(&c);
}
```

Here, pAccount is declared as a pointer to an Account. However, it's understood that when the function is called, it will be passed the address of some non-abstract subclass object such as Savings or Checking.

All objects received by fn() will be of either class Savings or class Checking (or some future non-abstract subclass of Account). The function is assured that you will never pass an actual object of class Account, because you could never create one to pass in the first place.

Declaring pure virtual functions — is it really necessary?

If withdrawal() can't be defined, why not leave it out? Why not declare the function in Savings and Checking where is can also be defined and keep it out of Account? In many object-oriented languages, you can do just that. But C++ wants to be able to check that you really know what you're doing.

Remember that declaring a function establishes its extended name including arguments while a definition includes the code to execute when the function is called.

I can make the following minor changes to Account to demonstrate the problem:

```
class Account
{
  // just like before but without
  // the declaration of withdrawal()
};

class Savings : public Account
{
 public:
  virtual void withdrawal(float amnt);
};

void fn(Account *pAcc)
{
  // withdraw some money
  pAcc->withdrawal(100.00F);
              // this call is not allowed
              // withdrawal( ) is not a member
              // of class Account
};

int main( )
```

```
{
  Savings s;  // open an account
  fn(&s);

  // ...continues on...
}
```

Suppose that you open a savings account s. You then pass the address of
that account to the function fn(), which attempts to make a withdrawal.
Because the function withdrawal() is not a member of Account, however,
the compiler generates an error.

Some languages wait to make that test when the function is actually called
during the execution of the program. In this case, the above code snippet would
work; main() calls the function fn() passing the object s. When fn() subse-
quently calls withdrawal(), the language would realize that withdrawal() is,
in fact, defined for the object given it. While flexible, this approach is slow
because the language has to make a number of tests during program execution.
It's also fraught with errors — if someone did pass an Account object without
the member function withdrawal() defined, the program would terminate if it
couldn't figure out what to do about it — this doesn't make users very happy.

See how pure virtual functions correct the problem. Here's the same situation
with Account declared as an abstract class:

```
class Account
{
 public:
  // just like preceding
  // declare withdrawal pure virtual
  virtual void withdrawal(float amnt) = 0;
};

class Savings : public Account
{
 public:
  virtual void withdrawal(float amnt);
};

void fn(Account *pAcc)
{
  // withdraw some money
  pAcc->withdrawal(100.00F); // now it works
};

int main( )
{
  Savings s;  // open an account
  fn(&s);
  // ...same as before...
}
```

The situation is the same except the class Account includes a member function `withdrawal()`. Now when the compiler checks to see whether `pAcc->withdrawal()` is defined, it sees the definition of `Account::withdrawal()` just as it expects. The compiler is happy. You're happy. That makes me happy, too. (Frankly, a football game and a cold beer are enough to make me happy.)

The pure virtual function is a placeholder in the base class for the subclass to override with its own implementation. Without that placeholder in the base class, there is no overriding.

Trying to Rationalize My Budget: BUDGET3.CPP

The chapter continues the metamorphosis of the purely functional Budget1 at the end of Part II through the object-based version Budget2 at the end of Part III into an object-oriented Budget3 program here.

The Budget programs handle bank deposits and withdrawals for a simulated bank. The user enters a series of bank accounts followed by the deposits and withdrawals for that account. Once the user has entered all of her transactions, the program displays the balances for each account plus the overall balance. Budget2 and Budget3 simulate both Checking and Savings accounts. Checking accounts charge a small fee for withdrawals when the balance is less that $500 while savings accounts charge a large fee after the first withdrawal irrespective of the balance.

Budget2 was an improvement over Budget1 in one sense: it isolated the details of account classes from the exterior functions that manipulate accounts. Unfortunately, Budget2 contained a large amount of redundancy between the two classes Savings and Checking, redundancies which we could have avoided using the inheritance principles.

Budget3 adds the following improvements over its predecessors:

- ✔ Use of inheritance to highlight the similarities between checking and savings accounts and to avoid redundancy
- ✔ Use of virtual member functions to increase readability and expandability
- ✔ Creation of a pure virtual class to capture the commonalties between checking and savings accounts
- ✔ Use of linked list rather than an array in order to relieve the limit on the number of bank accounts the program can hold

With the help of the new OO superhero inheritance and its sidekick polymorphism, we can rationalize the two account classes into a single class Account, which captures the commonalties between these two classes. The result is a much smaller and simpler program:

```cpp
// BUDGET3.CPP - Budget program with inheritance and
//               late binding (aka, polymorphism). Notice
//               how much smaller the program is compared
//               with Budget2 now that the redundancy
//               has been removed. A single function can
//               now handle both checking and
//               savings accounts (and any other accounts
//               that you might invent in the future).
//
//               In addition, this version stored accounts
//               in a linked list rather than a fixed array
//               in order to avoid the limitation of a
//               fixed maximum number of objects.
#include <iostream.h>
#include <stdlib.h>
#include <ctype.h>
#include <string.h>

class LinkedListObject
{
 public:
   LinkedListObject()
    {
       // add the current object to the end of the
       // linked list
       addToEnd();
    }

   // link list manipulation
   static LinkedListObject* first()
   {
    return pFirst;
   }
   LinkedListObject* next()
   {
    return pNext;
   }
   void addToEnd();

 protected:
   // keep accounts in a linked list
   // so there's no limit to the number of objects
   static LinkedListObject* pFirst;
        LinkedListObject* pNext;
};
```

```
// allocated the static pointer to the first
// object in the linked list
LinkedListObject* LinkedListObject::pFirst = 0;

// add the current object to the linked list of
void LinkedListObject::addToEnd()
{

  // add this to end of list and count it
  if (pFirst == 0)
  {
   pFirst = this;    // empty list; make it first
  }
  else
  {
   // search for the last element in the list
   LinkedListObject* pA;
   for (pA = pFirst; pA->pNext; pA = pA->pNext)
   {
   }
   pA->pNext = this;  // tack us onto end
  }
  pNext = 0;              // we're always last
}


// Account - this abstract class incorporates properties
//           common to both account types: Checking and
//           Savings. However, it's missing the concept
//           withdrawal(), which is different between the two
class Account : public LinkedListObject
{
 public:
  Account::Account(unsigned accNo,
                   double initialBalance = 0.0)
  {
    // initialize the data members of the object
    accountNumber = accNo;
    balance = initialBalance;

    // count it
    count++;
  }

  // access functions
  int accountNo()
  {
   return accountNumber;
  }
  double acntBalance()
```

```
   {
    return balance;
   }
   static int noAccounts()
   {
    return count;
   }

   // linked list functions which provide the proper
   // promotions, save a lot of hassle later
   static Account* first()
   {
       return (Account*)LinkedListObject::first();
   }
   Account* next()
   {
    return (Account*)LinkedListObject::next();
   }

   // transaction functions
   void deposit(double amount)
   {
    balance += amount;
   }
   virtual void withdrawal(double amount) = 0;

   // display function for displaying self on 'cout'
   void display()
   {
    cout << type()
        << " account " << accountNumber
        << " = "    << balance
        << "\n";
   }
   virtual char* type() = 0;

  protected:
   static int count;                    // number of accounts
   unsigned accountNumber;
   double   balance;
};

// allocate space for statics
int Account::count = 0;

// Checking - this class contains properties unique to
//            checking accounts. Not much left, is there?
class Checking : public Account
{
  public:
```

```
  Checking::Checking(unsigned accNo,
                     double initialBalance = 0.0) :
    Account(accNo, initialBalance)
  {
  }

  // overload pure virtual functions
  virtual void withdrawal(double amount);
  char* type()
  {
      return "Checking";
  }
};

// withdrawal - overload the Account::withdrawal() member
//              function to charge a 20 cents per check if
//              the balance is below $500
void Checking::withdrawal(double amount)
{
  if (balance < amount )
  {
   cout << "Insufficient funds: balance " << balance
        << ", check "                     << amount
        << "\n";
  }
  else
  {
   balance -= amount;

   // if balance falls too low, charge service fee
   if (balance < 500.00)
   {
     balance -= 0.20;
   }
  }
}

// Savings - same story as Checking except that it also
// has a unique data member
class Savings : public Account
{
 public:

  Savings::Savings(unsigned accNo,
                   double initialBalance = 0.0) :
    Account(accNo, initialBalance)
  {
   noWithdrawals = 0;
  }
```

```
  // transaction functions
  virtual void withdrawal(double amount);
  char* type()
  {
      return "Savings";
  }

 protected:
  int     noWithdrawals;
};

// withdrawal - overload the Account::withdrawal() member
//              function to charge a $5.00 fee after the
        first
//              withdrawal of the month
void Savings::withdrawal(double amount)
{
  if (balance < amount)
  {
    cout << "Insufficient funds: balance " << balance
      << ", withdrawal "          << amount
      << "\n";
  }
  else
  {
   if (++noWithdrawals > 1)
   {
     balance -= 5.00;
   }
   balance -= amount;
  }
}

// prototype declarations
unsigned getAccntNo();
void     process(Account* pAccount);
void     getAccounts();
void     displayResults();


// main - accumulate the initial input and output totals
int main(int argcs, char* pArgs[])
{
    // read accounts from user
    getAccounts();

    // display the linked list of accounts
    displayResults();
    return 0;
```

```
}

// getAccounts - load up the specified array of Accounts
void getAccounts()
{
  Account* pA;

  // loop until someone enters 'X' or 'x'
  char   accountType;      // S or C
  while (1)
  {
    cout << "Enter S for Savings, "
         << "C for Checking, X for exit:";
    cin >> accountType;
    switch (accountType)
    {
      case 'c':
      case 'C':
       pA = new Checking(getAccntNo());
       break;

      case 's':
      case 'S':
       pA = new Savings(getAccntNo());
       break;

      case 'x':
      case 'X':
       return;

      default:
       cout << "I didn't get that.\n";
    }

    // now process the object we just created
    process(pA);
  }
}

// displayResults - display the accounts found in the
//                  Account link list
void displayResults()
{
  // now present totals
  double total = 0.0;
  cout << "Account totals:\n";
  for (Account* pA = Account::first(); pA; pA = pA->next())
  {
   pA->display();
   total += pA->acntBalance();
```

```
  }
  cout << "Total worth = " << total << "\n";
}

// getAccntNo - return the account number entered
unsigned getAccntNo()
{
  unsigned accntNo;
  cout << "Enter account number:";
  cin  >> accntNo;
  return accntNo;
}

// process(Account) - input the data for an account
void process(Account* pAccount)
{
  cout << "Enter positive number for deposit,\n"
       << "negative for withdrawal, 0 to terminate\n";
  double transaction;
  do
  {
    cout << ":";
    cin >> transaction;

    // deposit
    if (transaction > 0)
    {
      pAccount->deposit(transaction);
    }
    // withdrawal
    if (transaction < 0) {
      pAccount->withdrawal(-transaction);
    }
  } while (transaction != 0);
}
```

I executed the program with the following data in order to demonstrate how the program works (or, as is so often the case with my programs, doesn't work). **Bold** characters indicate user input, while non-bold characters indicate output from the program.

```
Enter S for Savings, C for Checking, X for exit:S
Enter account number:123
Enter positive number for deposit,
negative for withdrawal, 0 to terminate
:200
:-20
:0
Enter S for Savings, C for Checking, X for exit:S
Enter account number:234
Enter positive number for deposit,
```

```
negative for withdrawal, 0 to terminate
:200
:-10
:-10
:0
Enter S for Savings, C for Checking, X for exit:c
Enter account number:345
Enter positive number for deposit,
negative for withdrawal, 0 to terminate
:200
:-20
:0
Enter S for Savings, C for Checking, X for exit:C
Enter account number:456
Enter positive number for deposit,
negative for withdrawal, 0 to terminate
:600
:-20
:0
Enter S for Savings, C for Checking, X for exit:x
Account totals:
Savings account 123 = 180
Savings account 234 = 175
Checking account 345 = 179.8
Checking account 456 = 580
Total worth        = 1114.8
Press any key to continue
```

The object oriented Budget3 begins with the base class LinkedListObject. This class contains the logic necessary to create a linked list. LinkedListObject contains the first and next pointers as well as the common first() and next() member functions. Any class derived from LinkedListObject can be used to create a linked list using the member functions it inherits.

The next class contained in Budget3 is Account. This class encapsulates all the things that we know about generic accounts:

✔ They are identified by account numbers.

✔ Each account carries a balance.

✔ Users can make deposits or withdrawals from a bank account.

We know how to perform a deposit for an Account, hence the member function deposit() is defined here. We don't know how to perform a withdrawal() since the different types accounts define a slightly different withdrawal process. This is reflected by declaring Account::withdrawal() pure virtual (this is indicated by the "= 0" at the end of the declaration).

The constructor for Account begins by automatically calling the constructor for LinkedListObject, which adds the current Account to the end of the linked list of account objects. The Account constructor then creates the unique account information by saving off the account number and the initial balance, which is assumed to be zero if not specified. It continues by incrementing the static data member count thereby keeping track of the number of Account objects in existence.

There is only one copy of a static object for the class. It is shared among all objects.

The accountNo() and acntBalance() functions defined next give the outside world the account number and balance information without giving them the ability to modify them directly.

The Account::first() and next() member functions override the LinkedListObject versions. Without these seemingly senseless functions, the users of Account would have to cast the objects returned from first() and next() themselves.

The object returned from first() and next() is a LinkedListObject and not an Account.

The display() and type() functions give all accounts a similar display format.

The Checking subtype of Account is fairly simple. The constructor for Checking does nothing more than pass its arguments to Account. The only real member function is withdrawal() which implements the rules of engagement for checking accounts.

The Savings class is identical to the Checking class in that all that it provides is the withdrawal() method.

Any subclass of Account which does not override withdrawal() would be virtual — you cannot create an instance of a virtual class.

The functions that make up the main program are now simplified. The function getAcounts() creates a Savings or a Checking account object depending upon the character entered by the user. This is the only place within the main program where the subclass of Account is referred to directly.

The displayResults() function loops through the linked list asking each Account object to display itself irrespective of the details of how a savings or checking account (or any other type of account for that matter) might accomplish this.

The process() function is even more impressive. This function performs deposits (handled by Account::deposit()) and withdrawals (handled by Savings::withdrawal() or Checking::withdrawal() depending upon the type of object pointed to by pAccount).

Notice how desirable the process() function has become. First, the redundancy of defining different versions of process() has been removed. Even more importantly, the logic of the process() function has been simplified. The programmer can now concentrate on how this function works without worrying about the internal details of different types of accounts.

The problem that Budget3 solves is fairly simple (and a lot contrived). Nevertheless, comparing the different versions of Budget may give you a feel for the differences between a purely functional program (Budget1) through an object-based program lacking inheritance (Budget2) to a fully object-oriented version (Budget3).

Part V
Optional Features

In this part . . .

*T*he goal of this book is not to turn you into a C++ language lawyer; it's to give you a solid understanding of the fundamentals of C++ and object-oriented programming.

The earlier parts in this book cover the essential features you need to know to produce a well-written, object-oriented C++ program. C++, however, is a big language (it has a serious case of feature-itis, if you ask me), and I have yet to discuss many features. In Part V, I present a summary of the additional features that I find most useful, along with my opinion as to when — and when not — to use them.

Chapter 24

Overloading Operators

● ●

In This Chapter

▶ Overview of overloading operators in C++

▶ Discussion of operator format versus function format

▶ Implementing operators as a member function versus as a non-member function

▶ The return value from an overloaded operator

▶ A special case: The cast operator

● ●

*T*he special little symbols that you use in C++ expressions (+, –, &, and so on) are called (smooth) operators. These operators are already defined for the intrinsic types like int, double, and char (not every operator is defined for every type). However, the existing operators are not defined for the classes that you invent yourself (the so-called user-defined classes).

Perhaps lucky for us, C++ allows you to define what the C++ operators would mean if they were applied to a user-defined class. This feature, called operator overloading, is the topic of this chapter.

I say, "perhaps this is lucky" for a reason. Normally, operator overloading is optional and usually not attempted by beginning C++ programmers. A lot of experienced C++ programmers don't think operator overloading is such a great idea, either. Therefore, if you're feeling a bit overwhelmed, you can skip this chapter and return to it when you feel curious and more at ease.

All warnings aside, you do need to know how to overload the assignment operator and it really helps to overload the ">>" and "<<" operators. Fortunately, there is a template that you can follow for these three operators that makes them easier to get right. Because I don't want you to get mixed up about different operators, I cover each of the three in its own chapter.

Let me say it one more time (I don't want irate e-mails questioning my lineage because someone overloaded some operator and he can't find his way back to safety): Operator overloading can introduce errors that are very difficult to find. Be sure that you know what you're doing before you plunge in.

Overloading Operators — Can't We Live Together in Harmony?

C++ considers user-defined types to be just as valid as intrinsic types, such as int and char. Because the operators are defined for the intrinsic types, why not allow them to be defined for user-defined types?

I realize that this is a weak argument, but operator overloading may have its uses. Consider a class USDollar that represents greenbacks. Some of the operators make no sense at all when applied to dollars. For example, what would it mean to invert (the ~ operator) a USDollar? Turn it upside down? (Does inverting the class Wallet make objects of class Dollar fall out? Probably not.) On the other hand, some operators definitely are applicable. For example, it makes sense to add a USDollar to or subtract a USDollar from a USDollar, the result being a USDollar. It also makes sense to multiply or divide a USDollar by a *double*. It probably doesn't make sense to multiply a USDollar by a USDollar.

Overloading the simple arithmetic operators for USDollar may improve the readability of your program. Compare the following two example code snippets:

```
// expense - calculate the amount of money paid
//           (including both principle and simple
//           interest)
USDollar expense(USDollar principle, double rate)
{
   // calculate the interest expense
   USDollar interest = principle.interest(rate);

   // now add this to the principle and return the
   // result
   return principle.add(interest);
}
```

With overloaded operators, the same function looks like the following:

```
// expense - calculate the amount of money paid
//       (including both principle and simple interest)
USDollar expense(USDollar principle, double rate)
{
   USDollar interest = principle * rate;
   return principle + interest;
}
```

Cool, no?

Before you investigate how to overload an operator, you need to understand the relationship between an operator and a function.

How Does an Operator Function and a Function Operate?

Think about this one for a second: An operator is nothing more than a built-in function with a peculiar syntax. For example, what's the difference between a+b and +(a,b)? Or, perhaps add(a,b)? None. In fact, that's exactly how addition is expressed in some languages.

C++ gives each operator a special functional name. The functional name of an operator is the operator symbol preceded by the keyword `operator` and followed by the appropriate argument types. For example, the + operator that adds an `int` to an `int` generating an `int` is called `int operator+(int, int)`.

The operator that adds two integers (`int operator+(int, int)`) is different from the operator that adds two doubles (`double operator+(double, double)`). This isn't too hard to accept when you realize that the internal format of an `int` variable and a `double` variable are completely different.

You can't invent new operators nor can you change the precedence or format of the operators. In addition, the operators can't be redefined when applied to intrinsic types — that is, you can't redefine what it means to add two integers (unless you have a Ph.D. in math).

The following examples demonstrate how the addition and increment operator might be defined for the class `USDollar` (I could have implemented the same functions for `CanadianDollar`, but who wants to put "eh?" in every comment?):

```
// USDollar - an object containing an integer number of
//            dollars plus an integer number of cents,
//            one hundred of which equals a complete
//            dollar
class USDollar
{
  friend USDollar operator+(USDollar&, USDollar&);
  friend USDollar& operator++(USDollar&);

 public:
  USDollar(unsigned int d, unsigned int c);

 protected:
  unsigned int dollars;
  unsigned int cents;
};

// constructor
USDollar::USDollar(unsigned int d, unsigned int c)
```

```
{
  dollars = d;
  cents = c;
  while (cents >= 100)
  {
    dollars++;
    cents -= 100;
  }
}

// operator+ - add s1 to s2 and return the result
//             in a new object
USDollar operator+(USDollar& s1, USDollar& s2)
{
  unsigned int cents   = s1.cents   + s2.cents;
  unsigned int dollars = s1.dollars + s2.dollars;
  USDollar d(dollars, cents);
  return d;
}

// operator++ - increment the specified argument;
//              change the value of the provided object
USDollar& operator++(USDollar& s)
{
  s.cents++;
  if (s.cents >= 100)
  {
    s.cents -= 100;
    s.dollars++;
  }
  return s;
}

int main(int argcs, char* pArgs[])
{
  USDollar d1(1, 60);
  USDollar d2(2, 50);
  USDollar d3(0, 0);
  d3 = d1 + d2;  // straightforward in use
  ++d3;
  return 0;
}
```

The class USDollar is defined as having an integer number of dollars and an integer number of cents that must be less than 100. The constructor enforces the latter rule by reducing the number of cents by 100 at a time and increasing the number of dollars appropriately.

Here operator+() and operator++() have been implemented as conventional non-member functions that are friends of USDollar.

Who's your friend?

The keyword `friend` is one that you haven't seen before. From within a class declaration you can declare an "outside function" to be a friend of the class. A friend function has all the rights and privileges of a class member. By declaring `operator+()` to be a friend, I'm giving it access to the protected members of `USDollar`.

The comparison between a class and a family works here as in our discussion of class access control. All of the members of the family have access to the fine silver (except that crazy aunt, but let's ignore that exception). Most people outside of the family are not allowed access unless they're specifically anointed by the family as friends. In this case, the family has decided to allow the family friend access to the fancy silver (and everything else, by the way — even the farmer's daughter) and that the first family trusts them not to abuse the privilege.

Notice that a person cannot declare himself to be a friend of the family — it must be the family that extends the invitation. The same applies here: A function can't declare itself to be the friend of a class. The `friend` keyword only makes sense within the class declaration.

It is possible for a family to invite a second family to be friends. This means that every member of the second family has access to the fancy silver. Similarly, a class can declare another class to be a friend, meaning that every member function in the second class is a friend. There is no reciprocal agreement: declaring class B to be a friend of A gives B access to the protected members of A but not the other way around.

Because `operator+()` is a binary operator (that is, it has two arguments), you see two arguments to the function (s1 and s2). The `operator+()` takes s1 and adds it with s2. The result of the expression is returned as a `USDollar` object from the function.

The unary operators, such as `operator++()`, take a single argument. `operator++()` increments the cents field. If it goes over 100, it increments the dollar field and zeros out the cents.

Nothing forces `operator+(USDollar&, USDollar&)` to perform addition. You could have `operator+()` do anything you like; however, doing anything else besides addition is a really bad idea. People are accustomed to their operators performing in certain ways. They don't like their operators dancing about willy-nilly performing other operations.

The operator += has nothing to do with the operators + or =. That is, each operator must be overloaded independently.

If you provide only one `operator++()` or `operator- -()`, it's used for both the prefix and postfix versions. The standard for C++ says that a compiler doesn't have to do this, but most do.

Originally there was no way to overload the prefix operator ++x separately from the postfix version x++. Enough programmers complained, so the rule was made that `operator++(ClassName)` refers to the prefix operator and `operator++(ClassName, int)` refers to the postfix operator. A zero is always passed as the second argument. Personally, I think that this syntax is silly, but it works. The same rule applies to `operator- -()`.

In use, the operators appear very natural. What could be simpler than d3 = d1 + d2 and ++d3?

Taking a More Detailed Look

Why does `operator+()` return the sum by value, but `operator++()` return the incremented object by reference? This is not an accident, but a very important difference.

We're starting to get into the part of operator overloading that is difficult to grasp, easy to screw up, and difficult to debug.

Considering the operator+ () case

The addition of two objects changes neither object. That is, a + b changes neither a nor b. `operator+()` cannot store the results of the addition into either a or b.:

```
// this is a really bad idea since it modifies
// s1 back in the calling function
USDollar& operator+(USDollar& s1, USDollar& s2)
{
  s1.cents += s2.cents;
  if (s1.cents >= 100)
  {
    s1.cents -= 100;
    s1.dollars++;
  }
  s1.dollars += s2.dollars;
  return s1;
}
```

The problem here is that a simple assignment such as u1 = u2 + u3; would modify u2 as well as u3.

Instead `operator+()` must generate a temporary object into which it can store the result of the addition. This is why `operator+()` constructs its own temporary object to return.

Specifically, the following would not work:

```
// this doesn't work
USDollar& operator+(USDollar& s1, USDollar& s2)
{
  unsigned int cents = s1.cents + s2.cents;
  unsigned int dollars = s1.dollars + s2.dollars;
  USDollar result(dollars, cents);
  return result;
}
```

Common screwup #1: Although this compiles without a squeak of complaint, it generates flaky results. The problem is that the returned reference refers to an object, `result`, whose scope is local to the function. Thus, `result` is out of scope by the time it can be used by the calling function.

Why not allocate a block of memory from the heap, as follows?

```
// this sort of works
USDollar& operator+(USDollar& s1, USDollar& s2)
{
  unsigned int cents = s1.cents + s2.cents;
  unsigned int dollars = s1.dollars + s2.dollars;
  return *new USDollar(dollars, cents);
}
```

Common screwup #2: You can return a reference to an object that was allocated off of the heap except that no mechanism exists to return the memory back to the heap. This type of error is called a *memory leak* and is very hard to track down. Although this operator works, it slowly drains memory from the heap each time an addition is performed.

Returning by value forces the compiler to generate a temporary object of its own on the caller's stack. The object generated in the function is then copied into the object as part of the return from `operator+()`.

How long does the temporary object returned from `operator+()` hang around? Originally this was vague, but the standards people got together and decided that such a temporary remains valid until the extended expression is complete. The extended expression is everything up to the semicolon. For example, consider the following snippet:

```
SomeClass f();
LotsAClass g();
void fn()
{
  int i;
  i = f() + (2 * g());
}
```

The temporary object returned by f() remains in existence while g() is invoked and while the multiplication is performed. This object becomes invalid at the semicolon.

Considering the operator++() case

Unlike operator+(), operator++() does modify its argument. Thus, you don't need to create a temporary or to return by value. You can save the calculated result in s. The argument provided can be returned to the caller:

```
// this works fine
USDollar& operator++(USDollar& s)
{
  s.cents++;
  if (s.cents >= 100)
  {
    s.cents -= 100;
    s.dollars++;
  }
  return s;
}
```

In fact, the following version, which returns by value has a subtle bug:

```
// this isn't 100% reliable either
USDollar operator++(USDollar& s)
{
  s.cents++;
  if (s.cents >= 100)
  {
    s.cents -= 100;
    s.dollars++;
  }
  return s;
}
```

Common screwup #3: By returning s by value, the function forces the compiler to generate a copy of the object. This works fine in expressions a = ++b, but what happens with an expression like ++(++a)? We would expect a to be incremented by 2. With the preceding definition, however, a is incremented by 1 and then a copy of a — not a itself — is incremented the second time.

The ++(++a) example is not a common construct, but it is legal. In any case, there are plenty of other examples that wouldn't work either.

The general rule is: If the operator changes the value of its argument, return the argument by reference. If the operator does not change the value of either argument, create a new object to hold the results and return that object by value. The input arguments should always be referential.

Coding Operators as Member Functions

An operator can be implemented as a non-static member function in addition to being a nonmember function. Implemented in this way, the example USDollar class appears as follows:

```
class USDollar
{
 public:
   USDollar(unsigned int d, unsigned int c);
   USDollar& operator++();
   USDollar operator+(USDollar& s);

 protected:
   unsigned int dollars;
   unsigned int cents;
};

USDollar::USDollar(unsigned int d, unsigned int c)
{
   dollars = d;
   cents = c;
   while (cents >= 100)
   {
     dollars++;
     cents -= 100;
   }
}

// operator+ - add this to s2 and return the result
//             in a new object
USDollar USDollar::operator+(USDollar& s2)
{
   // the "this->" is optional
   unsigned int c = this->cents  + s2.cents;
   unsigned int d = this->dollars + s2.dollars;
   USDollar t(d, c);
   return t;
}

// operator++ - increment the specified argument;
//              change the value of the provided object
USDollar& USDollar::operator++()
{
   this->cents++;
   if (this->cents >= 100)
   {
     this->cents -= 100;
     this->dollars++;
   }
```

```
    return *this;
}

int main(int argcs, char* pArgs[])
{
    USDollar d1(1, 60);
    USDollar d2(2, 50);
    USDollar d3(0, 0);
    d3 = d1 + d2;        // very straightforward in use
    ++d3;
    return 0;
}
```

I include the "this->" phrase in the above example in order to highlight the similarity between the member function and the nonmember function versions of the same operator. Obviously, this phrase is optional and understood by default.

Compare the declaration of USDollar::operator+(USDollar&) with ::operator+(USDollar&, USDollar&). At first glance, it appears that the member version has one less argument than the nonmember version. The following example compares the nonmember with the member versions of the function:

```
// operator+ - the non-member version
USDollar operator+(USDollar& s1, USDollar& s2)
{
    unsigned int cents   = s1.cents  + s2.cents;
    unsigned int dollars = s1.dollars + s2.dollars;
    USDollar d(dollars, cents);
    return d;
}
// operator+ - the member version
USDollar USDollar::operator+(USDollar& s2)
{
    unsigned int c = this->cents   + s2.cents;
    unsigned int d = this->dollars + s2.dollars;
    USDollar t(d, c);
    return t;
}
```

You can see that the functions are nearly identical. Where the nonmember version adds s1 and s2, however, the member version adds the "current object" — the one pointed at by this — to s2.

The member version of an operator always has one less argument than the nonmember version — the left-hand argument is implicit.

Suffering through Yet Another Overloading Irritation

Just because you've overloaded one version of an operator doesn't mean that you've overloaded them all: C++ considers operator*(double, USDollar&) to be different from operator*(USDollar&, double).

Common screwup #4: Each version of the operator must be overloaded separately.

This isn't as big a drag as it may appear at first blush. First, nothing keeps one operator from referring to the other. In the case of operator*(), you would probably do something like the following:

```
USDollar operator*(double f, USDollar& s)
{
   //...implementation of function here...
}
inline USDollar operator*(USDollar& s, double f)
{
   // use the previous definition
   return f * s;
}
```

The second version merely calls the first version with the order of the operators reversed. Making it inline avoids any extra overhead.

The machine code for inline functions is inserted at the point of the call.

When to make operators members or nonmembers

When should the programmer implement an operator as a member and when as a nonmember? The following operators must be implemented as member functions:

- = Assignment
- () Function call
- [] Subscript
- -> Class membership

Other than the operators listed, there isn't much difference between implementing an operator as a member or as a nonmember, with the following exception. An operator like the following could not be implemented as a member function:

```
USDollar operator*(double
    factor, USDollar& s);
```

```
void fn(USDollar& principle)
{
    USDollar interestExpense =
        interest * principle
    //...
}
```

To be a member function, `operator*()` would have to be a member of class `double`. Mere mortals cannot add operators to the intrinsic classes. Thus, operators such as the preceding must be nonmember functions.

If you have access to the class internals, make the overloaded operator a member of the class. This is particularly true if the operator modifies the object upon which it operates.

Overloading Operators Using Implicit Conversion

There is a second, entirely different approach to defining operators for user-defined classes. Think about the following expression for a second:

```
int i = 1;
double d = 1.0;

// expression #1
d = i + d;

// expression #2
i = i + d;
```

The first expression adds an `int` to a `double`. C++ does not define an `operator+(int, double)` function, but C++ does define an `operator+(double, double)`. In the absence of an `(int, double)` function, C++ converts the `int` i into a double (we say that *"i is promoted to a double"*) in order to use the `(double, double)` version. The same process occurs for both expressions, however, the situation is even worse in the second expression because `double` result must be demoted before being assigned to i.

Promoting user defined objects

If the programmer defines a promotion path from an intrinsic type to the user class, C++ will try to use it to make sense of an expression. Suppose, for example, that you provided a constructor to convert a double into a USDollar.

```
class USDollar
{
  friend USDollar operator+(USDollar& s1, USDollar& s2);

 public:
  USDollar(int d, int c);
  USDollar(double value)
  {
    dollars = (int)value;
    cents = (int)((value - dollars) * 100 + 0.5);
  }
  //...as before...
}
```

As far as C++ is concerned, you have provided a promotion path from double to USDollar. That is, anytime C++ finds itself in need of some cash, it can pawn a double.

We can use that conversion feature in order to piggyback on an existing operation:

```
void fn(USDollar& s)
{
  // all of the following use
  // operator+(USDollar&, USDollar&)
  s = USDollar(1.5) + s; // explicit conversion...
  s = 1.5 + s;   // ...implicit conversion...
  s = s + 1.5;   // ...in either order
  s = s + 1;     // even this works by converting the...
                 // ...int into a double and then...
                 // ...continuing as above
}
```

Now you need define neither operator+(double, USDollar&) nor operator+(USDollar&, double). C++ will convert the double into a USDollar and use the operator+(USDollar&, USDollar&) function already defined.

This conversion can be explicit, as shown in the first addition. It can also remain implicit, in which case C++ performs the conversion automatically.

Providing such conversion paths can save considerable effort by reducing the number of different operators the programmer must define.

Possible screwup #5: Allowing C++ to make these conversions, however, can be dangerous. If multiple possible conversion paths exist, mysterious compiler errors can arise.

Defining a Cast Operator

The cast operator can be overloaded as well. (The cast operator is not the person who puts those caste dots on Indian women's foreheads. The cast operator converts one type into another.) In practice, it looks like the following:

```
class USDollar
{
  public:
   USDollar(double value = 0.0);

   // the following function acts as a cast operator
   operator double()
   {
     return dollars + cents / 100.0;
   }
  protected:
   unsigned int dollars;
   unsigned int cents;
};

USDollar::USDollar(double value)
{
   dollars = (int)value;
   cents = (int)((value - dollars) * 100 + 0.5);
}
```

The cast operator `operator double()` provides a demotion path from `USDollar` to `double`. This cast creates a double equal to the number of dollars plus the number of cents divided by 100.

In practice, operators such as cast can be used as follows:

```
int main(int argcs, char* pArgs[])
{
   USDollar d1(2.0), d2(1.5), d3;

   // invoke cast operator explicitly...
   d3 = USDollar((double)d1 + (double)d2);

   //...or implicitly
   d3 = d1 + d2;
   return 0;
}
```

A cast operator is the word operator followed by the desired type. The member function `USDollar::operator double()` provides a mechanism for converting an object of class `USDollar` into a double. For reasons that are beyond me, cast operators have no return type. (The argument is, "You don't need it because you can tell the return type from the name." I prefer a bit of consistency.)

In the first expression, we convert the two `USDollar` values into double, use the existing `operator+(double, double)` and then use the constructor to convert the results back into a `USDollar`.

The second expression has exactly the same effect, but it's much sneakier. C++ tries to make sense out of the d3 = d1 + d2 by first converting d1 and d2 to doubles and then converting the sum back into a `USDollar`. The resulting logic is the same as in the first expression, but C++ figured it out this time.

This demonstrates both the advantage and disadvantage of providing a cast operator. Providing a conversion path from `USDollar` to `double` relieves programmers of the need to provide their own set of operators. `USDollar` can just piggyback on the operators defined for double.

On the other hand, providing a conversion path removes the ability of programmers to control which operators are defined. By providing a conversion path to `double`, `USDollar` gets all of `double`'s operators whether they make sense or not. In addition, going through the extra conversions may not be the most efficient process in the world. For example, the simple addition just noted involves three type conversions with all of the attendant function calls, multiplications, divisions, and so on.

Defining the rules for implicit conversions

With all this converting going on, how do you know what C++ will do with an expression such as the addition of a `USDollar` d1 and a `double` d2? The rules are straightforward:

1. C++ first looks for operator+(USDollar, double).
2. C++ next looks for an operator that can used by casting USDollar into a double.
3. Finally, C++ looks for an operator that can be used by casting both USDollar and double.

Number 1 is always unique; however, both Numbers 2 and 3 can be ambiguous.

Common screwup #6: It's a compile time error if there are more operation paths than one that could be used.

It's also an error if two conversions are provided for the same thing.

Common screwup #7: You can't provide two conversion paths to the same type. For example, the following is asking for trouble:

```
class A
{
 public:
   A(B& b);
};
class B
{
  public:
    operator A();
};
```

If asked to convert an object of class A into an object of class A, the compiler will not know whether to use B's cast operator B:operatorA() or A's constructor A::A(B&), both of which start out with a B and end up making an A out of it.

Perhaps the result of the two conversion paths would be the same, but the compiler doesn't know that. It must know which conversion path you really intended. If it can't determine this unambiguously, the compiler throws up its electronic hands and spits out an error.

Chapter 25

Overloading the Assignment Operator

• •

In This Chapter

▶ Introducing the assignment operator

▶ Overloading the assignment operator is necessary

▶ Similarities between the user defined assignment operator and the copy constructor

• •

Chapter 24 demonstrates how to go about overloading operators for classes that you define. Whether or not you start out overloading all operators, you need to learn how to overload the assignment operator fairly early.

In general overloading C++ operators is a dicey proposition. You shouldn't have any trouble overloading the assignment `operator=()` if you follow the pattern shown here.

Overloading the Assignment Operator Is Critical

C defines only one operator that can be applied to structure types: the assignment operator. In C, the following is legal and results in a bit-wise copy from source to destination:

```
void fn()
{
  struct MyStruct source, destination;
  destination = source;
}
```

To retain compatibility with C, C++ provides a default definition for `operator=()` for all user-defined classes. This default definition performs a member-by-member copy of each data member. However, this default member-by-member copy can be overloaded by an `operator=()` written specifically for the specified class.

The assignment operator is much like the copy constructor (see Chapter 19). In use, the two look almost identical:

```
void fn(MyClass& mc)
{
  MyClass newMC = mc;// this uses the copy constructor
  newMC = mc;    // this uses the assignment operator
}
```

The difference is that when the copy constructor was invoked on `newMC`, the object `newMC` didn't already exist. When the assignment operator was invoked, `newMC` was already a `MyClass` object in good standing.

The copy constructor is used when a new object is being created that's a copy of another. The assignment operator is used if the right-hand object is being copied over an existing argument on the left side of the assignment operator. Like the copy constructor, an assignment operator should be provided whenever a shallow copy isn't appropriate.

Finding Out How to Overload the Assignment Operator

Overloading the assignment operator is similar to overloading any other operator. For example, an assignment operator has been provided as an inline member function for the following class `Name`. (Remember, the assignment operator must be a member function of the class.)

```
#include <stdlib.h>
#include <string.h>
#include <ctype.h>

// Name - a simplistic example class
class Name
{
 public:
  Name()
  {
    pName = (char*)0;
  }
  Name(char *pN)
  {
```

```
   copyName(pN);
 }
 Name(Name& s)
 {
  copyName(s.pName);
 }
~Name()
 {
  deleteName();
 }

 // assignment operator
 Name& operator=(Name& s)
 {
  // delete existing stuff...
  deleteName();

  //...before replacing with new stuff
  copyName(s.pName);

  // return reference to existing object
  return *this;
 }

protected:
 // copyName - copy the source string pN to a locally
 //            allocated block of memory
 void copyName(char *pN)
 {
   int length = strlen(pN) + 1;
   pName = new char[length];
   strncpy(pName, pN, length);
 }

 // deleteName - return the pName memory to the heap
 void deleteName()
 {
   // if there is a block of heap memory...
   if (pName)
   {
     // ...return it to the heap...
     delete pName;

     // ...and flag the fact that the pointer is no
     // longer valid
     pName = 0;
   }
 }

 // pName points to a block of memory containing
 // the actual name as an ASCIIZ string
 char *pName;
};
```

```
int main(int argcs, char* pArgs[])
{
  Name s("Claudette");
  Name t("temporary");
  t = s;        // this invokes the assignment operator
  return 0;
}
```

The class `Name` retains a person's name in memory that is allocated from the heap in the constructor. The constructors and destructor for class `Name` are typical for a class containing a dynamic array of memory.

The assignment operator appears with the name `operator=()`. Notice that the assignment operator looks like a destructor followed by a copy constructor. This is also typical. Consider the assignment in the example. The object `t` already has a name associated with it (temporary). In the assignment `t = s`, you must first call `deleteName()` to return to the heap the memory that the original name occupies. Only then can you call `copyName()` to allocate new memory into which to store the new name.

The copy constructor did not need to call `deleteName()` because the object didn't already exist. Therefore, memory had not already been assigned to the object when the constructor was invoked.

In general, an assignment operator has two parts. The first part resembles a destructor in that it deletes the assets that the existing object already owns. The second part resembles a copy constructor in that it allocates new assets from the source object into the now-empty target object.

Creating shallow copies is a deep problem

Okay, so what's so wrong with a member-by-member copy? Often nothing, but not in the case of `Name`.

The class `Name` contains an asset that has been checked out for its use: namely, the block of heap memory pointed at by `pName`. If you didn't already know this, you could tell by looking at the constructors. Each of these (except for the default) calls the function `copyName()` shown here:

```
// copyName - copy the source string pN to a locally
//            allocated block of memory
void copyName(char *pN)
{
  int length = strlen(pN) + 1;
  pName = new char[length];
  strncpy(pName, pN, length);
}
```

Notice how the function allocates a string of memory equal to the length of the source char* string. (In a subsequent step, copyName() copies the contents of pN to the newly allocated string.)

The default government issue member-by-member copy blindly copies the data member to the target object. This results in two Name objects pointing at the same chunk of memory — a recipe for disaster. This called a shallow copy.

The assignment operator for Name must first return the existing pName memory to the heap (by calling deleteName()) before allocating its own chunk of memory (by calling copyName()) heap. This is known as a deep copy.

Going to C++ member-by-member

I've been very careful about saying "member-by-member copy." I avoid the simpler unqualified term "copy" because this implies a bit by bit just "moving over."

The significance of the member-by-member isn't obvious until you start looking at classes that themselves have class objects.

```
class MyClass
{
 public:
  Name name;
  int age;

  MyClass(char* pName, int newAge) : name(pName)
  {
    age = newAge;
  }
};
void fn()
{
  MyClass a("Kinsey", 16);
  MyClass b("Christa", 1);
  a = b;
}
```

(See Chapter 18 if you aren't familiar with the *:* name(pName) syntax for initializing the data member name.)

The default assignment operator works just fine in this case. The member-by-member copy assigns the int b.age to a.age — no problem so far. It continues by assigning the object b.name to a.name. This copy uses the Name::operator=() assignment operator.

Unless the class itself allocates resources (irrespective of what its member objects might do), it's unnecessary to overload the assignment operator.

Returning from over-C's assignments

Notice that the return type of operator=() is Name&. I could have made the return type void — C++ would have allowed it. If I did, however, the following would not work:

```
void otherFn(Name&);
void fn(Name& oldN)
{
  Name newN;

  // this wouldn't work
  otherFn(newN = oldN);

  // neither would this
  Name newerN;
  newerN = newN = oldN;
}
```

The results of the assignment newN = oldN would be void, the return type of operator=(). This means that there is no value to use in the subsequent operation, be it a function call or an expression.

Remember that the result of an assignment operator is the value of the right hand argument and the type of the left. Thus, the value of (i = 1) is 1. This is what allows expressions like i = j = 1;. The variable i is assigned the result of the assignment j = 1, which is 1.

Declaring operator=() to return a reference to the "current" object and returning *this retains the C++ semantics that you have all come to know and love.

The second detail to notice is that operator=() was written as a member function. Unlike other operators, the assignment operator cannot be over-loaded with a nonmember function.

The assignment operator must be a nonstatic member function. Interestingly enough, the special assignment operators, such as += and *=, have no special restrictions and can be nonmember functions.

Providing member protection

Writing an assignment operator isn't so difficult; however, sometimes you just don't want bother. If you don't want to bother writing an assignment operator, you may choose to just make it impossible to make assignments by overloading the default with a protected assignment operator.

For example:

```
class Name
{
  // ...just like before...
  protected:
    // assignment operator
    Name& operator=(Name& s)
    {
      return *this;
    }
};
```

With this definition, assignments such as the following are precluded:

```
void fn(Name& n)
{
  Name newN;
  newN = n;    // generates a compiler error -
               // function has no access to op=()
}
```

The function fn() doesn't have access to the now-protected assignment operator. This trick may save you the trouble of overloading the assignment operator.

Chapter 26

Using Stream I/O

C hapter 11 takes a quick look at stream I/O. If you compare Chapter 11 with the coverage of operator overloading presented in Chapter 25 you notice that stream I/O is not based on a new special set of symbols << and >> but just the right and left shift operators overloaded to perform input and output, respectively. (If you haven't read about operator overloading be sure to go over Chapter 25 before continuing.)

In this chapter, I describe stream I/O in more detail. I must warn you that stream I/O is too large a topic to be covered completely in a single chapter — entire books are devoted to this one topic. Fortunately for both of us, there isn't all that much that you need to write the vast majority of programs.

Diving into Stream I/O

The operators that make up stream I/O are defined in the include file iostream.h. This file includes prototypes for several operator>>() and operator<<() functions. The code for these functions is included in the standard library, which your C++ program links with.

```
// for input we have:
istream& operator>>(istream& source, char* pDest);
istream& operator>>(istream& source, int& dest);
istream& operator>>(istream& source, char& dest);
// ...and so forth...
```

```
// for output we have:
ostream& operator<<(ostream& dest, char* pSource);
ostream& operator<<(ostream& dest, int  source);
ostream& operator<<(ostream& dest, char source);
// ...and so it goes...
```

Buzzword time: When overloaded to perform I/O, `operator>>()` is called the *extractor* and `operator<<()` is called the *inserter*.

Look at what happens when I write the following:

```
#include <iostream.h>
void fn()
{
   cout << "My name is Stephen\n";
}
```

First, C++ determines that the left-hand argument is of type `ostream` and the right-hand argument is of type `char*`. Armed with this knowledge, it finds the prototype `operator<<(ostream&, char*)` in `iostream.h`. C++ generates a call to the function for the `char*` inserter, passing the function the string `"My name is Randy\n"` and the object `cout` as the two arguments. That is, it makes the call `operator<<(cout, "My name is Randy\n")`. The `char*` inserter function, which is part of the standard C++ library, performs the requested output.

How did the compiler know that `cout` is of class `ostream`? This and a few other global objects are also declared in `iostream.h`. A list is shown in Table 26-1. These objects are constructed automatically at program start-up, before `main()` gets control.

Table 26-1	Standard Stream I/O Objects	
Object	*Class*	*Purpose*
cin	istream	Standard input
cout	ostream	Standard output
cerr	ostream	Standard error output
clog	ostream	Standard printer output

But why the shift operators?

You may ask, "Why use the shift operators? Why not use another operator? Why use the operator overloading approach at all? Why not use another mechanism?" Why ask so many questions?

It didn't have to be the shift operators. The developers of C++ could have agreed on some standard function name such as `output()` to perform output and simply overloaded that function name for all the intrinsic types. Compound output would have looked something like the following:

```
void displayName(char* pName,
   int age)
{
   output(cout, "The name passed
     was ");

   output(cout, pName);

   output(cout, "; his age is
     ");

   output(cout, age);

   output(cout, "\n");
}
```

The left shift operator was chosen instead for several reasons. First, it's a binary operator. This means that you can make the `ostream` object the left-hand argument and the output object the right-hand argument. Second, left shift is a very low-priority operator. Thus, expressions such as the following work as expected:

```
#include <iostream.h>
void fn(int a, int b) {
   cout << "a + b" << a + b <<
     "\n";
// operator+ has higher prece-
   dence than
// operator<<
// so this expression is inter-
   preted as
// cout << "a + b" << (a + b)
   << "\n";
// and not interpreted as
// (cout << "a + b" << a) + (b
   << "\n");
}
```

Third, the left shift operator binds from left to right. This is what allows you to string output statements together. For example, the previous function is interpreted as follows:

```
#include <iostream.h>
void fn(int a, int b) {
   ((cout << "a + b") << a + b)
     << "\n";
}
```

But having said all this, the real reason is probably just that it looks really neat. The double less than, <<, looks like something is moving out of the code, and the double greater than, >>, looks like something is coming in. And, hey, why not?

And just what is an `ostream` anyway? An `ostream` object contains the members necessary to keep track of output. In a similar vein, `istream` describes an input stream.

The C equivalent is struct `FILE`, which is defined in `stdio.h`. The function `fopen()` opens a file for input and output. `fopen()` returns a pointer to a `FILE` object into which it has stored the information necessary for subsequent I/O operations. This object is returned in calls to the `fx()` functions, such as `fprintf()`, `fscanf()`, and `fgets()`.

Also defined as part of the stream I/O library are a number of subclasses of ostream and istream. These subclasses are used for input and output to files and internal buffers.

Examining the fstream Subclasses

The subclasses ofstream, ifstream, and fstream are defined in the include file fstream.h to perform stream input and output to a disk file. These three classes share a number of member functions that are used to control input and output, many of them inherited from istream and ostream. A complete list is provided with your compiler documentation, but let me get you started.

Class ofstream, which is used to perform file output, has several constructors, the most useful of which is

```
ofstream::ofstream(char*pFileName,
                   int  mode = ios::out,
                   int  prot = filebuff::openprot);
```

The first argument is a pointer to the name of the file to open. The second and third arguments specify how the file will be opened. The legal values for mode are listed in Table 26-2 and those for prot in Table 26-3. These values are bit fields that have the OR operator applied together. (The classes ios and filebuff are both parent classes of ostream.)

Table 26-2	Values for Mode in the ofstream Constructor
Flag	*Meaning*
ios::ate	Append to the end of the file, if it exists
ios::in	Open file for input (implied for istream)
ios::out	Open file for output (implied for ostream)
ios::trunc	Truncate file if it exists (default)
ios::nocreate	If file doesn't already exist, return error
ios::noreplace	If file does exist, return error
ios::binary	Open file in binary mode (alternative is text mode)

Table 26-3	Values for prot in the ofstream Constructor
Flag	*Meaning*
filebuf::openprot	Compatibility sharingmode
filebuf::sh_none	Exclusive; no sharing
filebuf::sh_read	Read sharing allowed
filebuf::sh_write	Write sharing allowed

For example, the following program opens the file MYNAME and then writes some important and absolutely true information into that file:

```
#include <fstream.h>

void fn()
{
  // open the text file MYNAME for writing - truncate
  // whatever's there now
  ofstream myn("MYNAME");

  // now write to the file
  myn << "Randy Davis is suave and handsome\n"
      << "and definitely not balding prematurely\n";
}
```

The constructor `ofstream::ofstream(char*)` expects only a filename and provides defaults for the other file modes. If the file MYNAME already exists, it is truncated; otherwise, MYNAME is created. In addition, the file is opened in compatibility-sharing mode.

A second constructor `ofstream::ofstream(char*, int)` enables the programmer to specify other file I/O modes. For example, if I wanted to open the file in binary mode and append to the end of the file if the file already exists, I would create the `ostream` object as follows. (In binary mode, new-lines are not converted to carriage returns and line feeds on output nor converted back to new-lines on input.)

```
#include <fstream.h>

void fn()
{
  // open the binary file BINFILE for writing; if it
  // exists, append to end of whatever's already there
  ofstream bfile("BINFILE", ios::binary | ios::ate);

  //...continue on as before...
}
```

The member function bad() returns 1 if the file object has an error. To check whether the file was opened properly in the earlier example, I would have coded the following:

```
#include <fstream.h>

void fn()
{
  ofstream myn("MYNAME");
  if (myn.bad())    // if the open didn't work...
  {
   cerr << "Error opening file MYNAME\n";
   return;           //...output error and quit
  }
  myn << "Randy Davis is suave and handsome\n"
      << "and definitely not balding prematurely\n";
}
```

All attempts to output to an ofstream object that has an error have no effect until the error has been cleared by calling the member function clear().

The destructor for class ofstream automatically closes the file. In the preceding example, the file was closed when the function exited.

Class ifstream works much the same way for input, as the following example demonstrates:

```
#include <fstream.h>

void fn()
{
  // open file for reading; don't create the file
  // if it isn't there
  ifstream bankStatement("STATEMNT", ios::nocreate);
  if (bankStatement.bad())
  {
   cerr << "Couldn't find bank statement\n";
   return;
  }

  // sit in a loop inputing from the file until
  // end-of-file reached
  while (!bankStatement.eof())
  {
   bankStatement > accountNumber > amount;
   //...process this withdrawal
  }
}
```

The function opens the file STATEMNT by constructing the object `bankStatement`. If the file does not exist, it is not created. (You assume that the file has information for you, so it wouldn't make much sense to create a new, empty file.) If the object is bad (for example, if the object was not created), the function outputs an error message and exits. Otherwise, the function loops, reading the accountNumber and withdrawal amount until the file is empty (end-of-file is true).

An attempt to read an `ifstream` object that has the error flag set, indicating a previous error, returns immediately without reading anything. Use the function `clear()` to clear an error in an input file.

The class `fstream` is like an `ifstream` and an `ofstream` combined. (In fact, it inherits from both.) An object of class `fstream` can be created for input or output or both.

Using the strstream Subclasses

The classes `istrstream`, `ostrstream`, and `strstream` are defined in the include file name either `strstrea.h` or `strstream.h`.

The original MS-DOS used on PCs limited file names to 8 characters followed by a three letter extension, hence the name 8.3 DOS file names. This limitation is long gone, however, many PC based C++ compilers, including Visual C++, stick with the 8.3-compatible name `strstrea.h`. The GNU C++ which comes on the enclosed CD-ROM sticks with the original `strstream.h` name.

The classes in `strstream.h` allow the operations defined for files by the `fstream` classes to be applied to character strings in memory. This is much like the `sx()` functions in C, `sprintf()` and `sscanf()`.

For example, the following code snippet parses the data in a character string using stream input:

```
// if in Visual C++ or most other PC compilers...
#ifdef _WIN32
// ...use the 8.3 name...
#include <strstrea.h>
// ...otherwise,...
#else
// ...use the full name
#include <strstream.h>
#endif
```

```
// parseString - demonstrate the string stream classes
//               by reading a passed buffer as if it were
//               an actual file
char* parseString(char* pString)
{
    // associate an istrstream object with the input
    // character string
    istrstream inp(pString, 0);

    // now input from that object
    int accountNumber;
    float balance;
    inp > accountNumber > balance;

    // allocate a buffer and associate an
    // ostrstream object with it
    char* pBuffer = new char[128];
    ostrstream out(pBuffer, 128);

    // output to that object
    out << "account number = " << accountNumber
        << ", balance = $" << balance;
    return pBuffer;
}
```

For example, pString might point to the following string:

```
"1234 100.0"
```

The object inp is associated with that string by the constructor for
istrstream. The second argument to the constructor is the length of the
string. In this example, the argument is 0, which means "read until you get to
the terminating NULL."

On the output side, the object out is associated with the buffer pointed to by
pBuffer. Here again, the second argument to the constructor is the length of
the buffer. A third argument, which corresponds to the mode, defaults to
ios::out. However, you can set this argument to ios::ate, if you want the
output to append to the end of whatever is already in the buffer rather than
overwrite it.

The input section extracts the value 1234 into the variable accountNumber
and the value 100 into balance. The output sections insert the string
"account number = " into the output buffer *pBuffer followed by the value
1234 stored in accountNumber and so on.

The buffer generated by this example input would contain the string

```
"account number = 1234, balance = $100.00"
```

The #ifdefs at the beginning of the previous code snippet are required in order to include the correct file. _WIN32 is always defined when building a program using Visual C++, but not when compiling using GNU C++. Thus, when compiling with Visual C++, the program #includes, strstrea.h, otherwise, the program uses the full name strstream.h.

Step back and examine this code snippet again. Other than the constructor, inp and out could have both pointed to files and the program would not have changed at all. Treating a memory buffer like an external file opens up the world of file manipulation functions to the common but frustrating world of string manipulation.

Manipulating Manipulators

You can use stream I/O to output numbers and character strings by using default formats. Usually the defaults are fine, but sometimes they don't cut it.

For example, I was less than tickled when the total from my favorite BUDGET program came back 249.600006 instead of 249.6 (or, better yet, 249.60). There must be a way to bend the defaults to my desires. True to form, C++ provides not one way but two ways to control the format of output.

Depending on the default settings of your compiler, you may get 249.6 as your output. Nevertheless, you really want 249.60.

First, the format can be controlled by invoking a series of member functions on the stream object. For example, the number of significant digits to display is set by using the function precision() as follows:

```
#include <iostream.h>
void fn(float interest, float dollarAmount)
{
   cout << "Dollar amount = ";
   cout.precision(2);
   cout << dollarAmount;
   cout.precision(4);
   cout << interest
     << "\n";
}
```

In this example, the function precision() sets the precision to 2 immediately before outputting the value dollarAmount. This gives you a number such as 249.60, the nice type of result you want. It then sets the precision to 4 before outputting the interest.

A second approach uses what are called manipulators. (Sounds like someone behind the scenes of the New York Stock Exchange, doesn't it? Well, manipulators are every bit as sneaky.) Manipulators are objects defined in the include file iomanip.h to have the same effect as the member function calls. (You must include iomanip.h to have access to the manipulators.) The only advantage to manipulators is that the program can insert them directly into the stream rather than resort to a separate function call.

If you rewrite the preceding example to use manipulators, the program appears as follows:

```
#include <iostream.h>
#include <iomanip.h>
void fn(float interest, float dollarAmount)
{
   cout << "Dollar amount = "
      << setprecision(2) << dollarAmount
      << setprecision(4) << interest
      << "\n";
}
```

The most common manipulators and their corresponding meanings are shown in Table 26-4.

Table 26-4	Common Manipulators and Stream Format Control Functions	
Manipulator	**Member Function**	**Description**
dec	flags(10)	Set radix to 10
hex	flags(16)	Set radix to 16
oct	flags(8)	Set radix to 8
setfill(c)	fill(c)	Set the fill character to c
setprecision(c)	precision(c)	Set display precision to c
setw(n)	width(n)	Set width of field to n characters*

* This returns to its default value after the next field is output.

Watch out for the width parameter (width() function and setw() manipulator). Most parameters retain their value until they are specifically reset by a subsequent call, but the width parameter does not. The width parameter is reset to its default value as soon as the next output is performed. For example, you might expect the following to produce two eight-character integers:

```
#include <iostream.h>
#include <iomanip.h>
void fn()
{
  cout << setw(8)     // width is 8...
       << 10          //...for the 10, but...
       << 20          //...default for the 20
       << "\n";
}
```

What you get, however, is an eight-character integer followed by a two-character integer. To get two eight-character output fields, the following is necessary:

```
#include <iostream.h>
#include <iomanip.h>
void fn()
{
  cout << setw(8)      // set the width...
       << 10
       << setw(8)      //...now reset it
       << 20
       << "\n";
}
```

Thus, if you have several objects to output and the default width is not good enough, you must include a setw() call for each object.

Which way is better, manipulators or member function calls? Member functions provide a bit more control because there are more of them. In addition, the member functions always return the previous setting so you know how to restore it (if you want). Finally, a query version of each member function exists to enable you to just ask what the current setting is without changing it. This is shown in the following example:

```
#include <iostream.h>
void fn(float value)
{
  int previousPrecision;
  // ...doing stuff here...
  // you can ask what the current precision is:
  previousPrecision = cout.precision();

  // or you can save the old value when you change it
  previousPrecision = cout.precision(2);
  cout << value;

  // now restore the precision to previous value
  cout.precision(previousPrecision);

  //...do more neat stuff...
}
```

Even with all these features, the manipulators are the more common, probably because they look neat. Use whatever you prefer, but be prepared to see both in other peoples' code.

Writing Custom Inserters

The fact that C++ overloads the left shift operator to perform output is really exciting because you are free to overload the same operator to perform output on classes you define. (Okay, really exciting is a bit extreme. I suppose finding out that you just won the lottery would be really exciting. This falls more in the category of syntactically satisfying.)

This is the much-vaunted extensibility of stream I/O that I have alluded to but avoided explaining until now. Consider, for example, the USDollar class introduced in Chapter 24, extended with a display() member function:

```
#ifdef _WIN32
#include <strstrea.h>
#else
#include <strstream.h>
#endif

#include <iomanip.h>
class USDollar
{
  public:
    USDollar(double v = 0.0)
    {
      dollars = v;
      cents = int((v - dollars) * 100.0 + 0.5);
    }

    operator double()
    {
      return dollars + cents / 100.0;
    }

    void display(ostream& out)
    {
      out << '$' << dollars << '.'
        // set fill to 0's for cents
        << setfill('0') << setw(2) << cents
        // now put it back to spaces
        << setfill(' ');
    }

  protected:
    unsigned int dollars;
    unsigned int cents;
```

```
};

// operator<< - overload the inserter for our class
ostream& operator<< (ostream& o, USDollar& d)
{
  d.display(o);
  return o;
}

int main(int argcs, char* pArgs[])
{
  USDollar usd(1.50);
  cout << "Initially usd = " << usd << "\n";
  usd = 2.0 * usd;
  cout << "then usd = " << usd << "\n";
  return 0;
}
```

The display() function starts by displaying $, the dollar amount, and the obligatory decimal point. Notice that output is to whatever ostream object it is passed and not necessarily just to cout. This allows the same function to be used on fstream and strstream objects, both of which are subclasses of ostream.

When it comes time to display the cents amount, display() sets the width to two positions and the leading character to 0. This ensures that numbers smaller than 10 display properly.

Notice how class USDollar, instead of accessing the display() function directly, also defines an operator<<(ostream&, USDollar&). The programmer can now output USDollar objects with the same ease and grace of the intrinsic types, as the example main() function demonstrates.

The output from this program is as follows:

```
Initially usd = $1.50
then usd = $3.00
```

You may wonder why the operator<<() returns the ostream object passed to it. This allows the operator to be chained with other inserters in a single expression. Because operator<<() binds from left to right, the following expression

```
void fn(USDollar& usd, float i)
{
  cout << "Amount " << usd << ", interest = " << i;
}
```

is interpreted as

```
void fn(USDollar& usd, float i)
{
    (((cout << "Amount ") << usd) << ", interest = ") << i;
}
```

The first insertion outputs the string "Amount" to cout. The result of this expression is the object cout, which is then passed to operator<< (ostream&, USDollar&). It is important that this operator return its ostream object so that the object can be passed to the next inserter in turn.

Had you declared the return type of the insertion operator void, a perfectly valid usage, such as the preceding example, would generate a compiler error because you can't insert a string into a void. The following error is worse because it's more difficult to find:

```
ostream& operator<<(ostream& os, USDollar& usd)
{
    usd.display(os);
    return cout;
}
```

Notice that this function returns not the ostream object it was given but the ostream object cout. This is easy to do because cout is far and away the most commonly referenced ostream object. (cout has already been voted into the ostream Hall of Fame.)

This problem doesn't become visible until the following comes along:

```
void storeAccounts(int account,
          USDollar balance,
          char* pName)
{
    ofstream outFile("ACCOUNTS", ios::ate);
    outFile << account << balance << pName;
}
```

The int account outputs to outFile through the function operator<< (ostream&, int&), which returns outFile. Then USDollar outputs to outFile through operator<<(ostream&, USDollar&), which incorrectly returns cout, not outFile. Now pName outputs to cout instead of to the file as intended.

Generating Smart Inserters

Many times, you would like to make the inserter smart. That is, you would like to say `cout << baseClassObject` and let C++ choose the proper subclass inserter in the same way that it chooses the proper virtual member function. Because the inserter is not a member function, you cannot declare it virtual directly. This is not a problem for the clever C++ programmer, as the following example demonstrates:

```cpp
#include <iostream.h>
#include <iomanip.h>
class Currency
{
 public:
   Currency(double v = 0.0)
   {
     unit = v;
     cent = int((v - unit)*  100.0 + 0.5);
   }

   virtual void display(ostream& out) = 0;

 protected:
   unsigned int unit;
   unsigned int cent;
};

class USDollar : public Currency
{
 public:
   USDollar(double v = 0.0) : Currency(v)
   {
   }

   // display format: $123.45
   virtual void display(ostream& out)
   {
     out << '$' << unit << '.'
       << setfill('0') << setw(2) << cent
       << setfill(' ');
   }
};

class DMark : public Currency
{
 public:
   DMark(double v = 0.0) : Currency(v)
   {
   }
```

```
    // display 123.00DM
    virtual void display(ostream& out)
    {
     out << unit << '.'
        // set fill to 0's for cents
        << setfill('0') << setw(2) << cent
        // now put it back to spaces
        << setfill(' ')
        << " DM";
    }
};
ostream& operator<< (ostream& o, Currency& c)
{
    c.display(o);
    return o;
}
void fn(Currency& c)
{
    // the following output is polymorphic because
    // operator(ostream&, Currency&) is through a virtual
    // member function
    cout << "Deposit was " << c
         << "\n";
}

int main(int argcs, char* pArgs[])
{
    // create a dollar and output it using the
    // proper format for a dollar
    USDollar usd(1.50);
    fn(usd);

    // now create a DMark and output it using its own format
    DMark d(3.00);
    fn(d);
    return 0;
}
```

The class Currency has two subclasses, USDollar and DMark. In Currency, the display() function is declared pure virtual. In each of the two subclasses, this function is overloaded with a display() function to output the object in the proper format for that type. The call to display() in operator<<() is now a virtual call. Thus, when operator<<() is passed USDollar, it outputs the object as a dollar. When passed DMark, it outputs the object as a deutsche mark.

Thus, although operator<<() is not virtual, because it invokes a virtual function the result is virtual perfection:

```
Deposit was $1.50
Deposit was 3.00 DM
```

This is another reason why I prefer to perform the work of output in a member function and let the non-member operator refer to that function.

Chapter 27

Handling Errors — Exceptions

● ●

In This Chapter

▶ Introducing an exceptional way of handling program errors

▶ Finding what's wrong with good ol' error returns

▶ Examining throwing and catching exceptions

▶ Packing more heat into that throw

● ●

I know that it's hard to accept, but occasionally functions don't work properly — not even mine. The traditional means of reporting failure is to return some indication to the caller. C++ includes a new, improved mechanism for capturing and handling errors called *exceptions*. An exception is "a case in which a rule or principle does not apply". Exception is also defined as an objection to something. Either definition works: An exception is an unexpected (and presumably objectionable) condition that occurs during the execution of the program.

The exception mechanism is based on the keywords try, catch, and throw (that's right, more variable names that you can't use). In outline, it works like this: A function *try*s to get through a piece of code. If the code detects a problem, it *throw*s an error indication that the calling function must *catch*.

The following code snippet demonstrates how that works in 1s and 0s:

```
#include <iostream.h>

// factorial - compute factorial
int factorial(int n)
{
  // you can't handle negative values of n;
  // better check for that condition first
  if (n < 0)
  {
    throw "Argument for factorial negative";
  }
```

```
    // go ahead and calculate factorial
    int accum = 1;
    while(n > 0)
    {
        accum *= n;
        n--;
    }
return accum;
}

int main(int argcs, char* pArgs[])
{
    try
    {
        // this will generate an exception
        cout << "Factorial of -1 is " << factorial(-1) << endl;

        // control will never get here
        cout << "Factorial of 10 is " << factorial(10) << endl;
    }
    // control passes here
    catch(char* pError)
    {
        cout << "Error occured: " << pError << endl;
    }
}
```

main() starts out by creating a block outfitted with the try keyword. Within this block, it can proceed on the way it would were the block not present. In this case, main() attempts to calculate the factorial of a negative number. Not to be hoodwinked, the clever factorial() function detects the bogus request and throws an error indication using the throw keyword. Control passes to the catch phrase, which immediately follows the closing brace of the try block. The second call to factorial() is not performed.

Justifying a New Error Mechanism?

What's wrong with error returns like FORTRAN used to make? Factorials cannot be negative, so I could have said something like "Okay, if factorial() detects an error, it returns a negative number. The actual value indicates the source of the problem." What's wrong with that? That's how it's been accomplished for ages.

Unfortunately, several problems arise. First, although it's true that the result of a factorial can't be negative, other functions aren't so lucky. For example, you can't take the log of a negative number either, but the negative return value trick won't work here — logarithms can be either negative or positive.

Second, there's just so much information that you can store in an integer. Maybe you can have –1 for "argument is negative" and –2 for "argument is too large." But if the argument is too large, I'd like to know what the argument was because it may help me to debug the problem. There's no place to store that type of information.

Third, the processing of error returns is optional. Suppose that someone writes `factorial()` so that it dutifully checks the argument and returns a negative number if the argument is out of range. If the code that calls that function doesn't check the error return, it doesn't do any good. Sure, I make all kinds of menacing threats like "You will check your error returns or else," but you all know that the language can't force anyone.

Even if I do check the error return from `factorial()` or any other function, what can my function do with the error? It can probably do nothing more than output an error message of my own and return another error indication to my caller, which probably does the same. Pretty soon, all code begins to have the following appearance:

```
// call some function, check the error return, handle it,
// and return
errRtn = someFunc();
if (errRtn)
{
  errorOut("Error on call to someFunc()");
  return MY_ERROR_1;
}
errRtn = someOtherFunc();
if (errRtn)
{
  errorOut("Error on call to someOtherFunc()");
  return MY_ERROR_1;
}
```

This mechanism has several problems:

- ✔ It's highly repetitive.
- ✔ It forces the user to invent and keep track of numerous error return indications.
- ✔ It mixes the error-handling code into the normal code flow, thereby obscuring the normal, non-error path.

These problems don't seem so bad in this simple example, but they become increasingly worse as the calling code becomes more complex. The result is that error-handling code doesn't get written to handle all the conditions that it should.

The exception mechanism addresses these problems by removing the error path from the normal code path. Further, exceptions make error handling obligatory. If your function doesn't handle the thrown exception, control passes up the chain of called functions until C++ finds a function to handle the error. This also gives you the flexibility to ignore errors that you can't do anything about anyway. Only the functions that can actually correct the problem need to catch the exception.

Examining the Exception Mechanism

Take a closer look at the steps that the code goes through to handle an exception. When the throw occurs, C++ first copies the thrown object to some neutral place. It then begins looking for the end of the current try block.

If a try block is not found in the current function, control passes to the calling function. A search is then made of that function. If no try block is found there, control passes to the function that called it, and so on up the stack of calling functions. This process is called *unwinding the stack*.

An important feature of stack unwinding is that as each stack is unwound, any objects that go out of scope are destructed just as if the function had executed a return statement. This keeps the program from losing assets or leaving objects dangling.

When the encasing try block is found, the code searches the first catch phrase immediately following the closing brace of the catch block. If the object thrown matches the type of argument specified in the catch statement, control passes to that catch phrase. If not, a check is made of the next catch phrase. If no matching catch phrases are found, the code searches for the next higher level try block in an ever-outward spiral until an appropriate catch can be found. If no catch phrase is found, the program is terminated.

Consider the following example:

```
#include <iostream.h>

class Obj
{
  public:
    Obj(char c)
    {
      label = c;
      cout << "Constructing object " << label << endl;
    }
    ~Obj()
```

```
    {
      cout << "Destructing object " << label << endl;
    }

  protected:
    char label;
};

void f1();
void f2();
int main(int, char*[])
{
  Obj a('a');
  try
  {
    Obj b('b');
    f1();
  }
  catch(float f)
  {
    cout << "Float catch" << endl;
  }
  catch(int i)
  {
    cout << "Int catch" << endl;
  }
  catch(...)
  {
    cout << "Generic catch" << endl;
  }
  return 0;
}

void f1()
{
  try
  {
    Obj c('c');
    f2();
  }
  catch(char* pMsg)
  {
    cout << "String catch" << endl;
  }
}
void f2()
{
  Obj d('d');
  throw 10;
}
```

The output from executing this program appears as follows:

```
Constructing object a
Constructing object b
Constructing object c
Constructing object d
Destructing object d
Destructing object c
Destructing object b
Int catch
Destructing object a
```

First you see the four objects a, b, c, and d being constructed as control passes through each declaration before f2() throws the int 10. Because no try block is defined in f2(), C++ unwinds f2()'s stack, causing object d to be destructed. f1() defines a try block, but its only catch phrase is designed to handle char*, which doesn't not match the int thrown. Therefore, C++ continues looking. This unwinds f1()'s stack, resulting in object c being destructed.

Back in main(), C++ finds another try block. Exiting that block causes object b to go out of scope. The first catch phrase is designed to catch floats that don't match our int, so it's skipped. The next catch phrase matches the int exactly, so control stops there. The final catch phrase, which would catch any object thrown, is skipped because a matching catch phrase was already found.

What Kinds of Things Can I Throw?

The thing following the throw keyword is actually an expression that creates an object of some kind. In the examples so far, I've always thrown integers, but throw can handle any type of object. This means that you can throw almost as much information as you want. Consider the following class definition:

```
#include <iostream.h>
#include <iostream.h>
#include <string.h>

// Exception - generic exception handling class
class Exception
{
  public:
    Exception(char* pMsg, char* pFile, int nLine)
    {
      strncpy(msg, pMsg, sizeof msg);
      msg[sizeof msg - 1] = '\0'; // make sure it's
                  // terminated
```

```
      strncpy(file, pFile, sizeof file);
      file[sizeof file - 1] = '\0';
      lineNum = nLine;
   }

   virtual void display(ostream& out)
   {
      out << "Error <" << msg << ">\n";
      out << "Occurred on line #" << lineNum
          << ", file " << file << endl;
   }
 protected:
 // error message
 char msg[80];

 // file name and line number where error occurred
 char file[80];
 int lineNum;
};
```

The throw looks like the following:

```
throw Exception("Negative argument to factorial",
                __FILE__,__LINE__);
```

FILE and *LINE* are intrinsic #*defines* that are set to the name of the source file and the current line number in that file, respectively.

The class `ostream` used by `display()` is the base class of the output stream classes. The object `cout` is an `ostream`, but so are `ofstream` and `ostrstream` objects. (See Chapter 26.)

The corresponding catch is straightforward:

```
void myFunc()
{
   try
   {
      //. . .whatever calls
   }
   // catch an Exception object
   catch(Exception x)
   {
      // use the built-in display member function
      x.display(cerr);
   }
}
```

The catch snags the Exception object and then uses the built-in display()
member function to display the error message.

The object cerr is the standard error output object — like cout but for error
output. The difference between cout and cerr is only important if you're an
accomplished Unix user.

The Exception class represents a generic error-reporting class. However,
this class can be extended by subclassing from it. For example, I can define
an InvalidArgumentException class that stores the value of the invalid
argument in addition to the message and location of the error:

```
class InvalidArgumentException : public Exception
{
 public:
   InvalidArgumentException(int arg, char* pFile, int nLine)
    : Exception("Invalid argument", pFile, nLine)
   {
     invArg = arg;
   }

   virtual void display(ostream& out)
   {
     Exception::display(out);
     out << "Argument was " << invArg << endl;
   }

 protected:
   int invArg;
};
```

The calling function automatically handles the new
InvalidArgumentException because an InvalidArgumentException is an
Exception and the display() member function is polymorphic.

Chapter 28

Inheriting Multiple Inheritance

*I*n the class hierarchies discussed elsewhere in this book, each class has inherited from a single parent. Such single inheritance is sufficient to describe more real-world relationship. Some classes, however, represent the blending of two classes into one.

An example of such a class is the sleeper sofa. As the name implies, it is a sofa and a bed (although not a very comfortable bed). Thus, the sleeper sofa should be allowed to inherit bed-like properties. To address this situation, C++ allows a derived class to inherit from more than one base class. This is called *multiple inheritance*.

Describing the Multiple Inheritance Mechanism

To see how multiple inheritance works, I can expand on the sleeper sofa example. Figure 28-1 shows the inheritance graph for class SleeperSofa. Notice how this class inherits from class Sofa and from class Bed. In this way, it inherits the properties of both.

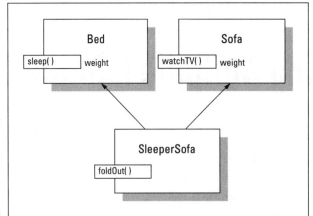

The code to implement class SleeperSofa looks like the following:

```
class Bed
{
 public:
  Bed();
  void sleep();
  int weight;
};

class Sofa
{
 public:
  Sofa();
  void watchTV();
  int weight;
};

// SleeperSofa - is both a Bed and a Sofa
class SleeperSofa : public Bed, public Sofa
{
 public:
  SleeperSofa();
  void foldOut();
};

int main(int argcs, char* pArgs[])
{
   SleeperSofa ss;

   // you can watch TV on a sleeper sofa like a sofa...
   ss.watchTV();      // Sofa::watchTV()
   //...and then you can fold it out...
   ss.foldOut();      // SleeperSofa::foldOut()
```

```
   //...and sleep on it like a bed (sort of)
   ss.sleep();      // Bed::sleep()
   return 0;
}
```

Here the class `SleeperSofa` inherits from both `Bed` and `Sofa`. This is apparent from the appearance of both classes in the class declaration. `SleeperSofa` inherits all the members of both base classes. Thus, both of the calls `ss.sleep()` and `ss.watchTV()` are legal. You can use a `SleeperSofa` as a `Bed` or a `Sofa`. Plus the class `SleeperSofa` can have members of its own, such as `foldOut()`. Is this a great country or what?

Straightening Out Inheritance Ambiguities

Although multiple inheritance is a powerful feature, it introduces several possible problems. One is apparent in the preceding example. Notice that both `Bed` and `Sofa` contain a member `weight`. This is logical because both have a measurable weight. The question is, "Which `weight` does `SleeperSofa` inherit?"

The answer is "both." `SleeperSofa` inherits a member `Bed::weight` and a separate member `Sofa::weight`. Because they have the same name, unqualified references to `weight` are now ambiguous. This is demonstrated in the following snippet:

```
#include <iostream.h>

void fn()
{
   SleeperSofa ss;
   cout << "weight = "
        << ss.weight    // illegal - which weight?
        << "\n";
}
```

The program must now indicate one of the two weights by specifying the desired base class. The following code snippet is correct:

```
#include <iostream.h>
void fn()
{
   SleeperSofa ss;
   cout << "sofa weight = "
        << ss.Sofa::weight  // specify which weight
        << "\n";
}
```

Although this solution corrects the problem, specifying the base class in the application function isn't desirable because it forces class information to leak outside the class into application code. In this case, fn() has to know that SleeperSofa inherits from Sofa. These types of so-called name collisions weren't possible with single inheritance but are a constant danger with multiple inheritance.

Adding Virtual Inheritance

In the case of SleeperSofa, the name collision on weight was more than a mere accident. A SleeperSofa doesn't have a bed weight separate from its sofa weight. The collision occurred because this class hierarchy does not completely describe the real world. Specifically, the classes have not been completely factored.

Thinking about it a little more, it becomes clear that both beds and sofas are special cases of a more fundamental concept: furniture. (I suppose I could get even more fundamental and use something like object with mass, but furniture is fundamental enough.) Weight is a property of all furniture. This relationship is shown in Figure 28-2.

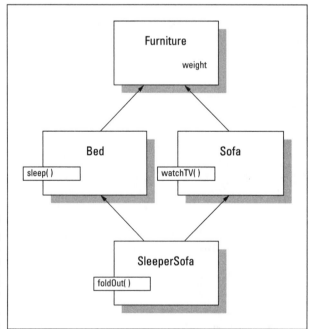

Figure 28-2:
Further factoring of beds and sofas (by weight).

Factoring out the class `Furniture` should relieve the name collision. With much relief and great anticipation of success, I generate the following C++ class hierarchy:

```
#include <iostream.h>

// Furniture - more fundamental concept; this class
//             has "weight" as a property
class Furniture
{
 public:
  Furniture();
  int weight;
};

class Bed : public Furniture
{
 public:
  Bed();
  sleep();
};

class Sofa : public Furniture
{
 public:
  Sofa();
  void watchTV();
};

class SleeperSofa : public Bed, public Sofa
{
 public:
  SleeperSofa();
  void foldOut;
};

void fn()
{
  SleeperSofa ss;
  cout << "weight = "
       << ss.weight    // problem solved; right?
       << "\n";
}
```

Imagine my dismay when I find that this doesn't help at all — `weight` is still ambiguous. (I wish my weight were as ambiguous!) "Okay," I say (not really understanding why weight is still ambiguous), "I'll try casting `ss` to a `Furniture`."

```
#include <iostream.h>

void fn()
{
  SleeperSofa ss;
  Furniture* pF;
  pF = (Furniture*)&ss; // use a Furniture pointer...
  cout << "weight = "    // ...to get at the weight
       << pF->weight
       << "\n";
};
```

Casting ss to a furniture doesn't work either. Now, I get some strange message that the cast of SleeperSofa* to Furniture* is ambiguous. What's going on?

The explanation is straightforward. SleeperSofa doesn't inherit from Furniture directly. Both Bed and Sofa inherit from Furniture and then SleeperSofa inherits from them. In memory, a SleeperSofa looks like Figure 28-3.

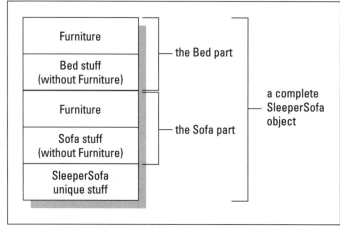

Figure 28-3:
Memory
layout of a
SleeperSofa.

You can see that a SleeperSofa consists of a complete Bed followed by a complete Sofa followed by some SleeperSofa unique stuff. Each of these subobjects in SleeperSofa has its own Furniture part, because each inherits from Furniture. Thus, a SleeperSofa contains two Furniture objects!

I haven't created the hierarchy shown in Figure 28-2 after all. The inheritance hierarchy I have actually created is the one shown in Figure 28-4.

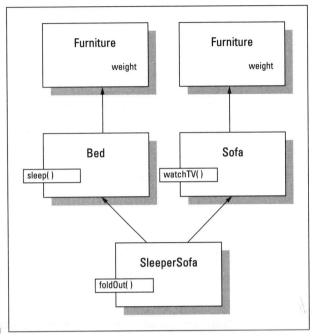

Figure 28-4:
Actual
result of my
first attempt.

But Sleepersofa containing two Furniture objects is nonsense.
SleeperSofa needs only one copy of Furniture. I want SleeperSofa to
inherit only one copy of Furniture, and I want Bed and Sofa to share that
one copy. C++ calls this *virtual inheritance* because it uses the virtual keyword.

I hate this overloading of the term *virtual* because virtual inheritance has
nothing to do with virtual functions.

Armed with this new knowledge, I return to class SleeperSofa and implement it as follows:

```cpp
#include <iostream.h>
class Furniture
{
 public:
  Furniture() {}
  int weight;
};

class Bed : virtual public Furniture
{
 public:
  Bed() {}
  void sleep();
};
```

```
class Sofa : virtual public Furniture
{
 public:
   Sofa() {}
   void watchTV();
};

class SleeperSofa : public Bed, public Sofa
{
 public:
   SleeperSofa() : Sofa(), Bed() {}
   void foldOut();
};

void fn()
{
   SleeperSofa ss;
   cout << "weight = "
      << ss.weight
      << "\n";
}
```

Notice the addition of the keyword virtual in the inheritance of Furniture in Bed and Sofa. This says, "Give me a copy of Furniture unless you already have one somehow, in which case I'll just use that one." A SleeperSofa ends up looking like Figure 28-5 in memory.

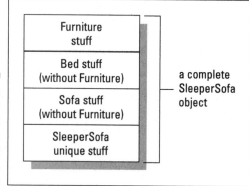

Figure 28-5:
Memory
layout of
SleeperSofa
with virtual
inheritance.

Here you can see that a SleeperSofa inherits Furniture, and then Bed minus the Furniture part, followed by Sofa minus the Furniture part. Bringing up the rear are the members unique to SleeperSofa. (Note that this may not be the order of the elements in memory, but that's not important for the purpose of this discussion.)

Now the reference in `fn()` to `weight` is not ambiguous because a `SleeperSofa` contains only one copy of `Furniture`. By inheriting `Furniture` virtually, you get the desired inheritance relationship as expressed in Figure 28-2.

If virtual inheritance solves this problem so nicely, why isn't it the norm? The first is because virtually inherited base classes are handled internally much differently than normally inherited base classes, and these differences involve extra overhead. The second reason is that sometimes you want two copies of the base class (although this is unusual).

As an example of the latter, consider a TeacherAssistant who is both a Student and a Teacher, both of which are subclasses of Academician. If the university gives its teaching assistants two IDs — a student ID and a separate teacher ID — class `TeacherAssistant` will need to contain two copies of class `Academician`.

Constructing the Objects of Multiple Inheritance

The rules for constructing objects need to be expanded to handle multiple inheritance. The constructors are invoked in the following order:

1. First, the constructor for any virtual base classes is called in the order in which the classes are inherited.

2. Then the constructor for any nonvirtual base classes is called in the order in which the classes are inherited.

3. Next, the constructor for any member objects is called in the order in which the member objects appear in the class.

4. Finally, the constructor for the class itself is called.

Notice that base classes are constructed in the order in which they are inherited and not in the order in which they appear on the constructor line.

Voicing a Contrary Opinion

I should point out that not all object-oriented practitioners think that multiple inheritance is a good idea. In addition, many object-oriented languages don't support multiple inheritance.

Multiple inheritance is not an easy thing for the language to implement. This is mostly the compiler's problem (or the compiler writer's problem). But multiple inheritance adds overhead to the code when compared to single inheritance, and this overhead can become the programmer's problem.

More importantly, multiple inheritance opens the door to additional errors. First, ambiguities such as those mentioned in the earlier section "Inheritance Ambiguities" pop up. Second, in the presence of multiple inheritance, casting a pointer from a subclass to a base class often involves changing the value of the pointer in sophisticated and mysterious ways. Let me leave the details to the language lawyers and compiler writers. I want to point out, however, that this can result in unexpected results. For example:

```
#include <iostream.h>

class Base1 {int mem;};
class Base2 {int mem;};
class SubClass : public Base1, public Base2 {};

void fn(SubClass* pSC)
{
  Base1* pB1 = (Base1*)pSC;
  Base2* pB2 = (Base2*)pSC;
  if ((void*)pB1 == (void*)pB2)
  {
    cout << "Members numerically equal\n";
  }
}

int main(int argcs, char* pArgs[])
{
  SubClass sc;
  fn(&sc);
  return 0;
}
```

pB1 and pB2 are not numerically equal even though they came from the same original value, pSC, and the message "Members numerically equal" doesn't appear. (Actually, if fn() is passed a zero because C++ doesn't perform these transmigrations on *null*, the message does appear; for any nonzero address, the message doesn't appear. See how strange it gets?)

I suggest that you avoid using multiple inheritance until you're comfortable with C++. Single inheritance provides enough expressive power to get used to. Later, you can study the manuals until you're sure that you understand exactly what's going on when you multiply inherit. One exception is the use of commercial libraries such as Microsoft's Foundation Classes (MFC), which use multiple inheritance quite a bit. These classes have been checked out and are safe.

Don't get me wrong. I'm not out and out against multiple inheritance. The fact that Microsoft and others use multiple inheritance effectively in their class libraries proves that it can be done. If multiple inheritance weren't worth the trouble, they wouldn't use it. However, multiple inheritance is a feature that you might want to hold off on using until you're ready.

Part VI
The Part of Tens

The 5th Wave   By Rich Tennant

WANDA HAD THE DISTINCT FEELING HER HUSBAND'S NEW SOFTWARE PROGRAM WAS ABOUT TO BECOME INTERACTIVE.

In this part . . .

What *For Dummies* book would be complete without a Part of Tens? In Chapter 29, I cover ten ways to avoid adding bugs to your C++ program. (Most of these suggestions work for C programs too at no extra charge.) Chapter 30 lists the ten most important compiler options (plus a few more) in Visual C++, the most popular commercial C++ development tool for the PC.

Chapter 29

Ten Ways to Avoid Adding Bugs to Your Program

● ●

In This Chapter

▶ Enabling all warnings and error messages

▶ Insisting on clean compiles

▶ Using a clear and consistent coding style

▶ Limiting the visibility

▶ Adding comments to your code while you write it

▶ Single-stepping every path at least once

▶ Avoiding overloaded operators

▶ Heap handling

▶ Using exceptions to handle errors

▶ Avoiding multiple inheritance

● ●

Enabling All Warnings and Error Messages

The syntax of C++ allows for a lot of error checking. When the compiler encounters a construct that it cannot decipher, it has no choice but to generate an error message. Although the compiler attempts to sync back up with the next statement, it does not attempt to generate an executable program.

Disabling warning and error messages is a bit like unplugging the red lights on your car dashboard because they bother you. Ignoring the problem doesn't make it go away. If your compiler has a Syntax Check from Hell mode, enable it. Both Microsoft and Borland have an Enable All Messages option — set it. You save time in the end.

During all its digging around in your source code, a good C++ compiler also looks for suspicious-looking syntactical constructs, such as the following code snippet:

```
#include "student.h"
#include "class.h"
Student* addNewStudent(Class class, char *pName, SSNumber ss)
{
  Student pS;
 if (pName != 0)
  {
   pS = new Student(pName, ss);
   class.addStudent(pS);
  }
  return pS;
}
```

Here you see that the function first creates a new Student object that it then adds to the Class object provided. (Presumably addStudent() is a member function of Class.)

If a name is provided (that is, pName is not 0), a new Student object is created and added to the class. With that done, the function returns the Student created to the caller. The problem is that if pName is 0, pS is never initialized to anything. A good C++ compiler, such as the Visual C++ compiler, can detect this path and generate a warning that there's a possibility that pS is never initialized when it's returned to the caller and maybe you should look into the problem, or words to that effect.

Insisting on Clean Compiles

Don't start debugging your code until you remove or at least understand all the warnings generated during compilation. Enabling all the warning messages if you then ignore them does you no good. If you don't understand the warning, look it up. What you don't know *will* hurt you.

Adopting a Clear and Consistent Coding Style

Coding in a clear and consistent style not only enhances the readability of the program but also results in fewer coding mistakes. Remember, the less brain power you have to spend deciphering C++ syntax, the more you have left over for thinking about the logic of the program at hand. A good coding style enables you to do the following with ease:

- ✔ Differentiate class names, object names, and function names
- ✔ Know something about the object based on its name
- ✔ Differentiate preprocessor symbols from C++ symbols (that is, #defined objects should stand out)
- ✔ Identify blocks of C++ code at the same level (this is the result of consistent indentation)

In addition, you need to establish a standard module header that provides information about the functions or classes in the module, the author (presumably, that's you), the date, the version of the compiler you're using, and a modification history.

Finally, all programmers involved in a single project should use the same style. Trying to decipher a program with a patchwork of different coding styles is confusing.

Limiting the Visibility

Limiting the visibility of class internals to the outside world is a cornerstone of object-oriented programming. The class is responsible for its own internals; the application is responsible for using the class to solve the problem at hand.

Specifically, limited visibility means that data membersshould not be accessible outside the class — that is, they should be marked as private or protected. In addition, member functions that the application software does not need to know about should also be protected.

A related rule is that public member functions should trust application code as little as possible. Any argument passed to a public member function should be treated as though it may cause bugs until it has been proven safe. A function such as the following is an accident waiting to happen:

```
class Array
{
  public:
    Array(int s)
    {
      size = 0;
      pData = new int[s];
      if (pData)
      {
        size = s;
      }
    }
```

```
~Array()
 {
  delete pData;
  size = 0;
  pData = 0;
 }
 //either return or set the array data
 int data(int index)
 {
  return pData[index];
 }
 int data(int index, int newValue)
 {
  int oldValue = pData[index];
  pData[index] = newValue;
  return oldValue;
 }
protected:
 int size;
 int *pData;
};
```

The function data(int) allows the application software to read data out of Array. This function is too trusting; it assumes that the index provided is within the data range. What if the index is not? The function data(int, int) is even worse because it overwrites an unknown location.

What's needed is a check to make sure that the index is in range. In the following, only the data(int) function is shown for brevity:

```
int data(unsigned int index)
{
  if (index >= size)
  {
   cout << "Array index out of range (" << index << ")\n";
   return 0;
  }
  return pData[index];
}
```

Now an out-of-range index will be caught by the check. (Making index unsigned precludes the necessity of adding a check for negative index values.)

Commenting Your Code While You Write It

I think you can avoid errors if you comment your code while you write it rather than wait until everything works and then go back and add comments.

I can understand not taking the time to write voluminous headers and function descriptions until later, but you always have time to add short comments while writing the code.

Short comments should be enlightening. If they're not, they aren't worth much and you should be doing something else instead. You need all the enlightenment you can get while you're trying to make your program work. When you look at a piece of code you wrote a few days ago, comments that are short, descriptive, and to the point can make a dramatic contribution to helping you figure out exactly what it was you were trying to do.

In addition, consistent code indentation and naming conventions make the code easier to understand. It's all very nice when the code is easy to read after you're finished with it, but it's just as important that the code be easy to read while you're writing it. That's when you need the help.

Single-Stepping Every Path at Least Once

As a programmer, it's important for you to understand what your program is doing. Nothing gives you a better feel for what's going on under the hood than single-stepping the program with a good debugger. (The debuggers included in the IDE of interactive compilers work just fine.)

Beyond that, as you write a program, you sometimes need raw material to figure out some bizarre behavior. Nothing gives you that material better than single-stepping new functions as they come into service.

Finally, when a function is finished and ready to be added to the program, every logical path needs to be traveled at least once. Bugs are much easier to find when the function is examined by itself rather than after it's been thrown into the pot with the rest of the functions — and your attention has gone on to new programming challenges.

Avoid Overloading Operators

Other than using the two stream I/O operators `operator<<()` and `operator>>()` and the assignment operator `operator=()`, you should probably hold off overloading operators until you feel comfortable with C++. Although a good set of overloaded operators can increase the utility and readability of a new class, overloading operators other than the three just listed is almost never necessary and can significantly add to your debugging woes as a new programmer. You can get the same effect by defining and using the proper public member functions instead.

After you've been C-plus-plussing for a few months, feel free to return and start overloading operators to your heart's content.

Heap Handling

As a general rule, programmers should allocate and release heap memory at the same "level." If a member function `MyClass::create()` allocates a block of heap memory and returns it to the caller, then there should be a member function `MyClass::release()` that returns the memory to the heap. Specifically, `MyClass::create()` should not require the parent function to release the memory itself. This certainly doesn't avoid all memory problems — the parent function may forget to call `MyClass::release()` — but it does reduce the possibility somewhat.

Using Exceptions to Handle Errors

The exception mechanism in C++ is designed to handle errors conveniently and efficiently. Now that this feature has been standardized, you should use it. The resulting code is easier to write, easier to read, and easier to maintain. Besides, other programmers have come to expect it — you wouldn't want to disappoint them, would you?

Avoiding Multiple Inheritance

Multiple inheritance, like operator overloading, adds another level of complexity that you don't need to deal with when you're just starting out. Fortunately, most real-world relationships can be described with single inheritance. (Some people claim that multiple inheritance is not necessary at all — I'm not one of them.)

Feel free to use multiple-inherited classes from commercial libraries, such as the Microsoft MFC classes. Microsoft has spent a considerable amount of time setting up its classes, and it knows what it's doing.

After you feel comfortable with your level of understanding of C++, experiment with setting up some multiple inheritance hierarchies. That way, you'll be ready when the unusual situation that requires multiple inheritance to describe it accurately arises.

Chapter 30

The Ten Most Important Microsoft Visual C++ Compiler Settings

● ●

In This Chapter
▶ Producing a command line program
▶ Changing your project settings
▶ Using the General Settings tab: MFC and directories
▶ Choosing debug factors
▶ Getting to the good stuff from the General tab
▶ Changing C++ language settings
▶ Controlling code generation
▶ Customizing your C++ language extensions
▶ Regulating compile optimizations
▶ Enabling precompiled headers

● ●

*T*his entire chapter should be considered a techie chapter. The default settings for most C++ compilers, including Visual C++, work for 99 percent of
all programs. However, you can use these modifications to default settings to
enhanced your programs in many cases.

Most programmers use the Microsoft Visual C++ compiler on the PC to generate applications. This chapter explains the ten most important Visual C++
compiler settings used to generate command line programs.

Note: The terms "switch settings," "switches," and "settings" are used syn-
onymously in the programming world.

Because this isn't a Windows programming book, I don't cover settings used
to generate Windows programs.

Generating a Command Line Program

Because the name Microsoft is so closely linked to Windows and because the Visual C++ compiler has some neat tools for generating Microsoft Windows applications, people often assume that Visual C++ won't generate a DOS-like command line type application. This simply isn't the case. In fact, I tested all the programs in this book using the Visual C++ 6 compiler (in addition to the GNU C++, which is included on the enclosed CD-ROM).

To create a command line program (what Microsoft calls a *console applica-tion*), choose File⇨New⇨Projects. From the list of program types, select Win32 Console Application. Enter a project name and then click OK. Each program that you create must have a project associated with it and each pro-ject goes into its own directory. The project describes the details of how the program was created (the flags are described in this chapter). (See Chapter 10 for a discussion of Project Files.) You can change the base directory for the project by editing the path specified in Location. Click OK to have Visual C++ create a project. At this point, you should be looking at an empty work-space (it's empty in the sense that there are no C++ source files associated with the project).

To create a new C++ source file, choose File⇨New⇨Files. From this, you should see a list of possible types of files that you can create. Select C++ Source File from the list of options and type in the filename of the new C++ source file. Selecting OK opens a new window into which you can type your program. In addition, Visual C++ automatically adds the new file to the cur-rently open project.

If you want to add previously created C++ source files to your project, choose Project⇨Add To Project⇨Files. The Files dialog box opens. Select the source files that you want to add to the project.

Changing Project Settings

To view the project settings, choose Project⇨Settings to reveal a screen like the one in Figure 30-1. Notice that Visual C++ allows you to maintain multiple, different project setting configurations. In fact, it creates two settings for you from the very beginning: Debug and Release. The difference between these settings is that Debug tends to be set to the value that's most convenient for the debugger. Because these settings are also the slowest possible, the Production setting is provided to produce the fastest, smallest executable program. These settings are used to create the final executable files prior to release of the program for use (perhaps by a customer).

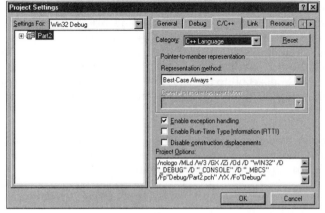

Figure 30-1:
The Project
Settings
window.

If the Project Settings window is not already open, choose Project⇨Settings. To change a setting, select the configuration for which you want the settings changed by clicking on the drop-down menu next to the Settings For label.

Choosing General Settings

The General Settings tab window, shown in Figure 30-2, contains two settings of interest. First, are you or are you not using MFC? MFC stands for *Microsoft Foundation Classes* and applies to Windows development, so the answer here is basically No.

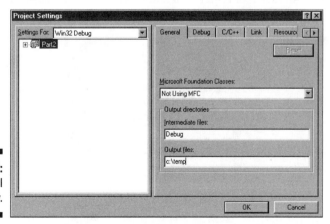

Figure 30-2:
The General
tab window.

The second question concerns directories. Visual C++ generates several intermediate files while both editing and compiling. Normally, these files go into the current directory. However, Visual C++ allows you to place these temporaries in a different directory if you want. About the only reason for this would be if the current directory were full (unlikely) or if you had a really fast disk (like a RAM disk) off to the side that you could use for temporary files. In this same section, Visual C++ allows you to place the file executable in any directory you want.

The directory name provided is relative, so if you want the output directory to be completely independent of the current directory, provide a full path (refer to Figure 30-2) for the Output directory.

Selecting Settings for Debug

The Debug Settings tab, shown in Figure 30-3, has four catchall questions. The second and third text fields are the only ones that affect much.

The second text field specifies the Working Directory. This directory is much the same as the Intermediate File directory specified under the General tab, which allows the user to direct intermediate debug files to a separate location.

The third text field allows the programmer to enter any arguments to the program during debug. These arguments would normally follow the program name when executing it from the command line prompt.

A second category under the Debug Settings tab is Additional DLL. Here DLL stands for *Dynamic Link Library*. You'll have little use for this setting.

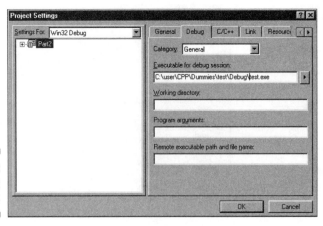

Figure 30-3:
The Debug
tab window.

Choosing General Options for C/C++

The C/C++ tab hides most of the "good stuff" starting right from the General category, as shown in Figure 30-4.

The Warning Level tells the compiler how hard to look for errors. A level of 0 says to overlook all but the most heinous infractions. Level 4 says don't let much of anything get by. The default is Level 3 (although I prefer Level 4).

Normally, the compiler continues with the link step after all the source files have compiled, even if warnings were generated. If the Warnings as Errors check box is selected, then Visual C++ will not continue with the link step if any warnings are generated during the compilation phase.

The Debug Info select box enables the user to select the form that the debug information takes. You probably don't have a reason to mess with this setting.

To browse variables during debug, you must have Visual C++ generate browser information during compilation. However, this is not the default because it increases the size of the object files while slowing down compilation a lot. To enable this, select the Generate Browse Info check box.

The Optimizations setting controls the amount of optimization that the compiler performs. During debug, you really don't want any optimizations performed because it can cause the debugger to do some confusing things. When you're ready to generate a "for release" version, enable either the Maximum Speed or Minimum Size options. If you prefer, you can select Customize and select the particular optimizations from the list provided that you would like to perform.

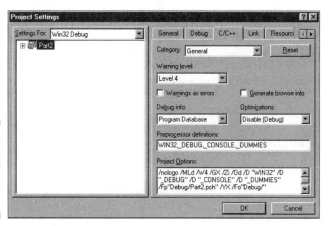

Figure 30-4:
The General category of the C/C++ tab window.

Finally, the Preprocessor Definitions window enables you to define any preprocessor #defines you want. For example, notice that I added the #define _DUMMIES. This enables me to control how my code is compiled via preprocessor directives within the code. You can add whatever you want, but be careful not to remove or modify any directives that are already there.

Controlling C++ Language Settings

The C++ language category enables the programmer to control those settings that are unique to C++. Some of these settings are rather confusing, so you may want to skip this category. This window is shown in Figure 30-5.

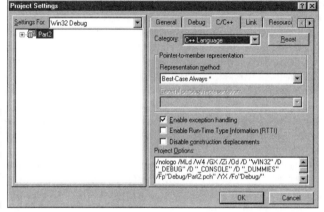

Figure 30-5: The C++ category of the C/C++ tab window.

Visual C++ supports different formats for the way that pointers to virtual member functions are handled. The default is Best-Case Always, which allows the compiler to select the virtual pointer type. However, if you want to control the pointer type, select General Purpose under Representation method and you're afforded three options: Point to Any Class; Point to Single- and Multiple-Inheritance Classes; and Point to Single-Inheritance Classes. The first two options generate more complicated code than the single-inheritance option. Select Single-Inheritance Classes if you have no intent of using multiple inheritance — the code generated will execute more quickly, but Visual C++ does not support multiple inheritance with this setting. (See Chapter 28 for a discussion of multiple inheritance.)

The next three check boxes also allow you to simplify the code generated by the compiler. If you are not using exception handing (you should be), click Exception Handling Off for a small decrease in the time to call a function. Leave the next two deselected — I don't cover those features.

Choosing Code Generation Settings

The Code Generation window, shown in Figure 30-6, controls the final step in the compilation process.

The Processor allows the user to select the type of CPU for which the compiled code is designed. The default Blend produces a blend of code that's optimized for most 80386 and later processors. You can select other specific variations of the Intel 80 x 86 processor; however, the resulting code may not execute on earlier processors.

The Calling Convention drop-down menu refers to the default way in which arguments are passed to functions. The default cdecl refers to the way in which most compilers pass arguments to C functions, by pushing arguments from left to right. The selection stdcall passes functions in the opposite direction. The third selection fastcall passes the first two arguments by caching them in a register. This can significantly speed up the performance of very small functions.

The third drop-down menu, Use Run-time Library, refers to the set of .lib functions you want to link with. Normally, you want to link with the Single-threaded or Debug Single-threaded. If you're creating multiple threads in your program (I didn't in this book), you'll need to select the Multi-threaded versions.

The final drop-down menu enables the user to select the alignment of structures. Making this number too large wastes a small amount of space but has no other effect. Making this number too small can slow down the execution speed of the program significantly. When you generate code for modern Intel processors, this number should certainly not be less than 4 and perhaps not even smaller than 8.

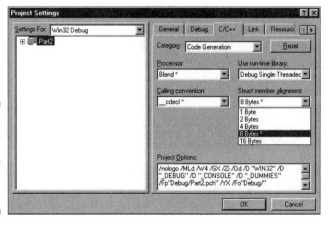

Figure 30-6:
The Code
Generation
category of
the C/C++
tab window.

Customizing with the Code Generation Window

The Code Generation window of the C/C++ tab window, shown in Figure 30-7, contains a series of individual check boxes.

Visual C++ enables a few language extensions to make Windows programming easier. It's a good idea to disable these language extensions if you're trying to write code that will be ported to a different environment.

Enabling Minimal Rebuild can save programmer time by relinking only those parts of the program that have changed since the last time the program was linked. Because this results in a larger executable file, you'll eventually want to perform a full relink, but it's worthwhile when you're in the constant compile/relink cycle common during development.

Enabling Incremental Compilation can also save time in that it recompiles only those functions that have changed since the last time the module has been compiled.

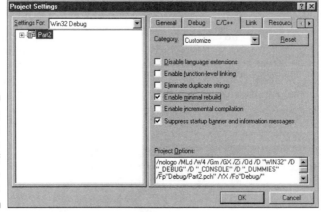

Figure 30-7:
The
Customize
category of
the C/C++
tab window.

Controlling Compile Optimizations

The Optimizations category allows the programmer to control the types of compile optimizations that are performed (see Figure 30-8).

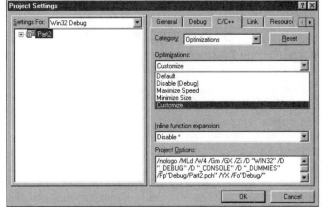

The three most common selections are Debug (meaning perform no optimiza-tions), Optimize for Speed, or Optimize for Size. A fourth option, Customize, enables the user to select the specific customizations that she would like to perform. I don't recommend this setting, however, because some of the opti-mizations aren't safe. Without knowing what you're doing, you can generate code that doesn't work from perfectly correct source code.

The Inline function expansion setting has three positions. In debug mode, the default is Disable, meaning that all functions are outlined whether they're declared inline or not. A second setting inlines functions that are specifically declared with the inline keyword, but none else. The final setting, Any Suitable, enables inlining for any function, which fulfills the requirements for inlining.

Selecting Precompiled Headers

The Standard C++ include files almost never change. Compiling these include files over and over again can result in a significant waste of time, because they seldom, if ever, change. To address this, the window shown in Figure 30-9 shows the support in Visual C++ for precompiled headers.

When precompiled headers are enabled the first time you compile your source file, the compiler writes the results of compiling the .H include files to a sepa-rate file, with the file extension .PCH. The next time you compile that module, or any other module that includes the same .H files, the compiler reads this saved information instead of recompiling the same files. Often, the Standard C++ include files are considerably larger than the application code, so enabling precompiled headers can increase compilation speed considerably.

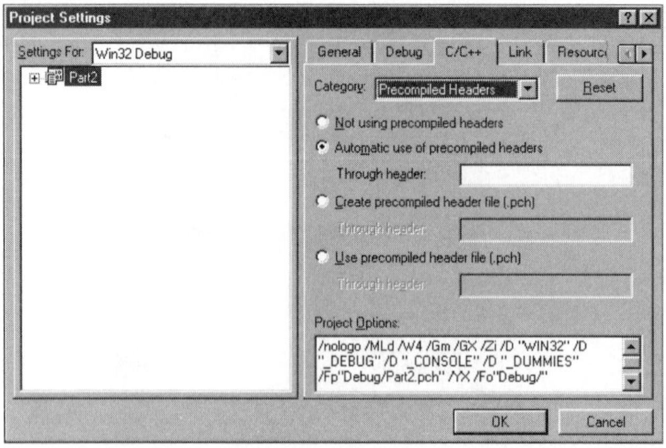

Figure 30-9:
The
Precompiled
Headers
category of
the C/C++
tab window.

To get the maximum benefit from precompiled headers, try to include the same .H files in the same order in each module. Enabling precompiled headers should have no effect on the executable file produced. When precompiled headers are turned on, they should sense a change to a header file automatically and cause the precompiled headers to rebuild. If you suspect otherwise, you can turn off precompiled headers.

Appendix A

About the CD-ROM

On the CD-ROM

▶ Getting your CD up and running

▶ Installing the GNU C++ development environment

▶ Installing the code for this book

System Requirements

Make sure that your computer meets the following minimum system requirements listed. If your computer doesn't match up to most of these requirements, you may have problems using the contents of the CD.

✔ A PC with a 486 or faster processor.

✔ Microsoft Windows 95 or later.

✔ At least 16MB of total RAM installed on your computer.

✔ At least 200KB of hard drive space available to install the GNU C++ development environment. The source code from the book takes a minimal amount of disk space.

✔ A CD-ROM drive.

If you need more information on the basics, check out *Windows 95 For Dummies* by Andy Rathbone, (IDG Books Worldwide, Inc.).

Using the CD with Microsoft Windows

C++ For Dummies, 4th Edition, comes with a public domain GNU C++ development environment, which can be used to compile and test each of the programs in this book. You do not need to install GNU C++ if you prefer to use a C++ package that you already own, such as Visual C++. However, the instructions for installing GNU C++ are detailed in Chapter 1.

To install the items from the CD to your hard drive, follow these steps.

1. **Insert the CD into your computer's CD-ROM drive.**

   Give your computer a moment to take a look at the CD.

2. **When the light on your CD-ROM drive goes out, double-click on the My Computer icon. (It's probably in the top-left corner of your desktop.)**

   This action opens the My Computer window, which shows you all the drives attached to your computer, the Control Panel, and a couple other handy things.

3. **Double-click on the icon for your CD-ROM drive.**

   Another window opens, showing you all the folders and files on the CD.

4. **Double-click the file called License.txt.**

   This file contains the end-user license that you agree to by using the CD. When you are finished reading the license, close the program, most likely NotePad, that displayed the file.

5. **Double-click the file called Readme.txt.**

   This file contains the most up-to-date information about the code.

6. **Copy individual folders from the CD to an appropriately named folder on your hard drive.**

The default location for the files to be installed is C:\CPP_For_Dummies, but you can use any name you like (just remember the name you chose and make the necessary mental changes when reading the book).

What You'll Find

The CD includes all the programs you find in this book. You can find the source code for each program (these end in a .CPP extension), an executable file for each program (these end in an .EXE extension, and an overlay file (these end in a .O extension).

In some folders, you'll find weird subfolders with names like DHbaaaa. These are created by the GNU compiler.

The programs are organized in folders that correspond to the chapters in which you find them.

In addition, you'll find the GNU C++ Compiler, which is free to use to compile your own C++ programs. You can find this in the GNU C++ Compiler folder.

If You've Got Problems (Of the CD Kind)

I tried my best to compile programs that work on most computers with the minimum system requirements. Alas, your computer may differ, and some programs may not work properly for some reason.

The two most likely problems are that you don't have enough memory (RAM) for the programs that you want to use, or you have other programs running that are affecting installation or running of a program:

✔ **Turn off any anti-virus software that you have on your computer.** Installers sometimes mimic virus activity and may make your computer incorrectly believe that it is being infected by a virus.

✔ **Close all running programs.** The more programs you're running, the less memory is available to other programs. Installers also typically update files and programs; if you keep other programs running, installation may not work properly.

✔ **In Windows, close the CD interface and run demos or installations directly from Windows Explorer.** The interface itself can tie up system memory, or even conflict with certain kinds of interactive demos. Use Windows Explorer to browse the files on the CD and launch installers or demos.

✔ **Have your local computer store add more RAM to your computer.** This is, admittedly, a drastic and somewhat expensive step. However, if you have a Windows 95 PC, adding more memory can really help the speed of your computer and enable more programs to run at the same time.

If you have problems using the GNU C++ compiler that comes with the enclosed CD-ROM, read through the installation instructions in Chapter 1 for a review of the most likely installation problems encountered.

If you still have trouble installing the items from the CD, please call the IDG Books Worldwide Customer Service phone number: 800-762-2974 (outside the U.S.: 317-572-3442).

Appendix B

Glossary

● ●

abstract class: A class that contains one or more pure virtual functions. Such a class cannot be instanced with an object.

abstraction: The concept of simplifying a real-world concept into its essential elements. Abstraction allows software classes to represent what would otherwise be hopelessly complicated real-world concepts.

analysis phase: The phase of development during which the problem is analyzed to determine its essential elements.

base class: A class from which another class inherits.

callback function: A function invoked by the operating system when a specific event occurs.

class member: Another term for static member.

classification: The grouping of similar objects. For example, warm-blooded, live-bearing, suckling animals are grouped into the classification *mammals.*

code segment: The part of a program containing executable instructions.

coding phase: The phase during which the results of the design phase are turned into code.

constructor: A special member function invoked automatically when an object is created.

copy constructor: A constructor whose argument is a reference to an object of the same class. For example, the copy constructor for class Z is declared `Z::Z(Z&)`.

data segment: The block of memory where C and C++ keep global and static variables. See *code segment* and *stack segment.*

deep copy: A copy made by replicating the object plus any assets owned by the object, including objects pointed at by data members of the object being copied.

default constructor: The constructor that has a *void* argument list.

derived class: A class that inherits from another class.

design phase: The phase of development during which the solution to the problem is formulated. The input to this phase is the result of the analysis phase.

disambiguation: The process of deciding which overloaded function a call refers to by comparing the use with the prototypes of the overloaded functions.

early binding: The normal, non-polymorphic calling method. All calls in C are bound early.

expression: A sequence of subexpressions and operators. A C or C++ expression always has a type and a value.

extensibility: The capability to add new features to a class without modifying existing code that uses that class.

friend: A function or class that is not a member of the class but is granted access to the private and protected members of the class.

function declaration: The description of a function giving its name, the name of the class with which the function is associated (if any), the number and type of any arguments, and the type of any value returned by the function.

function prototype declaration: A function declaration that contains no code.

function signature: Another name for the full function name (including argument types and return type).

global variable: A variable declared outside a function and therefore accessible to all functions.

heap: Memory allocated to the program through calls to `malloc()`. Such memory must be returned to the heap through calls to `free()`.

inheritance: The capability of a class in C++ to assume the properties of an existing class.

inline function: A function expanded at the point it is called, much like a macro definition.

instance member: Another term for a normal, nonstatic member.

instance of a class: A declared object of the specified type. For example, in the `int i` declaration, i is an instance of class `int`.

IS_A: The relationship between a subclass and its base class. For example, a Mallard IS_A Duck, meaning that an object of class Mallard is also a Duck.

late binding: The process by which polymorphism is accomplished in C++.

local variable: A variable declared in a function and therefore accessible to only that function.

member function: A function defined as part of a class in the same way that a data member is defined.

method: Another term for member function.

object-oriented programming: Programming that is based on the principles of data hiding, abstraction, inheritance, and polymorphism.

operator overloading: Defining a meaning for intrinsic operators when applied to a user-defined class.

outline function: A conventional function that is expanded at the point it is declared. Any subsequent references to the function generate a call to the point in memory where the function is expanded. See *inline function*.

overloading: Giving two different functions the same name. Such functions must be differentiable by the number or types of their arguments.

overriding: Providing a function in a subclass with the same name and arguments as a function in the base class. See *polymorphism* and *virtual member function*.

paradigm: A way of thinking; an approach to programming. Used in the context of the object-oriented paradigm or the functional programming paradigm. (Pronounced "pair-a-dime," as in 20 cents.)

pointer variable: A variable that contains an address.

polymorphism: The capability to decide which overloaded member function to invoke on the basis of the real-time type of the object, not the declared type of the object.

private: A class member accessible only to other members of the same class.

protected: A class member accessible to other members of the same class and members of any subclass. Protected members are not accessible publicly.

public: A class member accessible outside the class.

pure virtual function: A virtual member function that has no implementation.

reference variable: A variable that serves as an alias to another variable.

shallow copy: A binary, bit-for-bit copy.

short-circuit evaluation: A technique by which the right-hand subexpression of a binary expression is not evaluated if its value would not affect the value of the overall expression. This occurs with two operators: && and ||. For example, in the expression a && b, if the left-hand argument evaluates to 0 (false), there is no need to evaluate the right-hand argument because the result will still be 0.

signature field: A nonstatic data member that is given a particular value. This value can be checked in the member functions to determine whether this points to a valid object. This is a highly effective debugging technique.

stack segment: The part of a program in memory that contains the nonstatic, local variables.

static data member: A data member not associated with the individual instances of the class. For each class, one instance of each static data member exists, irrespective of how many objects of that class are created.

static member function: A member function that has no this pointer.

stream I/O: C++ input/output based on overloading operator<< and operator>>. The prototypes for these functions are in the include file iostream.h.

subclass: A class that inherits publicly from a base class. If Undergraduate is a subclass of Student, then Undergraduate IS_A Student.

this: The pointer to the current object. this is an implicit, hidden, first argument to all nonstatic member functions. this is always of type "pointer to the current class."

variable type: Specifies the size and internal structure of the variable. The built-in, or intrinsic, variable types are int, char, float, and double.

virtual member function: A member function that is called polymorphically. See *polymorphism*.

v_table: A table that contains the addresses of the virtual functions of a class. Each class that has one or more virtual member functions must have a v_table.

Index

• X •

• Y •

• Z •

IDG Books Worldwide, Inc., End-User License Agreement

READ THIS. You should carefully read these terms and conditions before opening the software packet(s) included with this book ("Book"). This is a license agreement ("Agreement") between you and IDG Books Worldwide, Inc. ("IDGB"). By opening the accompanying software packet(s), you acknowledge that you have read and accept the following terms and conditions. If you do not agree and do not want to be bound by such terms and conditions, promptly return the Book and the unopened software packet(s) to the place you obtained them for a full refund.

1. **License Grant.** IDGB grants to you (either an individual or entity) a nonexclusive license to use one copy of the enclosed software program(s) (collectively, the "Software") solely for your own personal or business purposes on a single computer (whether a standard computer or a workstation component of a multiuser network). The Software is in use on a computer when it is loaded into temporary memory (RAM) or installed into permanent memory (hard disk, CD-ROM, or other storage device). IDGB reserves all rights not expressly granted herein.

2. **Ownership.** IDGB is the owner of all right, title, and interest, including copyright, in and to the compilation of the Software recorded on the disk(s) or CD-ROM ("Software Media"). Copyright to the individual programs recorded on the Software Media is owned by the author or other authorized copyright owner of each program. Ownership of the Software and all proprietary rights relating thereto remain with IDGB and its licensers.

3. **Restrictions on Use and Transfer.**

   (a) You may only (i) make one copy of the Software for backup or archival purposes, or (ii) transfer the Software to a single hard disk, provided that you keep the original for backup or archival purposes. You may not (i) rent or lease the Software, (ii) copy or reproduce the Software through a LAN or other network system or through any computer subscriber system or bulletin-board system, or (iii) modify, adapt, or create derivative works based on the Software.

   (b) You may not reverse engineer, decompile, or disassemble the Software. You may transfer the Software and user documentation on a permanent basis, provided that the transferee agrees to accept the terms and conditions of this Agreement and you retain no copies. If the Software is an update or has been updated, any transfer must include the most recent update and all prior versions.

4. **Restrictions on Use of Individual Programs.** You must follow the individual requirements and restrictions detailed for each individual program in the "About the CD-ROM" section of this Book. These limitations are also contained in the individual license agreements recorded on the Software Media. These limitations may include a requirement that after using the program for a specified period of time, the user must pay a registration fee or discontinue use. By opening the Software packet(s), you will be agreeing to abide by the licenses and restrictions for these individual programs that are detailed in the "About the CD-ROM" section and on the Software Media. None of the material on this Software Media or listed in this Book may ever be redistributed, in original or modified form, for commercial purposes.

5. **Limited Warranty.**

   (a) IDGB warrants that the Software and Software Media are free from defects in materials and workmanship under normal use for a period of sixty (60) days from the date of purchase of this Book. If IDGB receives notification within the warranty period of defects in materials or workmanship, IDGB will replace the defective Software Media.

   (b) **IDGB AND THE AUTHOR OF THE BOOK DISCLAIM ALL OTHER WARRANTIES, EXPRESS OR IMPLIED, INCLUDING WITHOUT LIMITATION IMPLIED WARRANTIES OF MERCHANTABILITY AND FITNESS FOR A PARTICULAR PURPOSE, WITH RESPECT TO THE SOFTWARE, THE PROGRAMS, THE SOURCE CODE CONTAINED THEREIN, AND/OR THE TECHNIQUES DESCRIBED IN THIS BOOK. IDGB DOES NOT WARRANT THAT THE FUNCTIONS CONTAINED IN THE SOFTWARE WILL MEET YOUR REQUIRE-MENTS OR THAT THE OPERATION OF THE SOFTWARE WILL BE ERROR FREE.**

   (c) This limited warranty gives you specific legal rights, and you may have other rights that vary from jurisdiction to jurisdiction.

6. **Remedies.**

   (a) IDGB's entire liability and your exclusive remedy for defects in materials and workman-ship shall be limited to replacement of the Software Media, which may be returned to IDGB with a copy of your receipt at the following address: Software Media Fulfillment Department, Attn.: *C++ For Dummies,* 4th Edition, IDG Books Worldwide, Inc., 10475 Crosspoint Blvd., Indianapolis, IN 46256, or call 800-762-2974. Please allow three to four weeks for delivery. This Limited Warranty is void if failure of the Software Media has resulted from accident, abuse, or misapplication. Any replacement Software Media will be warranted for the remainder of the original warranty period or thirty (30) days, whichever is longer.

   (b) In no event shall IDGB or the author be liable for any damages whatsoever (including without limitation damages for loss of business profits, business interruption, loss of business information, or any other pecuniary loss) arising from the use of or inability to use the Book or the Software, even if IDGB has been advised of the possibility of such damages.

   (c) Because some jurisdictions do not allow the exclusion or limitation of liability for conse-quential or incidental damages, the above limitation or exclusion may not apply to you.

7. **U.S. Government Restricted Rights.** Use, duplication, or disclosure of the Software by the U.S. Government is subject to restrictions stated in paragraph (c)(1)(ii) of the Rights in Technical Data and Computer Software clause of DFARS 252.227-7013, and in subparagraphs (a) through (d) of the Commercial Computer–Restricted Rights clause at FAR 52.227-19, and in similar clauses in the NASA FAR supplement, when applicable.

8. **General.** This Agreement constitutes the entire understanding of the parties and revokes and supersedes all prior agreements, oral or written, between them and may not be modified or amended except in a writing signed by both parties hereto that specifically refers to this Agreement. This Agreement shall take precedence over any other documents that may be in conflict herewith. If any one or more provisions contained in this Agreement are held by any court or tribunal to be invalid, illegal, or otherwise unenforceable, each and every other pro-vision shall remain in full force and effect.

GNU GENERAL PUBLIC LICENSE

Version 2, June 1991
Copyright (C) 1989, 1991 Free Software Foundation, Inc.
59 Temple Place - Suite 330, Boston, MA 02111-1307, USA

Preamble

The licenses for most software are designed to take away your freedom to share and change it. By contrast, the GNU General Public License is intended to guarantee your freedom to share and change free software—to make sure the software is free for all its users. This General Public License applies to most of the Free Software Foundation's software and to any other program whose authors commit to using it. (Some other Free Software Foundation software is covered by the GNU Library General Public License instead.) You can apply it to your programs, too.

When we speak of free software, we are referring to freedom, not price. Our General Public Licenses are designed to make sure that you have the freedom to distribute copies of free software (and charge for this service if you wish), that you receive source code or can get it if you want it, that you can change the software or use pieces of it in new free programs; and that you know you can do these things.

To protect your rights, we need to make restrictions that forbid anyone to deny you these rights or to ask you to surrender the rights. These restrictions translate to certain responsibilities for you if you distribute copies of the software, or if you modify it.

For example, if you distribute copies of such a program, whether gratis or for a fee, you must give the recipients all the rights that you have. You must make sure that they, too, receive or can get the source code. And you must show them these terms so they know their rights.

We protect your rights with two steps: (1) copyright the software, and (2) offer you this license which gives you legal permission to copy, distribute and/or modify the software.

Also, for each author's protection and ours, we want to make certain that everyone understands that there is no warranty for this free software. If the software is modified by someone else and passed on, we want its recipients to know that what they have is not the original, so that any problems introduced by others will not reflect on the original authors' reputations.

Finally, any free program is threatened constantly by software patents. We wish to avoid the danger that redistributors of a free program will individually obtain patent licenses, in effect making the program proprietary. To prevent this, we have made it clear that any patent must be licensed for everyone's free use or not licensed at all.

The precise terms and conditions for copying, distribution and modification follow.

TERMS AND CONDITIONS FOR COPYING, DISTRIBUTION AND MODIFICATION

This License applies to any program or other work which contains a notice placed by the copyright holder saying it may be distributed under the terms of this General Public License. The "Program", below, refers to any such program or work, and a "work based on the Program" means either the Program or any derivative work under copyright law: that is to say, a work containing the Program or a portion of it, either verbatim or with modifications and/or translated into another language. (Hereinafter, translation is included without limitation in the term "modification".) Each licensee is addressed as "you".

Activities other than copying, distribution and modification are not covered by this License; they are outside its scope. The act of running the Program is not restricted, and the output from the Program is covered only if its contents constitute a work based on the Program (independent of having been made by running the Program). Whether that is true depends on what the Program does.

1. You may copy and distribute verbatim copies of the Program's source code as you receive it, in any medium, provided that you conspicuously and appropriately publish on each copy an appropriate copyright notice and disclaimer of warranty; keep intact all the notices that refer to this License and to the absence of any warranty; and give any other recipients of the Program a copy of this License along with the Program.

    You may charge a fee for the physical act of transferring a copy, and you may at your option offer warranty protection in exchange for a fee.

2. You may modify your copy or copies of the Program or any portion of it, thus forming a work based on the Program, and copy and distribute such modifications or work under the terms of Section 1 above, provided that you also meet all of these conditions:

    (a) You must cause the modified files to carry prominent notices stating that you changed the files and the date of any change.

    (b) You must cause any work that you distribute or publish, that in whole or in part contains or is derived from the Program or any part thereof, to be licensed as a whole at no charge to all third parties under the terms of this License.

    (c) If the modified program normally reads commands interactively when run, you must cause it, when started running for such interactive use in the most ordinary way, to print or display an announcement including an appropriate copyright notice and a notice that there is no warranty (or else, saying that you provide a warranty) and that users may redistribute the program under these conditions, and telling the user how to view a copy of this License. (Exception: if the Program itself is interactive but does not normally print such an announcement, your work based on the Program is not required to print an announcement.)

    These requirements apply to the modified work as a whole. If identifiable sections of that work are not derived from the Program, and can be reasonably considered independent and separate works in themselves, then this License, and its terms, do not apply to those sections when you distribute them as separate works. But when you distribute the same sections as part of a whole which is a work based on the Program, the distribution of the whole must be on the terms of this License, whose permissions for other licensees extend to the entire whole, and thus to each and every part regardless of who wrote it.

Thus, it is not the intent of this section to claim rights or contest your rights to work written entirely by you; rather, the intent is to exercise the right to control the distribution of derivative or collective works based on the Program. In addition, mere aggregation of another work not based on the Program with the Program (or with a work based on the Program) on a volume of a storage or distribution medium does not bring the other work under the scope of this License.

3. You may copy and distribute the Program (or a work based on it, under Section 2) in object code or executable form under the terms of Sections 1 and 2 above provided that you also do one of the following:

   (a) Accompany it with the complete corresponding machine-readable source code, which must be distributed under the terms of Sections 1 and 2 above on a medium customarily used for software interchange; or,

   (b) Accompany it with a written offer, valid for at least three years, to give any third party, for a charge no more than your cost of physically performing source distribution, a complete machine-readable copy of the corresponding source code, to be distributed under the terms of Sections 1 and 2 above on a medium customarily used for software interchange; or,

   (c) Accompany it with the information you received as to the offer to distribute corresponding source code. (This alternative is allowed only for noncommercial distribution and only if you received the program in object code or executable form with such an offer, in accord with Subsection b above.)

The source code for a work means the preferred form of the work for making modifications to it. For an executable work, complete source code means all the source code for all modules it contains, plus any associated interface definition files, plus the scripts used to control compilation and installation of the executable. However, as a special exception, the source code distributed need not include anything that is normally distributed (in either source or binary form) with the major components (compiler, kernel, and so on) of the operating system on which the executable runs, unless that component itself accompanies the executable.

If distribution of executable or object code is made by offering access to copy from a designated place, then offering equivalent access to copy the source code from the same place counts as distribution of the source code, even though third parties are not compelled to copy the source along with the object code.

4. You may not copy, modify, sublicense, or distribute the Program except as expressly provided under this License. Any attempt otherwise to copy, modify, sublicense or distribute the Program is void, and will automatically terminate your rights under this License. However, parties who have received copies, or rights, from you under this License will not have their licenses terminated so long as such parties remain in full compliance.

5. You are not required to accept this License, since you have not signed it. However, nothing else grants you permission to modify or distribute the Program or its derivative works. These actions are prohibited by law if you do not accept this License. Therefore, by modifying or distributing the Program (or any work based on the Program), you indicate your acceptance of this License to do so, and all its terms and conditions for copying, distributing or modifying the Program or works based on it.

6. Each time you redistribute the Program (or any work based on the Program), the recipient automatically receives a license from the original licensor to copy, distribute or modify the Program subject to these terms and conditions. You may not impose any further restrictions on the recipients' exercise of the rights granted herein. You are not responsible for enforcing compliance by third parties to this License.

7. If, as a consequence of a court judgment or allegation of patent infringement or for any other reason (not limited to patent issues), conditions are imposed on you (whether by court order, agreement or otherwise) that contradict the conditions of this License, they do not excuse you from the conditions of this License. If you cannot distribute so as to satisfy simultaneously your obligations under this License and any other pertinent obligations, then as a consequence you may not distribute the Program at all. For example, if a patent license would not permit royalty-free redistribution of the Program by all those who receive copies directly or indirectly through you, then the only way you could satisfy both it and this License would be to refrain entirely from distribution of the Program.

   If any portion of this section is held invalid or unenforceable under any particular circumstance, the balance of the section is intended to apply and the section as a whole is intended to apply in other circumstances.

   It is not the purpose of this section to induce you to infringe any patents or other property right claims or to contest validity of any such claims; this section has the sole purpose of protecting the integrity of the free software distribution system, which is implemented by public license practices. Many people have made generous contributions to the wide range of software distributed through that system in reliance on consistent application of that system; it is up to the author/donor to decide if he or she is willing to distribute software through any other system and a licensee cannot impose that choice.

   This section is intended to make thoroughly clear what is believed to be a consequence of the rest of this License.

8. If the distribution and/or use of the Program is restricted in certain countries either by patents or by copyrighted interfaces, the original copyright holder who places the Program under this License may add an explicit geographical distribution limitation excluding those countries, so that distribution is permitted only in or among countries not thus excluded. In such case, this License incorporates the limitation as if written in the body of this License.

9. The Free Software Foundation may publish revised and/or new versions of the General Public License from time to time. Such new versions will be similar in spirit to the present version, but may differ in detail to address new problems or concerns.

   Each version is given a distinguishing version number. If the Program specifies a version number of this License which applies to it and "any later version", you have the option of following the terms and conditions either of that version or of any later version published by the Free Software Foundation. If the Program does not specify a version number of this License, you may choose any version ever published by the Free Software Foundation.

10. If you wish to incorporate parts of the Program into other free programs whose distribution conditions are different, write to the author to ask for permission. For software which is copyrighted by the Free Software Foundation, write to the Free Software Foundation; we sometimes make exceptions for this. Our decision will be guided by the two goals of preserving the free status of all derivatives of our free software and of promoting the sharing and reuse of software generally.

NO WARRANTY

11. BECAUSE THE PROGRAM IS LICENSED FREE OF CHARGE, THERE IS NO WARRANTY FOR THE PROGRAM, TO THE EXTENT PERMITTED BY APPLICABLE LAW. EXCEPT WHEN OTHERWISE STATED IN WRITING THE COPYRIGHT HOLDERS AND/OR OTHER PARTIES PROVIDE THE PROGRAM "AS IS" WITHOUT WARRANTY OF ANY KIND, EITHER EXPRESSED OR IMPLIED, INCLUDING, BUT NOT LIMITED TO, THE IMPLIED WARRANTIES OF MERCHANTABILITY AND FITNESS FOR A PARTICULAR PURPOSE. THE ENTIRE RISK AS TO THE QUALITY AND PERFOR-MANCE OF THE PROGRAM IS WITH YOU. SHOULD THE PROGRAM PROVE DEFECTIVE, YOU ASSUME THE COST OF ALL NECESSARY SERVICING, REPAIR OR CORRECTION.

12. IN NO EVENT UNLESS REQUIRED BY APPLICABLE LAW OR AGREED TO IN WRITING WILL ANY COPYRIGHT HOLDER, OR ANY OTHER PARTY WHO MAY MODIFY AND/OR REDISTRIB-UTE THE PROGRAM AS PERMITTED ABOVE, BE LIABLE TO YOU FOR DAMAGES, INCLUDING ANY GENERAL, SPECIAL, INCIDENTAL OR CONSEQUENTIAL DAMAGES ARISING OUT OF THE USE OR INABILITY TO USE THE PROGRAM (INCLUDING BUT NOT LIMITED TO LOSS OF DATA OR DATA BEING RENDERED INACCURATE OR LOSSES SUSTAINED BY YOU OR THIRD PARTIES OR A FAILURE OF THE PROGRAM TO OPERATE WITH ANY OTHER PROGRAMS), EVEN IF SUCH HOLDER OR OTHER PARTY HAS BEEN ADVISED OF THE POSSIBILITY OF SUCH DAMAGES.

END OF TERMS AND CONDITIONS

Installation Instructions

To install the items from the CD to your hard drive, follow these steps:

1. **Insert the CD into your computer's CD-ROM drive.**

   Give your computer a moment to take a look at the CD.

2. **When the light on your CD-ROM drive goes out, double-click the My Computer icon. (It's probably in the top-left corner of your desktop.)**

   The My Computer window opens, showing you all the drives attached to your computer, the Control Panel, and a couple other handy things.

3. **Double-click the icon for your CD-ROM drive.**

   Another window opens, showing you all the folders and files on the CD.

4. **Double-click the file called License.txt.**

   This file contains the end-user license that you agree to when using the CD. After you read the license, close the program (most likely Notepad) that displayed the file.

5. **Double-click the file called Readme.txt.**

   This file contains the most up-to-date information about the code.

6. **You can copy individual folders from the CD to an appropriately named folder on your hard drive, or you can run the self-extractor, CODE.EXE.**

The self-extractor places all the files on your hard drive and maintains the folder structure of the CD. The default location for the files to be installed is C:\C++ FD CODE, but you can change the name of this folder in the self-extractor dialog box.

IDG BOOKS WORLDWIDE BOOK REGISTRATION

Register This Book and Win!

We want to hear from you!

Visit **http://my2cents.dummies.com** to register this book and tell us how you liked it!

✔ Get entered in our monthly prize giveaway.

✔ Give us feedback about this book — tell us what you like best, what you like least, or maybe what you'd like to ask the author and us to change!

✔ Let us know any other *For Dummies*® topics that interest you.

Your feedback helps us determine what books to publish, tells us what coverage to add as we revise our books, and lets us know whether we're meeting your needs as a *For Dummies* reader. You're our most valuable resource, and what you have to say is important to us!

Not on the Web yet? It's easy to get started with *Dummies 101*®: *The Internet For Windows*® *98* or *The Internet For Dummies*® at local retailers everywhere.

Or let us know what you think by sending us a letter at the following address:

For Dummies Book Registration
Dummies Press
10475 Crosspoint Blvd.
Indianapolis, IN 46256

™

...FOR DUMMIES

BESTSELLING
BOOK SERIES